Mom's Secret Recipe File

Mom's Secret Recipe File

More than 125 Treasured Recipes from the
Mothers of Our Great Chefs

EDITED BY

Chris Styler

HYPERION

NEW YORK

A portion of the proceeds from the sale of this book is being donated to the Women's Commission for Refugee Women and Children.

Library of Congress Cataloging-in-Publication Data

Mom's secret recipe file : more than 125 treasured recipes from the mothers of our great chefs / edited by Chris Styler.
    p. cm.
  ISBN 1-4013-0754-X
  1. Cookery. 2. Cooks—Biography. I. Styler, Christopher.

TX714.M65 2004
641.5—dc22

                                   2003067536

Hyperion books are available for special promotions and premiums. For details, contact Michael Rentas, Manager, Inventory and Premium Sales, Hyperion, 77 West 66th Street, 11th floor, New York, New York 10023, or call 212-456-0133.

Book design by Richard Oriolo

FIRST EDITION

10 9 8 7 6 5 4 3 2 1

Contents

First and foremost I would like to thank the chefs, writers, and restaurateurs who have taken the time and energy to contribute to this book. Their stories, passion for food, and recipes add up to more than the sum of their parts. They are a testament to the willingness of people to share and help others less fortunate than themselves.

Acknowledgments

I would also like to thank all the people who helped get me in touch and keep in touch with all the contributors, many of whom were opening restaurants, writing books, and taping television shows (sometimes all on the same day!): Miguelina Polanco; Shelly Burgess; Norma Galehouse; Louise Holland; Zoe Wales; Sarah Hearn; Emily Burdick; Chris Whaley; Jocelyn Morse; Gina Gargano; Tiffani Faison; Teresa General; Carollynn Bartosh; Drew Gillaspie; Carol Lalli Music; Jennie Andersson; Katie Barr; and also Gladys Bourdain and Sally Oliver.

Thanks to the folks at Hyperion: Will Schwalbe developed this idea, entrusted it to me, and then kept me stoked with his enthusiasm—I look forward to working with him in the future; Leslie Wells and Elisa Lee helped me handle the logistics.

Ellen Jorgensen, Roxanne Saucier, and Megan McKenna from the Women's Commission for Refugee Women and Children lent invaluable assistance.

My agent, Kim Yorio, did more than bring this project to my attention. She crashed my quiet Sunday morning at home and mapped out three years of my life.

Amy Searfoss made the calls (and the recalls), sent the emails, and kept me up to speed.

Carl from Village Camera in South Orange, New Jersey, handled treasured family photos from contributors as if they were his own.

Last, I would like to thank Joseph Seoane. When I got cranky he un-cranked me. I could not have done this, and a whole lot more, without him.

—*Chris Styler*

The Women's Commission for Refugee Women and Children would like to thank the many people who made this project possible, especially all of the fabulous chefs, and other moms, who participated.

We send our heartfelt gratitude to Chris Styler for all of his work, and the creativity and dedication he brought to it.

Our thanks go to all the people at Hyperion for everything they did to make this such a special book.

Also, a special tribute to Mary Anne Schwalbe, the mother of the Women's Commission, whose secret ingredient is a gentle yet strong guiding hand.

Finally, to the women refugees who inspire us with their strength and courage, and with whom it is a privilege to work. We are particularly honored to be a beneficiary of this project, for it brings to mind the cooking expertise of women throughout the world who, even when fleeing war or disaster in their home country, bring with them their cooking traditions—the recipes they learned from their mothers and grandmothers—to share with their families and maintain a community in their uprooted lives. Our own country, in turn, has been made richer by the recipes and cooking traditions that refugees and other immigrants have brought here.

—*Mary Diaz, executive director, the Women's Commission for Refugee Women and Children*

"I'm always surprised when I hear about a chef who *didn't* grow up with great food," Jasper White writes in the introduction to his chapter. That simple statement is given weight by the marvelous, diverse, and extremely personal collection of recipes contributed to this book by America's top chefs, cookbook authors, and television personalities.

Introduction

The source of these recipes, as we made clear to contributors, was theirs to decide, as long as that source was a woman (or women) whose cooking and personality had inspired them. Barbara Kafka writes—candidly and beautifully as always—about her mother's utter inability to boil water. (I knew Barbara's mother. She didn't cook, nor could she be bothered to learn.) But had Barbara's mother learned her way around a kitchen, Rachel's Perfect Chocolate Dessert would never have made it into Barbara's repertoire, nor would it appear in this and no other book.

Along with the recipes, you'll find stories of extraordinary women, such as Jacques Pépin's mother, who pedaled a bicycle through France's war-ravaged countryside to barter with farmers to put food on the table, and women who did the most ordinary things to keep a family nourished, happy, and together.

I have worked in the food and restaurant business for thirty years and have seen the generosity and kindness exhibited by this community as they battled hunger, helped the homeless, and volunteered to teach less fortunate members of the community. But even I was stunned by the response when I asked for contributions to this book. Give a bunch of chefs a worthy cause, and there they are—tying on an apron, firing up a burner, ready to go. As Sara Moulton, one of the first people I contacted for this project, put it, "What can I do?"

What Sara and the other contributors did, in addition to sharing their treasured recipes, childhood memories, and stories, was reach out to women and children in some of the most troubled parts of the world. The Women's Commission for Refugee Women and Children, the cause that brought this remarkable collection of talented chefs together, cares for these people, offering them education, empowerment, and a voice in their own future. Every copy sold contributes money that will benefit this extraordinary organization.

It is most appropriate that we asked our contributors to share with us recipes and stories from women who have inspired them. These recipes represent more than food; they embody tradition, a link with the past and family and community. To these chefs a kitchen is more than a room with a stove; it is the center of the home and a haven, as Michael Lomonaco points out in the introduction to his chapter. Sadly, tradition, security, and ties to family and home are all destroyed when women and children are displaced. These recipes and reminiscences will help women and children who have lost that security and continuity—hopefully only for a short while—to regain them.

One look at the roster of contributors, and it's no surprise that the recipes in this book are wonderful. What may come as a surprise is the variety, the absolute individuality of the choices that make this collection such a joy. Delicately seasoned shrimp grilled and served over Swiss chard flavored with fermented black beans may not have been your childhood comfort food, but it was Martin Yan's. And after I tried Martin's recipes, they became mine. Whatever the ingredients, whatever the seasonings, these recipes convey the warmth and comfort of a freshly baked after-school cookie.

Most of the recipes gathered here have never been published before. I may be wrong, but Rozanne Gold has probably been waiting a long time for a chance to get her mother's recipe "Tunk-a-lee" into print. I am glad she did. "Tunk-a-lee"—softly scrambled eggs with slowly cooked tomato and onion piled high on lightly toasted wheat bread—was my breakfast for a week straight after I first tried it.

Some recipes in this collection may be found elsewhere in one version or another. Lidia Bastianich sent a recipe for gnocchi, a version of which has appeared in *all* her books. Should that surprise anyone? For many chefs the foods of their childhood are inexorably linked with the way they cook and think about food as professionals. I hope that however many books Lidia writes, each contains a recipe for gnocchi just so people who haven't experienced them before will discover the miracle of fluffy dumplings that have their origins in two of the most decidedly unfluffy ingredients around: flour and potatoes. Take an hour to make Lidia's gnocchi. Better yet, take the time to make them with your children or grandchildren, as Lidia does.

I learned a lot in the six months I worked on this book. I had never used a pressure cooker before trying Rose Levy Beranbaum's grandmother's lamb stew with prunes. I'd never eaten (let alone made) Pound Pudding until I tried Jamie Oliver's version of this classic steamed pudding.

And I remembered much, too. Talking to Nick Malgieri about his Italian-American grandmother brought back memories of my own. Even stories that took place in other parts of the world and with unfamiliar foods resonated for me. Mollie Katzen's grandmother working the dough, nudging it, as Mollie puts it, reminded me of my grandmother covering her bed with a clean tablecloth and covering that with freshly filled ravioli. The ingredients, the dishes, and the locations may be different from household to household, but the joy, the generosity, and the warmth behind all these recipes is constant.

I have known some of the people who so willingly contributed recipes to this collection for twenty-five years. Others I met through phone calls and emails exchanged while working on this project. I counted on a lot of good meals as I worked my way through these recipes, and that was, in fact, the case. The genuine concern and warmth I experienced working with the contributors to this book were, so to speak, the icing on an already beautiful cake.

List of Recipes

LIDIA MATTICCHIO BASTIANICH was born in Pola on the Istrian Peninsula that juts into the Adriatic Sea. She emigrated to the United States with the help of Catholic Charities in 1958.

"The First Lady of Italian Cuisine" is best known for her two public television series, *Lidia's Italian American Kitchen* and *Lidia's Italian Table*, each of which was accompanied by a cookbook of the same name. She was one of five television chefs featured on *An American Feast*, a cooking special hosted by Julia Child that aired nationally in December 2000.

Lidia opened her first restaurant in Queens, New York, in 1971. She made the move to Manhattan to open the acclaimed Felidia restaurant in 1981. With her son, Joseph, Lidia runs the very popular Manhattan theater district eatery Becco. Their first venture outside of New York City was Lidia's Kansas City (with managing partner David Wagner, a native of Kansas City). Lidia's Pittsburgh followed soon after, with plans for more restaurant openings in the works.

Lidia's expertise extends beyond the realms of television and restaurants. She developed her own line of pasta sauces, Lidia's Flavors of Italy. She teamed up with her daughter, Tanya, to start Esperienze Italiane, which specializes in high-end trips to Italy. Lidia's website, *www.lidiasitaly.com*, was launched in 1998 and is now visited by about

Lidia Matticchio Bastianich

forty thousand people monthly. She lives in Douglaston, New York, and is the proud grandmother of five.

━━━━━

F amily is everything to me, and my mother, Erminia, is the matriarch of four generations of our family. And, of course, when those generations get together, there is always plenty of food. Dishes such as chicken with po-tatoes, breaded cutlets, and meatballs were on the menu when I was young and are still favorites for lunches and Sunday dinners.

Lidia Matticchio Bastianich and her mother, Erminia.

When I started in the restaurant business, my mother was very supportive even though she wanted me to be more academic. It was tough starting out in my own restaurant and raising two kids, but my mother was always there for me. She took care of the kids while I spent long hours try-ing to get the restaurant going. Sometimes she would bring them in to Buonavia, our first restau-rant, and do some prep work for me while she watched them. Even up until a couple of years ago she came into Felidia to take reservations in the mornings and then work the coat room dur-ing lunch.

My mother still helps me out. Sometimes when things are busy at the restaurants, I'll come home to find that she has prepared all the ingredients for a big pot of vegetable or lentil soup. All I have to do is pull out my soup pot and get cooking. I love making the food that my mother really enjoys, like those big pots of soup that perk away on the stove. Or my version of linguine with clam sauce or lobster *brodetto*—a cut-up lobster simmered in a spicy, vinegar-seasoned tomato sauce. I make manicotti for her, too. It isn't a part of our traditional cooking, but she loves anything with fresh ricotta in it.

To me, food is a way to pass traditions and togetherness from generation to generation. It makes me very happy to see my grandchildren lined up and waiting for the warm crepes to come from the pan, just as I did when I was a child.

Gnocchi POTATO DUMPLINGS

Everything goes in circles. When I was a little girl, I loved making these feather-light *gnocchi* with my mother. Now my grandchildren can't wait to get their hands in the dough and make their own. Gnocchi freeze well, but they don't keep for long once you make them. So freeze any gnocchi you don't plan to eat right away.   MAKES ABOUT 10 SERVINGS

6 large Idaho or russet potatoes (about 4 pounds), scrubbed but unpeeled

2 tablespoons plus 1 teaspoon salt

Freshly ground white pepper

2 large eggs, beaten

4 cups unbleached flour, or as needed

Grated Parmigiano-Reggiano cheese for serving

MOM'S TIP

Boil the potatoes just until tender but not until the skins split. If they do, the potatoes will soak up water, and your gnocchi will be heavy.

1.   Boil the potatoes in plenty of water until easily pierced with a skewer, about 40 minutes. Drain them and, when cool enough to handle, peel them. While still quite warm, rice the potatoes onto a cool, smooth surface, preferably marble. Spread them out (with a fork to prevent them from clumping) to expose as much surface as possible to the air. (When the potatoes are spread out, more steam will escape, and you'll need less flour to make the gnocchi, which will keep the gnocchi light.)

2.   Bring 6 quarts of water to a boil in a large, heavy pot. Toss in 2 tablespoons of salt.

3.   Gather the cooled potatoes into a mound and form a well in the center. Stir the remaining 1 teaspoon of salt and a dash of the pepper into the beaten eggs and pour the mixture into the well. Work the potatoes and eggs together with both hands, gradually adding enough flour, about 3 cups, to make a firm but moist dough. Scrape up the dough from the work surface with a knife as often as necessary while working in the flour. Mixing the dough should take no

longer than 10 minutes. The longer the dough is worked, the more flour it will require, and the heavier it will become.

4. Dust the dough, your hands, and the work surface lightly with flour and cut the dough into 6 equal parts. Continue to dust the dough, your hands, and the surface when the dough starts to feel sticky.

5. Roll each piece of dough with the palms of both hands into a rope ½ inch thick. Cut the ropes crosswise into ½-inch pieces. Indent each piece with a thumb or use the tines of a fork to produce a ribbed effect. (This facilitates adhesion of the sauce.)

6. Drop the gnocchi into boiling water, a few at a time, stirring gently and continuously with a wooden spoon, and cook for 2–3 minutes, until they rise to the surface. Remove the gnocchi with a slotted spoon or skimmer, transfer to a warm platter, and add a little sauce of choice. Boil the remaining pieces in batches until all are done. Sauce as desired, add pepper and cheese to taste, and serve immediately.

Variations: A few ways to serve gnocchi

- Scoop the gnocchi into a large serving bowl and drizzle some olive oil over them. Toss them with pesto and pass grated Parmigiano-Reggiano cheese at the table.

- Toss the gnocchi with your favorite tomato sauce enriched with chopped olives, some roughly torn fresh basil leaves, and chopped fresh Italian parsley.

- Melt butter over low heat so that it doesn't separate. Warm a generous amount of fresh sage leaves in the butter. Toss the sage butter with the cooked gnocchi and pass grated cheese separately.

Palacinke SWEET CREPES

When I was young, these crepes were sometimes a snack, but very often, spread with marmalade and served with milk, they were dinner. Now when my grandkids come over, I have some batter ready. *Palacinke* are a good fall-back position if one of the kids isn't crazy about what's on the menu.

MAKES ABOUT 10 SERVINGS

2 large eggs	I teaspoon vanilla extract
2 cups milk	2 cups all-purpose flour
½ cup club soda	3 tablespoons olive oil
¼ cup sugar	Grated zest of I lemon
¼ teaspoon salt	Grated zest of I orange
I tablespoon dark rum	Vegetable oil for frying

I. Whisk the eggs in a medium mixing bowl until blended. Stir in the milk, club soda, sugar, salt, rum, and vanilla until the sugar has dissolved. Gradually sift in the flour, stirring constantly to make a batter the consistency of melted ice cream. Stir in the olive oil and lemon and orange zests.

> **MOM'S TIP**
>
> *The secret to making thin, even crepes is to flex your wrist quickly, covering the bottom of the pan with batter as quickly as possible.*

2. Heat I tablespoon of vegetable oil in a 6- to 7-inch crepe pan or nonstick skillet over medium-high heat. Tilt the pan to coat the bottom with oil, then pour off the excess. Pour about 2 tablespoons of batter into the pan and tilt and swirl it to distribute the batter as thinly and evenly as possible. Return the pan to the heat, lower the flame to medium, and cook the crepe until lightly browned, 30 to 40 seconds. Flip it carefully with a spatula and cook the second side until brown spots appear. Remove from the pan to a warmed platter and repeat the process with the remaining batter.

The finished crepes are best served warm in any of the following ways:

- Sprinkled with granulated or confectioners' sugar

- Spread with marmalade and then folded into quarters

- Topped with a spoonful of whipped cream and some fresh berries or orange segments

- Spread with 1 tablespoon of Nutella or melted bittersweet chocolate and then folded into quarters and topped with whipped cream. Drizzle a little warm melted chocolate over the whipped cream if you like.

Pollastrella alla Campagnola con Cipolle, Patatine Rosse, ed Olive

COUNTRY-STYLE SPRING CHICKEN WITH ONIONS, POTATOES,

AND OLIVES

This is one of the dishes we always ask my mother to make for us. I think her version of this dish is the best I've ever had. Maybe it's the motherly love that goes into it, but it takes me right to the comfort zone every time I eat it.

MAKES 6 SERVINGS

4 pounds spring chicken parts (see Note)

¼ cup extra virgin olive oil

Salt

Freshly ground black pepper

1½ pounds small (about 1½ inches) red potatoes, halved

3 small yellow onions (about 6 ounces), cut into quarters

2 sprigs fresh rosemary

1 whole *peperoncino* (dried hot red pepper), broken in half, or ½ teaspoon crushed hot red pepper

20 pitted Kalamata olives

2 tablespoons chopped Italian parsley leaves

1. Toss the chicken pieces together with the oil in a large bowl. Season with salt and pepper, and toss again. Heat 2 large (at least 12 inches) nonstick or well-seasoned cast-iron pans over medium heat. Add the chicken pieces, skin side down, and cover the skillets. Cook the chicken, turning it once, until light brown on both sides, 5 to 7 minutes.

2. Move the chicken pieces to one side of each skillet. Add the potato halves, cut side down, to the clear side of the skillet and cook over medium heat for 15 minutes, turning them and the chicken pieces often, until evenly browned. (At this point both the chicken and the potatoes should be crisp and brown.) Adjust the

heat to medium-low and divide the onions, rosemary, *peperoncino*, and olives between the skillets and cook, covered, until the onions have softened and the flavors have blended, about 15 minutes. Stir the contents of the skillets gently several times as they cook.

3. Drain the oil from the pans, sprinkle everything with the chopped parsley, and serve.

NOTE: Spring chickens, sometimes called *poussins*, are available in specialty grocery stores. Cut each chicken into four pieces: two breast/wing and two leg pieces.

Riso e Patate RICE AND POTATO SOUP

MAKES 6 SERVINGS

3 tablespoons olive oil

2 baking potatoes, peeled and cut into ½-inch dice

2 carrots, peeled and shredded

2 celery stalks, halved crosswise

2 teaspoons tomato paste

10 cups hot homemade chicken stock or reduced-sodium canned chicken broth

2 bay leaves

Salt

Freshly ground pepper

1 cup long-grain rice

Grated Parmigiano-Reggiano cheese

1.   Heat the oil in a deep, heavy pot or large saucepan. Add the potatoes and cook, turning occasionally, until browned, about 5 minutes. Add the carrots and celery, and cook for 2 to 3 minutes over medium heat, stirring with a wooden spoon. The potatoes may stick slightly to the bottom of the pan as they cook. No harm done. In fact, they'll take on added flavor. Just don't let them burn.

2.   Add the tomato paste, stock, bay leaves, and salt and pepper to taste. Bring to a boil, then adjust the heat so the liquid is simmering. Cover the pot and simmer for 40 minutes over medium-low heat. The soup can be prepared to this point and refrigerated up to 3 days. Bring to a simmer before serving.

3.   Add the rice and cook until tender, about 12 minutes. Remove and discard the celery and bay leaves, adjust the seasoning, and serve sprinkled with grated cheese.

AFTER GRADUATING FROM the University of Michigan in 1975, Sara Moulton pursued her passion for cooking by attending the Culinary Institute of America in Hyde Park, New York. Sara has since worked in restaurants in Boston and New York, most notably as a chef-tournant at Manhattan's La Tulipe.

Sara Moulton

Accepting a job in the test kitchen at *Gourmet* magazine in 1984 led four years later to a position as the magazine's executive chef, which she holds to this day. Sara's television experience began when she worked with the team in the "back kitchen" for public television's *Julia Child and More Company* in 1979 and continued with a stint as executive chef at ABC-TV's *Good Morning America*. She is currently *GMA*'s food correspondent. Sara's *Cooking Live* show on Food Network ran for six years and some twelve hundred shows, until March 31, 2002. Her new show, *Sara's Secrets*, began the next day. Sara's first cookbook, *Sara Moulton Cooks at Home*, was published in 2002.

Sara cofounded the New York Women's Culinary Alliance, an organization devoted to creating opportunities for women in the culinary field. She lives in New York City with her husband, Bill, and their two children, Ruth and Sam.

≈≈≈

As long as I can remember, I've been surrounded by good food. My dad's mom, Ruth, was a great New England cook. We spent all summer every summer in a house we rented across from hers in northeastern Massachusetts. Granny made Johnnycakes, bread from scratch, and something she called raspberry vinegar. It wasn't really vinegar but raspberries fermented with sugar for a few days, and it was delicious. All the kids loved to hang out with Granny, making bread and cookies. When my parents and aunt and uncle bought an old farmhouse down the road from Granny's, I was introduced to my aunt's great cooking. I remember she made the most amazing pies. It didn't matter what fruit was in season, her pies were always the best.

Sara Moulton and her mom, Elizabeth, c. 1982.

Even with all this good food, I ate only hot dogs as a kid. Around the seventh grade all that changed. I think it had to do with the fact that we started eating together as a family every night. My mother made salads with Belgian endive—that was really something back in the late fifties. We had fresh fennel, creamed spinach with béchamel sauce, shad roe, and really great fresh ingredients just about every night. We never had bottled dressing; it was always freshly made vinaigrette. (I still think my mother makes the best vinaigrette.)

My mom was a very big influence on my choice of career. She and I ate together and dined out a lot when I was growing up. When I was in junior high, she bought *The New York Times Cook Book* by Craig Claiborne, and she and I cooked our way through it. (That was our "veal and sauce" phase.) After she finally made it to Europe—it had been her lifelong dream—our cooking got even better. Every time she came home from Greece, Italy, or wherever, she'd practically race into the kitchen to get going.

I went to the University of Michigan thinking at the time I would be a lawyer, a doctor, or a biological medical illustrator. Or maybe I'd teach. Through it all, though, I always had cooking jobs. I worked in the kitchen of a local bar and cooked for two of the university professors and their kids.

But it was my mom who pushed me into cooking as a career. She wrote to Craig Claiborne and Julia Child to ask their advice. It was Craig who suggested I go to the CIA.

I still think of my mother every time I make a veal scaloppine dish or Greek food, such as moussaka. Some of her recipes, like Mom's Brushed Egg-

Sara Moulton with her big sister, Anne, and her mom, Elizabeth.

plant, were in my first cookbook, *Sara Moulton Cooks at Home*. And I make things for my kids that she used to make for us, like meatball stroganoff and blueberry pudding. Now we take *our* kids up to Massachusetts for the last two weeks in August. My uncle, the gardener of the family, passed away, but my aunt carries on the tradition. We make dinner based on what's in the garden. There's a group of about twenty cousins and family when we all get together. We're all obsessed with food. It's all about exercising so we can have another big meal.

Mom's Meatball Stroganoff

This was one of my favorite dishes as a kid, a less expensive version of the classic dish created and named for Count Stroganov in late-nineteenth-century Russia. Very popular in America during the sixties and seventies, the original recipe for beef stroganoff called for thin slices of pricey beef fillet. Although my mom used meatballs instead, it seemed luxurious to me. Eventually my mom (and my aunt Jean and my grandmother) stopped making it, maybe because it finally seemed too old-fashioned. By the time I wanted to demonstrate it on my show, beef stroganoff was so antique that none of my relatives could come up with a recipe—and all I remembered of it were bouillon cubes, tomato paste, and cultivated mushrooms.

When I recreated the recipe, I lost the bouillon cubes (too chemical tasting to me now) and the tomato paste but kept the cultivated mushrooms—although you would get a more elegant dish if you used such flavorful mushrooms as shiitakes or chanterelles. The ground beef of choice is chuck because it has the most flavor (and the most fat, too, alas). If you want to make a lighter version of this dish, you can substitute ground sirloin or ground round and low-fat sour cream.   MAKES 4 TO 6 SERVINGS

1 pound ground chuck meat

1 medium onion, finely chopped

2 cloves garlic, minced

Kosher salt

Freshly ground black pepper

½ cup fresh bread crumbs

2 large egg yolks

2 tablespoons extra virgin olive oil

½ pound cultivated white mushrooms, thinly sliced

½ cup dry sherry

2 cups chicken stock, preferably homemade

2 tablespoons unsalted butter, softened

2 tablespoons all-purpose flour

2 tablespoons chopped fresh dill

½ cup sour cream

1.   Combine the chuck, half of the chopped onion, the garlic, 1 teaspoon of salt, 1 teaspoon of pepper, the bread crumbs, egg yolks, and ½ cup of water in a large bowl. Mix well and form meatballs that measure about 1 inch in diameter.

2.   Heat the oil in a large nonstick skillet over medium-high heat. Add the meatballs and cook, shaking and turning, until well browned, about 5 minutes. Don't crowd the pan; work in batches if necessary. Transfer to paper towels to drain.

3.   Pour off any excess fat from the skillet, leaving 3 tablespoons in the pan, and add the remaining onion. Cook, stirring often, until softened, about 5 minutes. Add the mushrooms and cook, stirring, until the liquid they give off has evaporated, 7 to 10 minutes. Pour in the sherry, raise the heat to high, and boil until almost all the liquid has evaporated. Pour in the stock and bring to a boil.

4.   Mix the butter with the flour in a small bowl until it forms a smooth paste. Pinch off pea-size pieces and add little by little to the boiling sauce, whisking constantly for 3 minutes. Add the meatballs, stir in the dill and sour cream, season with salt and pepper, and cook over low heat until the meatballs are just heated through. Serve hot.

Stuffed Mushrooms

This is my version of my mother's stuffed mushrooms, which I've updated by adding pancetta—an Italian cured-pork product similar to unsmoked bacon—and freshly grated Parmigiano-Reggiano cheese. I did not put a cup measurement on the cheese. Depending on whether you use a traditional cheese grater or one of those new microplanes that make the cheese very light and fluffy, the measurements can be completely different.

My mom serves these mushrooms with the meal, not before it, which I think is a cool idea.   MAKES 4 SERVINGS

8 large mushrooms (about 2 inches in diameter), cleaned

1 tablespoon extra virgin olive oil, plus extra for coating the mushroom caps

Salt and freshly ground pepper

2 ounces pancetta, diced

1 large shallot, minced (about ¼ cup)

1 teaspoon fresh thyme leaves

¼ cup red wine

2 tablespoons fresh bread crumbs

1 walnut-size piece of Parmigiano-Reggiano or Parmesan cheese, freshly grated

1.   Preheat the oven to 425° F. Remove the stems from the mushrooms and finely chop them. Coat the caps with oil and season with salt and pepper. Arrange the mushrooms, gill side down, in a shallow baking pan and bake until a knife easily pierces the mushrooms, about 25 minutes. Take the baking pan out of the oven and turn the mushrooms over.

2.   Cook the pancetta in the oil in a large skillet over moderately low heat until crisp, about 6 to 8 minutes. Transfer with a slotted spoon to a plate lined with paper towels. Add the shallot to the skillet and cook, stirring occasionally, until tender, about 3 minutes. Add the chopped mushroom stems and cook over

medium heat until all the liquid the mushrooms give off has evaporated, about 5 minutes. Add the thyme and wine, and cook until almost dry. Remove from the heat and stir in the bread crumbs, cheese, and salt and pepper to taste.

3. Divide the stuffing among the mushroom caps and top each with some of the pancetta. Return to the oven and bake for 10 minutes, or until heated through.

Chicken Tarragon

Chicken tarragon is something my mom used to make using a recipe from *The New York Times Cook Book*. She probably would have used vermouth because that is what "Julia" used on TV. MAKES 4 SERVINGS

2 tablespoons vegetable oil

1 tablespoon unsalted butter

Flour, preferably Wondra

Salt and freshly ground pepper

4 boneless, skinless chicken breast halves (about 1¾ pounds total)

1 large shallot, minced (about ¼ cup)

½ cup dry vermouth or white wine

1 cup chicken broth

½ cup heavy cream

2 teaspoons finely chopped fresh tarragon

1. Heat the oil and butter in a large skillet over medium heat. Season the flour with salt and pepper. Coat the chicken with the flour, shaking off the excess. Add the coated chicken to the pan and cook until lightly browned, about 3 minutes per side.

> **MOM'S TIP**
>
> *Cooking the chicken over gentle heat just until it is cooked through will prevent it from becoming tough.*

2. Transfer the chicken with tongs to a platter. Add the shallot to the pan and cook, stirring, for 1 minute. Pour in the vermouth and simmer until almost dry. Add the chicken broth, return the chicken to the pan, and bring the liquid to a boil. Cover and simmer gently until the chicken is just cooked through, about 10 minutes.

3. Remove the chicken with tongs and return to the platter. Pour the heavy cream into the skillet, add the tarragon, and simmer until thickened, about 5 minutes. Season with salt and pepper to taste. Return the chicken to the skillet just long enough to heat through. Serve each breast topped with some of the sauce.

BARBARA KAFKA'S most recent book, *Soup: A Way of Life*, has been on the best-seller list of the *Los Angeles Times*. *Roasting: A Simple Art* won the IACP/Julia Child Cookbook Award and was a Book-of-the-Month Club main selection, as was her preceding book, *Party Food*.

Barbara wrote on a regular basis for *The New York Times* and has written a monthly column, "The Opinionated Palate," for *Gourmet* and other columns for *Family Circle* and *Vogue*.

Other books include *The New York Times* best-seller *Microwave Gourmet* and *Microwave Gourmet Healthstyle Cookbook*. Both were Book-of-the-Month Club main selections and sold out in paperback in America and England. Both were winners of the Tastemaker Award, presented by the International Association of Culinary Professionals.

In the past, Barbara was active as a consultant to restaurants and industry, and as a product designer. For many years she taught with James Beard as well as around the country on her own. The winner of many awards, Barbara has served on the boards of culinary organizations and educational boards. She is currently at work on a new book, *Vegetable Love*.

Barbara Kafka

As far as anyone can remember, my mother's side of the family consists of non- or bad cooks. My mother was a conscientious objector to women's work. In any case, it was no exaggeration to say, "She couldn't boil water." When this arduous task was once assayed as she strove to make herself a cup of tea, she scalded herself quite badly.

Her mother was merely a bad cook. She understood hospitality and would share with all and sundry. She didn't understand food. There was only one dish that I remember her making that was eagerly anticipated by the family: Romanian eggplant dip. I loved it and would sneakily poke a finger into the refrigerated bowl for a mouthful. Clearly, it was my first dip. It is extremely easy and good. I used it in my book *Party Food*.

I never tasted my paternal grandmother's food. By the time I came along, she was too old for cooking. By all accounts she was a better cook than my other grandmother. For my father's sake, I strove to recreate some of the recipes that he remembered fondly. I made many versions of borscht. The cold borscht in *Soup: A Way of Life* is very traditional. Be sure to have plenty of the add-ins available. With lots of them this can be a whole meal on a hot summer's evening when served with a salad and good bread, preferably rye.

In a way, the nearest thing I had to a mother's cooking was that of Rachel Wellman, who cooked for us until just before I went off to college. She was a truly gifted cook and baker. When my uncle Abe, who stayed a bachelor until World War II, stayed over after a night on the town, she always left him a chocolate cake. He would eat half of the whole thing, washed down with a bottle of milk. Perhaps the most sensational cake she made was the one with liquid ganache poured over very cold whipped cream. How she managed it in the refrigerator we had then—with its tiny freezer compartment that could house only two diminutive ice trays—I will never know.

Today I cook and am the only "mom" in the house.

Romanian Eggplant Dip

This simplest of eggplant dips, also known as baba ghanouj, is very good and easily multiplied. MAKES ABOUT 3 CUPS

1 medium eggplant (about 1 pound)

¼ cup olive oil

2 tablespoons fresh lemon juice

1 to 2 medium cloves garlic, or to taste, smashed, peeled, and minced

2 teaspoons kosher salt

Freshly ground black pepper to taste

¼ cup loosely packed chopped fresh Italian parsley leaves (optional)

1. Place the oven rack in the center position. Preheat the oven to 400° F. Roast the eggplant on a heavy, ungreased baking sheet (not an air-cushioned cookie sheet) until it bursts and the center becomes very tender. This will take about 1½ hours. Smaller—not baby—eggplants will take less time. It is done when the skin is dark and the eggplant looks a bit like a deflated balloon.

2. Remove from the oven. Using 2 forks, immediately tear the eggplant open and scrape out the pulp onto the hot baking sheet. Let it sizzle and brown. This will help some of the liquid evaporate. Discard the dry skin.

3. Transfer the pulp to a bowl and continue to pull it apart with the 2 forks until it is very finely shredded. Beat in the remaining ingredients. Store, covered, in the refrigerator at least overnight to let the flavors develop. Prepare up to 1 week ahead.

[Adapted from *Party Food;* William Morrow, 1992.]

Cold Beet Borscht

This may be one of the world's most glamorous-looking soups. It turns a brilliant magenta when the cream is added to the cooked beets and beet liquid. I like to serve it in a large white bowl surrounded by smaller bowls that contain the toppings. I ladle out the soup and invite the eaters to serve themselves the toppings.

I frequently double or treble the recipe and keep it in the refrigerator. A large bowl of soup plus bread and a salad is an ideal summer lunch. MAKES 6 FIRST-COURSE SERVINGS (OR MORE, DEPENDING ON THE AMOUNT OF TOPPINGS USED)

I pound beets, scrubbed well and all but I inch of stems removed	TOPPINGS
2 teaspoons distilled white vinegar, or to taste	Chopped onion
	Chopped cucumber
4 teaspoons fresh lemon juice	Chopped dill
¾ teaspoon citric acid powder (see Note)	Lemon wedges
	Sour cream
½ cup plus I tablespoon sugar	Heavy cream
I½ teaspoons kosher salt	Grated beets
½ cup sour cream	Cold, boiled, very small potatoes
⅔ cup heavy cream	Chopped hard-boiled egg

1. Bring the beets and 5 cups of water to a boil in a small saucepan. Lower the heat and simmer until the beets are tender when pierced with the tip of a knife, about 45 minutes.

2. Drain the beets in a damp cloth–lined sieve and reserve the cooking liquid. Run the beets under cold water to cool, then peel. In a food processor, grate the beets using the grating disc (this can also be done on a box grater).

3.   Return half of the grated beets to the cooking liquid. Reserve the rest as a topping or for another use. Season the soup with the vinegar, lemon juice, citric acid, sugar, and salt. Chill.

4.   Before serving, whisk in the sour cream and heavy cream. Pass small bowls of the suggested toppings.

> NOTE: Citric acid used to be readily available in crystals in pharmacies, and in some it still is, or you can find citric acid in powder form where home-canning supplies are sold.

[Adapted from *Soup: A Way of Life*; Artisan, 1998.]

The Perfect Chocolate Dessert

MAKES 8 TO 10 SERVINGS

18 ounces good-quality semisweet chocolate, coarsely grated

¼ pound (1 stick) unsalted butter

6 large eggs, separated

1 cup plus 5 teaspoons sugar

1 teaspoon vanilla extract

1½ teaspoons unflavored gelatin

3 cups heavy cream

1. Place the rack in the lower third of the oven. Preheat the oven to 375° F. Butter and flour an 8-inch springform pan.

2. Using a double boiler, put water in the bottom pan but make sure the water does not touch the bottom of the upper pan. Bring the water to a simmer and turn off the heat. Check the temperature of the water with a thermometer. It should not be hotter than 140° F.

> **MOM'S TIP**
>
> *Refrigerate leftover chocolate glaze until firm. Using a melon baller, form small, round "truffles" and coat them lightly with cocoa powder, confectioners' sugar, or ground nuts.*

3. While the water is heating, put 10 ounces of the semisweet chocolate in a food processor and process until all the pieces are the size of lentils.

4. When the water has reached the right temperature, put the chocolate in the upper pan set over the steaming water. Stir with a wooden spoon. When the chocolate has almost melted, add the butter and continue stirring. When both the butter and the chocolate have melted, keep them warm by replacing the water in the bottom of the pan with warm tap water or leaving the water if it's still warm enough.

5. Put the egg yolks in the bowl of an electric mixer. Begin beating and gradually beat in ¾ cup of sugar. Beat until the mixture is pale yellow and quite thick. Add the chocolate mixture and beat until completely combined and smooth. Beat in the vanilla until blended.

6. In another bowl, beat the egg whites until they form soft peaks. Gradually add ¼ cup of sugar. Continue to beat just until the whites form soft peaks; be careful not to overbeat them. Stir some of the whites into the chocolate mixture to lighten it. Fold in the rest. Pour the batter into the prepared pan and smooth the top.

7. Bake for 15 minutes, then lower the temperature to 300° F and bake for another 15 minutes. Lower the temperature to 250° F and bake for another 30 minutes. Turn off the oven and leave the oven door ajar. Let the cake cool in the oven for another 30 minutes. Remove the cake to a cooling rack and cover the top with a damp cloth. Let stand 5 minutes. Remove the towel and let the cake cool on the rack. Remove the sides of the pan. The cake will have a crust that cracked and collapsed as the temperature in the oven was lowered. Remove that crust gently. Set the cake aside and let it cool completely.

8. In the meantime, prepare the stabilized whipped cream: Place the gelatin in a pot with ¼ cup of cold water. Set aside for a few minutes until the gelatin is absorbed. Place the pot over simmering water and stir until the gelatin is dissolved. Let cool but do not let the gelatin harden. In a separate bowl, whip 2 cups of the heavy cream until about doubled in bulk, or until it forms soft peaks. Gradually beat in the 5 teaspoons of sugar and the gelatin. Beat until the cream is stiff. Refrigerate for 10 minutes.

9. When the cake has cooled completely, cut it in half horizontally to make 2 equal layers. Place the bottom layer on a plate and spread it with ½ inch of the whipped cream. Place the other layer on top and cover the entire cake, top and sides, with ½ inch of the whipped cream. Make the surface as smooth as possible.

10. Place the cake in the freezer long enough for the whipped cream to harden but not for the cake to freeze.

11. In the meantime, prepare the chocolate glaze. Heat the remaining cup of heavy cream in a small saucepan over medium-low heat just until bubbles begin to form around the edges (about 140° F). Coarsely grate the remaining 8 ounces

of semisweet chocolate. Pour the hot cream over the chocolate in a mixing bowl. Whisk until the chocolate is completely melted and the mixture is thickened. Let stand at room temperature until cool enough to mound very slightly on a spoon, about 95° F.

12. Remove the cake from the freezer. Spoon or pour the chocolate glaze slowly over the center of the cake, allowing it to spread out and cover the top of the cake. As the glaze trickles down the side of cake, you have 2 options: Leave the glaze as is, with some of the whipped cream showing, or, working very quickly, spread the glaze evenly over the sides of the cake with a flexible spatula to completely cover the whipped cream. If you choose to cover the sides, "patch" any exposed whipped cream with some of the remaining glaze. Refrigerate for at least 1 hour to set the chocolate. When the chocolate is set, clean up any glaze that has dripped down onto the plate. Serve the cake chilled.

JACQUES PÉPIN is a contributing editor to *Food & Wine* magazine and one of America's best-known chefs, cookbook authors, and cooking teachers. Jacques' memoir, *The Apprentice: My Life in the Kitchen*, was published in 2003. It was followed by a special companion program, also called *The Apprentice*, which aired on PBS-TV stations nationwide the following summer. He is currently hosting, with his daughter, Claudine, the acclaimed public television series *Jacques Pépin Celebrates*. The most recent of his twenty published cookbooks, *Jacques Pépin Celebrates*, is a companion book to that series. On the horizon for 2004 are a new series and cookbook showcasing simple, satisfying food that can be prepared easily and quickly.

Jacques serves as dean of special programs at The French Culinary Institute in New York City and teaches at Boston University. Born in Bourg-en-Bresse, France, he was the personal chef to three French heads of state, including Charles de Gaulle, before moving to the United States in 1959. He resides in Madison, Connecticut, with his wife, Gloria.

Jacques
Pépin

My mother, Jeanne, has never been afraid of hard work. She made clothes for the entire family and pedaled her bicycle from farm to farm—sometimes forty miles in a day—to keep my brothers and me fed while my father was away fighting with the Resistance during World War II. She was always a real free spirit, not afraid to try anything, but the war made her even more so.

Jeanne and Jacques Pépin at the James Beard House, c. 1991.

After the war she had an opportunity to open a restaurant, and she took it, even though she had never run a restaurant before and didn't have any formal training as a chef. She was a very instinctive cook, not at all bound by tradition or afraid of mixing one thing with another, and the food she served in the restaurant was simple and good. The menu was limited by what was in season and available right after the war, and that wasn't very much.

Well before I started my formal apprenticeship, I worked with Maman in her restaurants. (She owned and ran four consecutively.) My two brothers and I left for the market with her very early every day. There was no refrigeration then, so we bought what we needed for the day, and the four of us carried it home. It was on those trips to the market that I learned about quality and price—I saw what Maman was buying and what she paid for it.

Cleaning vegetables took most of my time in Maman's kitchen, but I also helped to plate the hors d'oeuvres—pâté, anchovies, and the like. Years later, in 1983, when my wife, Gloria, and I ran Gloria's French Café in Madison, Connecticut, the roles were reversed. My mother, who was then in her late sixties, prepared the hors d'oeuvres that arrived at each table as part of the café's set menu. At the café we served the same kind of simple country dishes we did at my mother's restaurants.

Jacques and Jeanne Pépin teaching a class, c. 1980.

I still cook some of the same dishes my mother made at home and in her restaurants, such as her *gateaux de foies de volailles,* a chicken liver "cake" seasoned with chopped parsley and garlic, and chicken *chasseur,* simmered with white wine, tomato, and tarragon. Here I am offering recipes for a few simple and delicious dishes that taste as good to me today as they did when I was a boy.

Gratin of Eggs

A favorite family recipe when I was a child, this egg gratin is still popular with children and adults alike. The ingredients are always on hand, so it is a real savior when unexpected guests arrive for dinner. The gratin sauce (an onion-flavored white sauce) can be used to make gratins out of all kinds of leftovers, such as cooked cauliflower, zucchini, or carrots. MAKES 6 SERVINGS

6 or 7 hard-cooked eggs
2 tablespoons unsalted butter
1½ cups sliced onions
1 tablespoon all-purpose flour
1½ cups milk

½ teaspoon salt
¼ teaspoon freshly ground black pepper
½ cup grated Swiss cheese

1. Preheat the oven to 400° F. Slice the eggs with an egg slicer or a knife and arrange them on the bottom of a 4- to 6-cup gratin dish. Melt the butter in a saucepan, and when it is hot but not smoking, add the onions. Cook them over medium to high heat, stirring occasionally, for 2½ to 3 minutes, or until they sizzle and just start to brown. Add the flour, mix well with a wooden spatula, and cook for about 30 seconds. Add the milk, salt, and pepper, stirring constantly, and bring the mixture to a boil. Lower the heat and let the sauce simmer gently for about 1 minute. Pour it over the eggs and mix in gently.

2. Sprinkle the Swiss cheese on top of the eggs and bake until the edges are bubbling, 10 to 12 minutes. Place under the broiler for 4 to 5 minutes to make a brown crust on top. Serve immediately.

Parisienne Gnocchi

Parisienne gnocchi are marvelous little dumplings made of *pâte à choux* dough. They are poached in water and then finished in the oven. I grew to love them growing up because my mother always made them at Le Pélican, her restaurant in Lyon. They can be served as a first course, side dish, or main course. There are two other types of gnocchi, one of German origin that is made with potato and is poached in the same manner, and another called (in France) Roman gnocchi, which are made with hard-wheat semolina—the same flour used to make pasta. The semolina is cooked with water or milk into a mush or a type of polenta and then spread on a tray, cooled, cut into shapes, and fried or baked with cheese or tomato sauce. MAKES 6 TO 8 SERVINGS

½ teaspoon salt

⅓ teaspoon grated nutmeg

3 tablespoons unsalted butter

I cup all-purpose flour

¼ cup plus I tablespoon grated Parmesan cheese

3 large eggs

I. Bring I cup of water, the salt, nutmeg, and 2 tablespoons of the butter to a boil in a heavy saucepan. As soon as the mixture boils, drop the entire cup of flour into the pan and mix it in quickly with a sturdy wooden spoon. Keep stirring until the mixture forms a smooth mass that separates easily from the sides of the saucepan. Cook and stir about 30 seconds more to dry the mixture further.

2. Transfer the dough to the bowl of an electric mixer or to a regular bowl if you plan to mix it by hand. Beat at low speed or by hand for 5 to 10 minutes, until the mixture is a bit cooler. Add the ¼ cup of cheese and I of the eggs. Mix at low speed or by hand until the egg is incorporated. At first the mixture will seem to separate, but keep mixing. Eventually the mixture will become tight and thick. Add

the second egg and mix again until smooth. Repeat with the third egg. Cover the dough with an oiled piece of plastic wrap and let it cool.

3. Heat about 3 inches of water to 180° F in a large saucepan. It should not boil. (If the mixture boils, the dumplings will cook too fast, expand, and eventually deflate. The dumplings should poach without expanding; they will expand later in the oven.)

4. Mold the dumplings with a teaspoon, using 1½ to 2 teaspoons of dough for each dumpling. Push the dough off the spoon with your index finger, holding it close enough to the water so it does not splash. Alternatively, fill a pastry bag fitted with a 1-inch plain tip with the dough, rest the tip on the edge of the saucepan, press the mixture out, and cut it off at the tip to form small gnocchi, each about 1½ inches long. (If concerned about overcrowding, poach the gnocchi in 2 batches.)

5. Poach the gnocchi about 3 minutes. They will sink to the bottom initially but will rise to the surface when they are done. Carefully lift the gnocchi (they will not be completely cooked inside) with a slotted spoon and drop them into a bowl of ice water to cool. They will sink to the bottom of the bowl when cool. Drain and use right away or refrigerate for up to a few hours for later use.

6. To finish the dish, preheat the oven to 350° F. Butter a large gratin dish with the remaining tablespoon of butter and arrange the gnocchi in 1 layer in the dish. (They should have enough room—about 1 inch between them—to expand, so use 2 gratin dishes if necessary.) Sprinkle on the remaining tablespoon of cheese and bake until puffed and lightly browned, about 25 minutes. Serve immediately.

Potato Lace

My mother especially liked this dish served with a salad, and it is ideal for unexpected guests or when you need a filler to complete a family meal. There is only a slight drawback to it: It should be eaten immediately after it is cooked, when it is most savory and crisp. Leftovers can be crisped under the broiler, but they are never as good as when they have just come out of the skillet.

I shred the potatoes into little strips for this recipe, but they could also be grated like the onions to give a different texture and taste. If you make the batter ahead, refrigerate it, covered tightly with a piece of plastic wrap, to lessen discoloration. The top of the batter will discolor anyway, but as you stir it, the discoloration will disappear, and it doesn't change the taste. Don't prepare the batter more than a few hours ahead, or it will become watery.

MAKES 12 TO 14 PANCAKES

I large or 2 medium onions (enough to make ½ cup grated onion)

3 to 4 potatoes (1½ pounds), peeled

2 large eggs

3 tablespoons all-purpose flour

¼ cup chopped fresh parsley

I teaspoon salt

½ teaspoon freshly ground black pepper

I cup vegetable oil, preferably corn or cottonseed

1. Peel the onions and grate them with a hand grater using the small side that seems to have been perforated with nails. These tiny holes abrade in any direction and liquefy the onions to a smooth puree.

2. Shred the potatoes on the side of the grater with the oblong holes that cut in one direction, downward. Hold the potato with the palm of your hand only,

to avoid cutting your fingertips. You should have about 3 cups of grated potatoes. Put them in a clean kitchen towel and twist the towel with one hand while you press on it with the other to extrude the juice. Most of the starch is released with the juice, so the potatoes will be airy and crisp.

3. Combine the grated onion, squeezed potatoes, eggs, flour, parsley, salt, and pepper in a bowl, preferably glass or stainless steel to prevent discoloration, and mix thoroughly. The batter will be fairly loose.

4. Heat 2 to 3 tablespoons of the oil in a nonstick skillet over medium heat. For each potato pancake, spoon about 3 tablespoons of the mixture into the skillet. (In an 8-inch-diameter pan you will be able to fry 3 at a time.) Spread the mixture immediately with the back of a spoon so that the pancakes are very thin and have little holes throughout. Cook over medium to high heat for about 1½ minutes on each side. The potatoes should be thin and crispy. Use a large spatula to flip them over. Add additional oil as necessary.

5. Remove the pancakes with the spatula. Notice that the edges are jagged and quite crisp. Serve as soon as possible.

JASPER WHITE was born in New Jersey, where he spent a good amount of his childhood on a farm near the Jersey shore. He credits his love of good food to his family, especially his grand-mother from Rome, Italy. Jasper began his cooking ca-reer in 1973, and after graduating from the Culinary Institute of America, he spent a few years working and traveling around the United States. Before settling in Boston, Jasper worked in New York, Florida, San Francisco, Seattle, and Montana.

Jasper
White

Jasper White is the acclaimed chef behind the renowned Jasper's restaurant, a Boston landmark famous for seafood and other New En-gland specialties that opened in 1983 in a nineteenth-century molasses warehouse on the Boston waterfront. The restaurant was owned and op-erated in partnership with his wife, Nancy, a graphic artist by trade. During the twelve-year run, Jasper's and Jasper White received numerous awards and were featured extensively in national and local media.

In May 2000, Jasper made a bold statement with his new restau-rant, Summer Shack, located in Cambridge, Massachusetts. Summer Shack is a big, funky dining hall that seats more than three hundred people and has lobster tanks and steam kettles taking center stage. This cooking area, the Lobster Line, is so unique that Jasper received a U.S. Patent protecting its design. In 2001, Summer Shack was nominated for a James Beard Foundation Award for Best New Restaurant (one of five in the United States and the only casual restaurant in that category). More recently, Jasper opened Summer Shacks at Mohegan Sun Resort and Casino in Connecticut and in Back Bay, Boston.

Jasper lives in Lincoln, Massachusetts, with his wife and three children: JP (Jasper Paul), Mariel, and Hayley.

———

I'm always surprised when I hear about a chef who didn't grow up with great food. I give all the credit for my passion for food to my family, especially my father's mother, Ida. My paternal grandmother came from Rome when she was six or seven. She must have always been surrounded by excellent food: Her father was a chef in New York City, and her mother, from everything I hear, was an unbelievable cook.

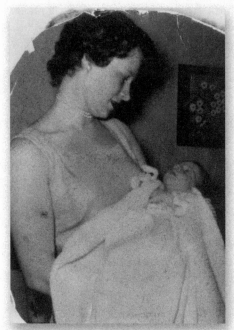

Newborn Jasper White and his mother.

My grandmother's cooking is my gold standard. When all of us young chefs were working in the late seventies, before the beginning of the American Food Revolution, it was all about cooking technique, but there was a little voice in my head that said, "Don't forget about the ingredients." That's what it was all about with my grandmother—the ingredients. We took trips to the specialty stores to buy aged provolone and other ingredients we couldn't get locally. But what really got us all excited were the crabs we caught in Barnegat Bay, and the woodcocks and pheasants my father shot while hunting.

Even though she came here from Italy, my grandmother didn't cook what I think of as Italian food. She made the best apple fritters I've ever eaten, and she had Jersey corn down to a science. We'd drive to the farm just before dinner and pick our own. The corn was in the pot about half an hour after it was on the stalk. But in a way that is the essence of Italian cooking: taking the best ingredients you can find and preparing them simply.

A much more recent shot of Jasper and his mom.

My grandmother always got me excited about food. If I was headed to her house for the weekend, I'd call first and we'd plan the menu together. In the summer we'd pick vegetables from her garden for every meal. When I close my eyes to think of beautiful, clean food, I think of those weekends at my grandmother's house.

My mother is first-generation Irish without a strong cooking tradition. When she married my Irish-Italian father, the pressure was really on. But my mother rose to the occasion. She had my grandmother not only as a role model but as a willing teacher, and that helped a lot. Of course we kids put pressure on her, too. You can't send the kids away on the weekend where they would be eating string beans and mint from the garden and then put a can of peas on the table.

I don't remember my grandmother ever making the ham recipe I'm including here, so it must be something my mother figured out on her own. It's still one of my favorite Sunday dinners. I hope it becomes one of yours.

My Grandmother's Pecan Pie

¼ pound (1 stick) butter, at room temperature

¾ cup light brown sugar

3 large eggs

1 cup chopped pecans

¾ cup dark corn syrup

1 teaspoon vanilla extract

¼ teaspoon salt

One 9-inch fluted unbaked pie crust, either store-bought or homemade, chilled

About 1 heaping cup fancy pecan halves, enough to top the pie

1. Preheat the oven to 375° F. Beat the butter and sugar together in the bowl of an electric mixer until light and fluffy, about 3 minutes, or longer if using a handheld mixer. Add the eggs, 1 at a time, and continue to beat until incorporated.

2. Add the chopped pecans, corn syrup, vanilla, and salt, and mix well. Pour the filling into the pie shell, place in the oven, and bake for 15 minutes.

3. Remove the pie, lower the oven temperature to 350°, and close the oven door. Working very quickly, arrange the pecan halves on top of the pie in a circular design. Return the pie to the oven and bake until the filling is set and the top is well browned, 30 to 35 minutes. Cool completely before serving.

Shrimp with Thyme Butter

My mother made this quick dish with dried thyme. I don't remember the quantities she used, but there was always plenty of shrimp for everybody. This recipe is updated a little, with fresh thyme instead of dried and a little bit of white wine. Serve it with plain white rice.   MAKES 3 TO 4 SERVINGS

I pound large (about 25 per pound) shrimp, shelled and deveined

¾ teaspoon salt, or to taste

¼ teaspoon freshly ground pepper

2 tablespoons chopped fresh thyme

2 tablespoons olive oil

¼ cup dry white wine or 2 tablespoons fresh lemon juice

2 tablespoons butter, cut into small pieces

I.   Toss the shrimp with the salt, pepper, and thyme until coated. (You can season the shrimp up to several hours in advance. Cover them and refrigerate until needed.)

2.   Heat the oil in a large skillet over medium-high heat. Add the shrimp and stir until bright pink and almost fully cooked, about 3 minutes. Remove the skillet from the heat and scoop the shrimp into a bowl. Pour the wine into the skillet and return the pan to medium-low heat. Bring to a boil, scraping up the little brown bits that stick to the pan. Put the butter in the skillet and swirl the pan to melt the butter. Return the shrimp to the skillet and stir until they're coated with sauce and cooked through, about 2 minutes. Serve hot with boiled rice.

Mom's Fresh Ham Sunday Dinner

MAKES 12 SERVINGS, WITH LEFTOVERS

I fresh ham (about 14 pounds)

10 cloves garlic

6 sprigs fresh thyme

6 branches fresh rosemary

3 tablespoons cracked black pepper

2 tablespoons vegetable oil

Kosher salt

I large or 2 medium onions, finely chopped

2 medium carrots, finely chopped

3 tablespoons all-purpose flour

4 cups chicken stock or water

Freshly ground black pepper

1. Take the fresh ham out of the refrigerator about an hour before cooking to allow it to come to room temperature.

2. Preheat the oven to 350° F. Carefully score the ham by making long slits about I inch apart through the skin but not into the meat. Turn the ham and make more long slits, creating a crisscross of I-inch squares or diamonds in the skin. Cut only the skin; cut into the fat as little as possible and do not touch the meat.

3. Chop the garlic, thyme, and rosemary, and combine with the cracked pepper and oil. Rub this into the meaty section of the leg, and a little on the skin as well. Coat the entire leg with a very thin layer of salt. Place the leg, skin side down, in a roasting pan and put in the oven.

4. After about I hour, turn the leg and baste with the fat that has rendered into the pan. Baste the skin every 20 to 30 minutes; the last basting should take place about 20 minutes before the ham is done. (A 14-pound fresh ham will take about 3 hours to cook. Allow 15 minutes per pound if your roast is a different size.)

5. About I hour before the ham is done, sprinkle the onions and carrots around the ham. The little squares of crackling (skin) should be very crisp by the end of the roasting time.

6. Remove the fresh ham to a platter in a warm place and allow it to rest at least 30 minutes while you prepare the gravy. Pour off any excess fat, leaving about 3 tablespoons in the pan. Place the roasting pan over low heat on top of the stove. Sprinkle the flour into the pan and cook slowly for 3 to 4 minutes, stirring frequently. Add the stock, a little at a time, allowing the gravy to thicken each time before adding more. Be sure to scrape the bottom of the pan lightly to loosen up anything that is stuck there; these little particles are full of flavor. At this point the gravy can be simmered in the roasting pan or transferred to a saucepan with all the vegetables and other particles in it. Simmer for at least 20 minutes or, even better, 30 minutes. Strain through a coarse strainer and correct the seasoning with salt and pepper.

7. Stand up the ham so that the small end with the leg bone is sticking up. Carve the ham as thin as possible. Hold the blade of the knife in a slightly upward position and alternate slices from each side, working toward the bone. The bone running through the center is angled forward, so as you get toward the bottom, most of the meat will be behind the bone, not in front. When you get to this point, simply turn the ham around. Serve with the gravy on the side.

MOM'S TIP

To make delicious roast potatoes to serve with the ham, peel 2½ pounds of medium Maine potatoes and cut them into 1½-inch pieces. Spoon off 2 tablespoons of fat from the roasting pan after the ham has been roasting an hour. Grease a separate roasting pan with the fat, scatter the potatoes in the pan, and season them with salt and pepper. Roast, stirring the potatoes every 10 minutes, until golden brown and crispy, about 1 hour.

[Adapted from Jasper White's *Cooking from New England;* Harper & Row, 1989.]

NICK MALGIERI, former executive pastry chef at Windows on the World, is a 1996 inductee into the James Beard Foundation's Who's Who of Food and Beverage in America. He is the author of *Chocolate: From Simple Cookies to Extravagant Showstoppers*, which won an IACP/Julia Child Cookbook Award for best baking book of 1998 and was included in *Food & Wine* magazine's *Best of the Best* for 1998. Nick has written several other books, including *How to Bake* (recipient of a James Beard Foundation Book Award for best baking book of 1995), *Nick Malgieri's Perfect Pastry*, *Great Italian Desserts*, and *Cookies Unlimited*. His most recent book, *Perfect Cakes*, was published in 2003.

Nick
Malgieri

A graduate of the Culinary Institute of America, Nick was voted one of the ten best pastry chefs in America by *Chocolatier* and *Pastry Art and Design* magazines in 1998 and 1999. Currently, Nick directs the baking program at the Institute of Culinary Education (formerly Peter Kump's New York Cooking School) and frequently serves as a guest teacher at many cooking schools. Nick's recipes have been published in *The New York Times*, *Cuisine*, *Restaurant Business*, *Family Circle*, *McCall's*, *Ladies' Home Journal*, and other magazines and newspapers. His monthly column, "Ask the Baker," is syndicated throughout the United States by the *Los Angeles Times*. Nick has appeared on local television throughout the United States as well as on all the national morning shows. Other television credits include appearances with Julia Child on *Baking with Julia*, with Martha Stewart, and with Vincent Schiavelli in the PBS series *The Chefs of Cucina Amore*.

⁓

G rowing up in our Newark, New Jersey, neighborhood in the 1950s, I was immersed in a completely Italian world. My grandmother, Clotilde LoConte, lived with us and did most of the cooking. Dinner almost always started out with a *minestra*, or first course. Sometimes it was string beans in tomato sauce, or broccoli or cabbage cooked in oil and garlic. Other times the *minestra* was a pasta or simple soup, such as dandelions or chicory cooked in broth, or a version made with broccoli rabe that I describe in the recipe that follows. It was the "American" foods like meat loaf—which my mother surrounded with potatoes and peas before baking—that seemed exotic to us.

My mother, Antoinette, didn't start cooking until she was in her forties. She worked as a lining maker in the garment industry but always had dinner on the table every night within a few hours of getting home from work. I don't think my grandmother taught her any specific dishes; she just picked up good cooking from being around it all her life. The funny thing is how much my mother's food tasted like my grandmother's. It's very rare that two people cook the same dish and get the same results.

My mother and grandmother made certain things on certain days. Of course, Fridays for Catholics in that era meant fish. Sunday dinner was macaroni with what Italian Americans called "gravy"—a big pot of tomato sauce filled with sausages, meatballs, and a variety of meats such as veal knuckle, beef chuck, and beef or pork *braciole*—thin cutlets rolled around stuffing and tied into neat bundles. There was even a *braciola di cotica*, which was a square of pork skin with some of the fat left on that was rolled around Parmesan cheese, chopped parsley, raisins, and pine nuts. Delicious. Monday was always chicken soup and veal cutlets. Tuesday we had the leftover macaroni from Sunday.

But then there were the holidays. Christmas Eve at our house—like most Italian-American households—meant seafood: pasta with crab sauce, fried fish fillets, baked lobster and *baccalà* among them. Christmas day we had soup and a big pasta course followed by, believe it or not, a full turkey dinner with stuffing, cranberry sauce—the works.

Here are a few recipes I remember from my childhood meals and ones that I still enjoy today. I hope you enjoy them as well.

Peperoni a Giambotella

BELL PEPPERS IN TOMATO SAUCE

This is a great side dish or sandwich condiment: bell peppers stewed in a garlic-scented tomato sauce. If you'd like to double or triple the recipe, rub the pepper strips lightly with olive oil and bake instead of frying them for the initial cooking. MAKES 4 SIDE-DISH SERVINGS

4 large green bell peppers	One 8-ounce can tomato sauce
1/3 cup olive oil	1/2 teaspoon dried oregano
2 cloves garlic, peeled	Salt

I. Rinse and halve the peppers. Pull the cores, seeds, and stems from the pepper halves and discard them. Cut the peppers into 1-inch strips.

2. Heat half of the oil in a wide skillet over medium heat and add the peppers. Cook, tossing frequently, until they are softened and beginning to color, about 10 minutes. Remove from the pan with a slotted spoon.

3. Add the remaining oil and the garlic to the pan and cook until the garlic is golden, about 4 minutes. Scoop the garlic from the pan with a slotted spoon and discard it. Remove the pan from the heat and let the oil cool slightly.

4. Return the pan to low heat and add the tomato sauce, oregano, and salt to taste. Cook for about 15 minutes, or until the oil rises to the top.

5. Stir in the peppers and cook until tender, about 15 minutes. Serve hot, warm, at room temperature, or cold.

Pasta e Piselli

PASTA AND PEAS

This is definitely a southern Italian interpretation of this dish, of which many versions exist throughout Italy. MAKES 3 OR 4 SMALL FIRST-COURSE SERVINGS

3 tablespoons olive oil	2 cups frozen petite peas
I small onion, peeled and thinly sliced	Salt and pepper
One 8-ounce can tomato sauce	8 ounces thin pasta, such as linguini fini or spaghettini, broken in fourths
I sprig parsley	

1. Heat the oil in a saucepan over medium heat. Add the onion and cook over low heat until the onion has softened and just begins to color, about 6 minutes. Add the tomato sauce and parsley, and bring to a simmer. Cook over low heat until the oil rises to the surface, about 15 minutes. Remove and discard the parsley.

2. Add the peas, season with salt and pepper, and cook over low heat about 10 minutes.

3. Meanwhile, cook the pasta in boiling salted water, until almost *al dente*. Drain the pasta and add it to the sauce and peas along with enough pasta cooking water to make the sauce the consistency of a thin soup, about 1½ cups.

4. Simmer the pasta in the sauce until *al dente*, about 3 minutes. Serve immediately, making sure to serve the peas with the pasta; they have a tendency to sink to the bottom.

Broccoli Rabe in Aglio e Olio

BROCCOLI RABE WITH GARLIC AND OIL

I am always mystified when I see broccoli rabe served as a hot vegetable dish with a main course or when it is served in summer. We always had it as a *minestra*, or first course, as in the recipe here. Or we cooked it quickly in boiling water and added it to a frittata or made it into a very vinegary salad. We ate broccoli rabe only during the period between the first and last frost.

Using a dried cherry pepper, which is no longer as easy to find as it once was, imparts a slightly bitter, nutty flavor to the oil, unlike the crushed red pepper, which adds heat alone. By the way, we never add salt to the water when cooking broccoli rabe. Tradition states that salt in the water intensifies the broccoli's bitterness. MAKES 6 FIRST-COURSE SERVINGS

2 bunches broccoli rabe

¼ cup olive oil

2 large cloves garlic, peeled and sliced

1 dried cherry pepper or crushed red pepper to taste

Salt

1. Bring a large pan of water to a boil. Do not salt the water.

2. Rinse and pick over the broccoli rabe, removing yellow and wilted leaves. Trim off and discard an inch from the bottom of the stems. Add the broccoli rabe to the water and return to a boil. Lower the heat and simmer gently so that the broccoli rabe doesn't break apart. Cook until just tender, about 3 minutes.

3. While the broccoli is cooking, heat the oil in a small saucepan and add the garlic and dried cherry pepper, if using. Cook until the garlic is light golden, about 3 minutes, then remove the pan from the heat.

4. Allow the oil to cool slightly (the garlic will continue coloring for a minute longer). Pour in 1 cup of the broccoli rabe cooking water and add 1 teaspoon of salt and a little crushed red pepper if the dried pepper was not used. Stir to dissolve the salt in the water.

5. Pour off all but about 1 cup of water from the broccoli rabe. Pour the broccoli rabe and liquid into a serving bowl. Add the oil and water mixture to the bowl and toss to mix. Taste for seasoning and serve with lots of crusty bread.

MOM'S TIP

If some of the broccoli rabe stems are thick, split a few inches of stem starting at the bottom and leaving the stem attached to the leaves. This will prevent the leaves from overcooking before the stems are tender.

ROSE HAS BEEN CALLED the "diva of desserts" and "the most meticulous cook who ever lived." Rose's first book, *The Cake Bible*, was the 1988 winner of the IACP/Seagram Book of the Year and the NASFT Showcase Award for the cookbook that has contributed most to educating the consumer about specialty foods. A culinary best-seller, *The Cake Bible* is currently going into its thirtieth printing. *The Pie and Pastry Bible*, published in 1998, received many kudos, including Food & Wine Books' *Best of the Best: The Best Recipes from the 25 Best Cookbooks of the Year* and Coffee & Cuisine "Best Cookbook" Award. *Rose's Christmas Cookies* was the 1990 winner of the James Beard Foundation Book Award in the dessert and baking category. Her latest book, *The Bread Bible*, was published in 2003.

Rose is a contributing editor to *Food Arts* magazine and a frequent contributor to the food pages of *The Washington Post*. She is also a popular guest on major television shows, including the *Today* show, *The Early Show*, *Martha Stewart*, *Charlie Rose*, and Food Network. An internationally known food expert, Rose also has been a featured presenter in the highly regarded Melbourne Food & Wine Festival.

Rose Levy Beranbaum

My grandmother was born Sarah Horowitz on Yom Kippur in Minsk, Russia. The daughter of a rabbi and one of eight children and two stepchildren, she was gifted intellectually, but unlike her older sister—who moved to America and became a dentist—she was not given the opportunity for higher education.

Rose Levy Beranbaum and her mother, Lillian, c. 1990.

Grandma Sarah's sister and brother, both of whom did well in America, sent for the rest of the family around 1901. My grandmother arrived in America with her family when she was sixteen years old. (Rumor has it that during the crossing an Arab sheik offered to make her number one of his ten wives. Her father, the rabbi, was unimpressed.) It's hard for me to imagine her as a young, romantic girl wooed by sheiks; I knew her as a stern, no-nonsense woman with—so I thought when I was young—amazing power. Maybe I was right. On the day she died, Big Ben stopped beating for the first time in its history. But my grandmother had a softer side, a side that loved to tell stories. We shared a room until I went away to college, so I was privy to all sorts of old-country wisdom, family stories, and tales of czarist Russia. In effect she passed on the history of our roots. I have become the family chronicler, the storyteller, and the one who remembers more about family members than they remember about themselves!

During the time my grandfather worked in Manhattan's main post office, Grandma Sarah opened a candy store to help support the family. She also cooked to feed the family. If by chance something she prepared tasted good, she had no objection, but the goal of Grandma Sarah's time in the kitchen was no-nonsense nourishment. So it always struck me as odd, if not outright contradictory to her stern character, that she would occasionally take valuable time to make rock candy, a confection made by adding string to sugar dissolved in water. When done right, the sugar transmutes into large, transparent crystals that resemble chunks of quartz and cling to the string.

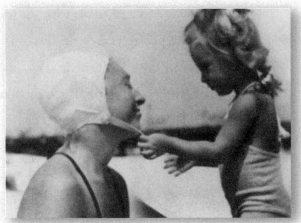

Rose Levy Beranbaum and her mother.

My mother, Lillian, contracted polio at three years of age and needed countless operations, resulting in permanent disabilities. But like all the women in our family, she was feisty. She was feisty enough as a young girl to use her crutches to defend her older brother against other children who threatened him and to go on to attain a full scholarship to Cornell University. After Cornell she attended Pitt dental school in Rochester, where she was the only woman, and did postgraduate work at Tufts in Boston. Mother became an orthodontist and dentist, and never did any cooking until her retirement, when, much to my astonishment, she exhibited a great talent for home cooking.

I offer you a recipe from each of these remarkable women and one for rock candy—my tribute to my dear grandma Sarah.

Rock Candy

One day as a young girl I watched my grandmother lower what appeared to be string into a saucepan full of the sugar solution she used to make rock candy. I idly asked her what she was doing. "Adding dental floss" was the succinct, put-an-end-to-the-discussion reply. This grabbed my attention. "Why dental floss?" I queried. "Vell," she said in her endearing Yiddish accent that I grew up believing all grandmothers had, "I neeted schtring to make it vurk ahnd dere's zo much dental fluss arunt." I roared with laugher. There she was, mother of a dentist, making the sort of candy that is designed to dissolve very slowly in the mouth—a surefire tooth rotter—using dental floss, the very purpose of which is to help prevent tooth decay. The irony eluded her, however, and I laughed alone.

A few years ago I decided to make rock candy for the holidays for the first time. My cookbook library contains well over seven hundred books, but specific rock candy instructions appeared in only one—a book that had never let me down. The instructions were quite detailed, and soon I was visualizing neat rods of rock candy just like my grandmother's. But to make a long story short, it took several weeks and twenty pounds of sugar to get it right. My husband saved the day when he suddenly remembered that during his one and only attempt at making rock candy, he first dipped the strings in the syrup and then rolled them in sugar before resubmerging them in syrup. Apparently the undissolved sugar speeds up the crystallization process.

All those years I had assumed that rock candy was very easy to make because if it hadn't been, Grandma would not have taken the trouble. But as with many things, I guess, it's easy if you know what you're doing. I finally realized it must have been one of the things she learned as the owner of a candy store. (Another unexplored irony.)

I recounted the above story to my father, who was then reminded of a drink from his childhood called "rock and rye." It was administered by *his* grandmother for colds and contained rye whiskey with rock candy. These days I wouldn't dream of sucking rock candy. My plan is to offer the swizzle sticks to company as a festive way to stir sugar into coffee. And if I get a cold, I just might try the rock and rye! MAKES 4 ROCK CANDY COFFEE STIRRERS

4 wooden skewers or ⅛-inch wooden sticks	**I cup water**
2½ cups sugar, plus more for the skewers	

I. Wipe the skewers with a damp paper towel. Dip in sugar to coat about 3 inches of one end. Set aside.

2. In a small saucepan, stir together the sugar and water until all the sugar is moistened and most of it is dissolved. Bring to a boil over medium heat, stirring constantly. Be careful not to allow any sugar crystals to form on the sides of the pan. If they do, wet a pastry brush and brush them back into the solution. Stop stirring as soon as the mixture starts to boil. Pour into a 4-cup glass measure. Insert the sugar-coated skewers in the syrup so they are not touching each other and set the measure aside, undisturbed, for about I week. When the skewers are coated with translucent sugar crystals, remove them from the syrup and dry on lightly greased racks.

Grandma Sarah's Lamb and Prune Stew
(Pressure Cooker Method)

This unusual combination of lamb and prune is so succulent and flavorful that it has always been one of my favorite recipes. The truth is, Grandma came up with it as a way to get the family to eat prunes. Although it was originally a stew, I like to boil down the liquid and juices until just enough remains to glaze the lamb and potatoes. Another enrichment I've made is the optional addition of ruby port.

Grandma simmered the meat in a large pot on top of the stove for what seemed like hours, but in the pressure cooker it cooks to a perfection of melting tenderness in only thirty minutes.   MAKES 6 TO 8 SERVINGS

3 tablespoons all-purpose flour

I tablespoon salt

¼ teaspoon freshly ground black pepper

2 large pinches of cayenne pepper

5 to 6 pounds lamb shanks, cut into 2- to 3-inch pieces

3 tablespoons vegetable oil

3 cups thinly sliced onions

1½ cups thinly sliced celery, including the leaves

3 cloves garlic, minced

27 ounces pitted prunes (4½ cups firmly packed)

I tablespoon fresh thyme

I large bay leaf

1½ cups water

½ cup ruby port or extra water

21 to 24 small (1½-inch diameter) red-skin potatoes or 6 larger ones (about 2 pounds), scrubbed and cut in half

I. In a gallon-size plastic bag, combine the flour, salt, black pepper, and cayenne pepper, and shake to mix. Add a few pieces of the lamb and shake to coat with the flour mixture. Remove the coated lamb to a baking sheet and repeat until all the lamb pieces are coated. If any of the flour mixture remains, set it aside.

2. Heat a large, heavy frying pan, preferably cast-iron, until hot. Add I tablespoon of the oil, and when a film appears on the oil, add only as much lamb as

will fit without crowding. Brown the lamb on all sides, in batches, over medium-high heat, adding more oil as necessary to keep the lamb from sticking. Remove the lamb to a bowl and set aside.

3. Pour any remaining oil into the same pan. Add the onions and celery, and cook until the onions are golden brown, about 8 minutes. Sprinkle any remaining flour mixture over the vegetables, stir in the garlic, and cook, stirring, for about 30 seconds. Spoon the mixture into the pressure cooker. Top with the lamb, about one-third of the prunes, the thyme, and bay leaf.

4. Return the pan to the heat and pour in about half of the water. Bring to a boil, scraping up the brown bits from the pan. Add the pan liquid along with the remaining water and port to the pressure cooker.

5. Cook at full pressure for 20 minutes. Release the pressure and check for doneness. The meat should be tender but not falling off the bone. If necessary, return the pot to the heat, and after it reaches full pressure, cook for another 5 to 10 minutes. Meanwhile, steam the potatoes about 20 minutes or just until tender, then peel them if desired.

6. Release the pressure and, using a skimmer, remove the meat to a large serving plate and cover with aluminum foil to keep warm. Tilt the pan and skim off any fat from the top of the liquid. Mash the cooked prunes into the liquid and add the remaining prunes and the cooked potatoes.

7. Bring to a boil and, stirring often, reduce the liquid until very thick, about 5 to 10 minutes. Spoon the potatoes and prunes onto the meat, plus any remaining sauce for a rich burnished color and fabulous flavor.

8. Serve with syrah or zinfandel (although Grandma certainly didn't).

Traditional Method

Increase the water to 4 cups. Proceed as above, but after bringing to a boil, lower the heat and simmer, partly covered, for 1 hour, or until the meat is almost completely tender. Add the potatoes and the remaining prunes and cook 30 minutes more, until the potatoes are tender.

Reducing the liquid will take about 15 minutes.

Mom's Healthful but Delicious Coleslaw

When I was growing up, "good for you" invariably applied to things I did not want to eat. There were, however, a few exceptions to my reluctance to eat healthy foods, the main one being our family's special version of coleslaw, invented by my grandmother, who lived with us and did the cooking. Rather than the usual creamy dressing, it was prepared with equal parts of freshly squeezed lemon juice and oil. It wouldn't be the same without the minced garlic, and in recent years my mother's much appreciated additions were both currants, for little bursts of sweetness, and chopped avocado, which adds a slight creaminess and lusciousness of flavor. Two generations removed, my cousin Alexandra Bush now makes the coleslaw with red cabbage, which has a more assertive flavor and a beautiful color, combined with carrots.

Years ago I bought my mother a food processor to ease the preparation by speeding the grating of the cabbage and carrots. She tried it several times, but we all agreed that the hand grating added something to the texture. She returned to the old way, and I breathed a sigh of relief.

When I was a child, this coleslaw often accompanied family meals, and we all enjoyed it on top of buttered rye bread. But because it was such a family favorite, it always appeared (and still does) at all holiday dinners as well. Its savory freshness and lightness in face of all the heavier fare makes it an ideal side dish.

Any leftover coleslaw is still delicious, though less crisp, the following day, but that's the storage limit once the dressing has been added. (I know because I always went home with a jar of the leftover slaw, which traditionally went onto sandwiches made with rye bread.) I guess I must have grown up; the fact that it's healthful actually pleases me now.   MAKES 6 SERVINGS

3 cups (10 ounces) cabbage, shredded with a knife or 4 mm Cuisinart slicing disc

4 medium carrots (about 5 ounces), coarsely shredded (about 1½ cups)

½ cup chopped green pepper

¼ cup dried currants

¼ cup olive oil, preferably light

¼ cup freshly squeezed lemon or lime juice

1 large clove garlic, minced (about 1½ teaspoons)

½ cup diced avocado (optional)

1.   Place the cabbage, carrots, green pepper, and currants in a large bowl. Measure the oil and juice into a glass measuring cup, add the garlic, and mix lightly. Pour on top of the cabbage mixture and toss to combine. Add the avocado and toss lightly.

2.   Cover tightly and refrigerate for at least 1 hour before serving. The coleslaw is best eaten the same day.

MOM'S TIPS

The vegetable mixture, except for the avocado, can be prepared several hours ahead.

Don't be tempted to make a garlic-free version. Professed garlic haters ignore it and go for the one with the garlic!

CHRIS STYLER, experienced chef, restaurant consultant, and author, has more than twenty-five years of experience in the food world. Chris grew up in Clark, New Jersey, watching family and friends cook, and turned his fascination with food into a career. Chris's love for food has taken him to the test kitchens of *Cuisine* and *Food & Wine*, to restaurants in Italy for study, and all across North and South America for consultation, menu design, and food journalism.

Chris was the chef of Metro C.C. in Manhattan and the Black Dog Tavern on Martha's Vineyard. He was also the chef/owner of Blue Collar Food, a Manhattan-based catering company.

Author of *Primi Piatti*, a cookbook of Italian first courses, and *Smokin'*, a guide to home-smoked foods, Chris is also the coauthor of two books, *Sylvia's Soul Food* with Sylvia Woods and *Blue Collar Food* with Bill Hodge. Chris's most recent publishing projects were collaborating on *Lidia's Italian-American Kitchen*, written by Lidia Matticchio Bastianich (recipient of the IACP Award for Best Cookbook, Chef and Restaurant Category), and recipe development and testing for *The Mushroom Lover's Mushroom Cookbook*, written by Amy Farges. Additionally, Chris has written for a variety of publications that include *Family Circle*, *Woman's Day*, *New York* magazine, New York *Daily News*, *Good Food*, and *Food Arts*. In January 1999, he was named editor-at-large for *Food Arts* magazine.

In the last five years, Chris has served as culinary producer/chef for five PBS television series: *Lidia's Italian Table* and *Lidia's Italian-American Kitchen* (airing from Fall 1998 through Winter 2004); *Julia and Jacques: Cooking at Home* (Fall 1999); *Savor the Southwest* (Spring 1999); and *America's Test Kitchen* (Spring 2001). On the other side of the camera, Chris has had numerous appearances on *Good Morning America*, *The Rosie O'Donnell Show*, *Good Day New York*, *Our Home*, and *The Home Show*.

Chris graduated cum laude from the Culinary Division of Johnson & Wales University in Providence, Rhode Island, and is currently at work on two cookbooks as well as keeping active in television production.

~~~

I don't know how she did it. There were five of us kids, with the three oldest—all boys—into just about every kind of trouble you can imagine. (Either my two younger sisters were not as badly behaved as we were, or by that time my parents were too exhausted to probe into their daily routines and turn up evidence of wrongdoing.)

My mother—"Babe" to anyone who has known her longer than five minutes—instilled a sense of responsibility in us at an early stage. Age-appropriate chores were assigned, starting with dusting around age six and moving on to laundry as soon as we could reach the dial on the washer. Preschool breakfast was pretty much a free-for-all, where the competition was tough and the last Pop-Tart went to the strongest. It worked. We all had and kept jobs by the time we were twelve or thirteen. Today my sister, who is raising four kids—five if you count her husband—holds

Chris Styler, center, with his sister, Beth Ann, on his lap; his brother, Richie, on the left; and his mom in the chair.

down a demanding job for her local watershed association and volunteers at a foster home.

But when it came to cooking, it was my mother's show all the way. If fact, we were "encouraged" not to hang around the kitchen while she was doing her thing. There were occasional forays into the exotic, but usually it was a meat-and-potatoes kind of household: Excellent pot roast and dumplings prepared in an ancient cast-aluminum Dutch oven with a glass lid; porcupine meatballs (the grains of rice that protruded were supposed to be the quills); and chicken soup were in heavy rotation. Generally speaking, my mother steered clear of the Italian specialties her mother turned out day after day. Why compete with the master? But she did make a mean eggplant parmigiana. I can still picture her standing at the stove, frying two pans of breaded eggplant slices, with brown paper bags arranged on the side for draining the eggplant after it came out of the pan.

Between the exercise classes and the day trips, my mother doesn't cook much anymore, but we can still get her to turn out a pot roast with dumplings or a pot of soup from time to time—if we're lucky.

Babe's Potato Salad

This is one of the simplest recipes you'll come across for potato salad, but it is also one of the best. The secret for success lies in peeling the potatoes *after* they're cooked, so they don't get waterlogged. My father once told me—when I was young enough to believe him—that he had a hard time deciding whether to marry Sophia Loren or my mother. In the end, he said, my mother's potato salad was what swayed him. Sorry, Sophia. MAKES 6 SERVINGS

4 Idaho potatoes (about 2½ pounds)

I small yellow onion, finely diced (about 3¼ cup)

2 stalks celery, trimmed, washed, and finely diced (about I cup)

I cup Hellmann's mayonnaise

I teaspoon white vinegar

Salt

Freshly ground pepper

I. Scrub the potatoes well and put them in a 4- or 5-quart pot. Pour in enough water to cover them by at least 3 inches. Bring to a boil over high heat, then adjust the heat so the water is at a gentle boil. Cook until they are tender at the center when poked with a knife, about 35 minutes. Scoop them out with a slotted spoon and cool to room temperature.

2. Scrape off the skins with a butter knife and cut the potatoes into I-inch pieces. Toss the potatoes and the onion, celery, mayonnaise, vinegar, salt, and pepper in a medium bowl until the potatoes are coated. If the mayonnaise is too thick to evenly coat the potatoes, add I or 2 tablespoons of water. Cover and refrigerate at least a few hours. This is better the next day.

Cream Puffs

For years my mother brought a batch of these to every family gathering, party, and barbecue she went to. This eventually prompted one of the kids to say, "Ma, enough with the cream puffs already," every time she reached for the mixing bowl. Double batches required someone to come into the kitchen and relieve her of the stirring after the fifth or sixth egg. Once, about twenty-two years ago, I persuaded her to make the dough in a food processor. Although there was no discernible difference in the dough, she still hasn't forgiven me for what she saw as a breach in her code of ethics. Neither was she impressed when I pointed out that *pâte à choux*, which is what the dough is called in French, is one of the staples of classic pastry making. It can be transformed into éclairs, made into miniature puffs for a soup garnish, or, with the addition of Gruyère cheese, turned into *gougères*. To her this was and always will be cream puff dough.   MAKES ABOUT 24

I stick (8 tablespoons) unsalted butter

½ teaspoon salt

I cup sifted unbleached all-purpose flour

4 large eggs

2 cans evaporated milk

2 packages vanilla pudding, *not* instant

Confectioners' sugar

1.   Preheat the oven to 450° F. If you are not using a nonstick baking sheet, coat your baking sheet with nonstick cooking spray or line it with a sheet of parchment paper.

2.   Bring the butter, salt, and I cup of water to a boil in a heavy medium saucepan. Remove it from the heat and add the flour all at once. Stir vigorously until the flour is incorporated and the mixture is smooth. Return the pan to the heat and stir for a minute or so, until the mixture leaves the sides of the pan. Scrape the

dough into a mixing bowl and beat for 1 or 2 minutes to cool it slightly. Add the eggs, 1 at a time, beating vigorously after each one. Use the pastry right after making it.

3.   Drop the batter by rounded tablespoonfuls onto the baking sheet to form 12 rounds, each about 1½ inches in diameter. Set the baking sheet on the oven rack, lower the heat to 350° F, and bake until puffed and golden brown, about 20 minutes. The pastries should feel very light when you lift one from the sheet. Cool the puffs completely on a wire rack.

4.   While the pastries are baking and cooling, make the filling: Pour the evaporated milk into a 4-cup glass measure. Pour in enough cold water to measure 3¾ cups of liquid. Pour into a heavy saucepan and stir in the pudding mix. Bring to a boil, stirring often. Scrape into a bowl, apply a piece of plastic wrap directly to the surface to prevent a skin from forming, and chill in the refrigerator.

5.   Split the cooled puffs in half horizontally. Pull out any dough from the halves and mound a heaping tablespoonful of the chilled pudding in the bottom half. Top with the other half and sprinkle with the sugar.

Spinach and Sun-dried Tomato Strata

Strata is the perfect dish when you're having guests for brunch because it must be made ahead. If you keep the proportion of bread, milk, and eggs more or less the same, you can add just about anything you like. Make sure, though, that the ingredients aren't too wet, or the eggs won't set. MAKES 6 SERVINGS

One 10-ounce bag spinach, stemmed

2 tablespoons olive oil

1 medium yellow onion, finely diced (about 1 cup)

Salt

Freshly ground pepper

½ cup soaked, drained, and finely chopped sun-dried tomatoes

6 cups 1-inch day-old bread cubes

3 cups milk

7 eggs

½ teaspoon ground nutmeg

2 cups (about 6 ounces) shredded Monterey Jack cheese

1. Fill a sink with cool water, add the spinach, and swish it around gently. Allow the grit to settle to the bottom of the sink, then scoop out the spinach to a colander. Drain the spinach thoroughly or, better yet, spin it dry in a salad spinner. Stack several of the leaves and cut them into ½-inch strips. Cut the rest of the spinach this way.

2. Heat the oil in a large skillet over medium heat. Stir in the onion and cook, stirring, just until it begins to brown, about 10 minutes. Scatter a big handful of the spinach into the pan and stir until wilted. Add the remaining spinach in batches, waiting for it to wilt before adding the next, until all the spinach is in the pan. Season very lightly with salt and pepper. Stir in the tomatoes and cook until the spinach is tender, about 2 minutes. Drain in a colander, squeezing lightly to remove excess liquid.

3. Coat a 9 × 11-inch baking dish with nonstick cooking spray. Spread the bread cubes on the bottom of the dish, and top with an even layer of spinach and

onions. Beat the milk, eggs, I teaspoon of salt, ½ teaspoon of pepper, and the nutmeg together in a bowl until smooth. Pour the egg mixture into the baking dish, cover the dish with plastic wrap, and refrigerate at least 6 hours, or as long as overnight.

4.   Bring the strata to room temperature 30 minutes before baking and preheat the oven to 350° F. Sprinkle the cheese evenly over the spinach. Bake until the center is firm and a knife inserted in the center comes out clean, about 40 minutes. Let stand 15 to 20 minutes before cutting into squares and serving.

Tuesday Night Meatball Soup

My mother usually served this soup with what was known in our house as "Mary." (Don't ask.) You make Mary by frying onions and potatoes lightly in oil and butter until tender, then adding some of the reserved chicken meat from step four of this recipe at the last minute. Serve the Mary along with the soup, and either mix it into each bowl or eat it separately.   MAKES 8 SERVINGS

FOR THE MEATBALLS

¼ cup finely chopped fresh Italian parsley leaves

1 egg

2 tablespoons grated Romano cheese

½ teaspoon kosher salt

Freshly ground black pepper

8 ounces ground beef or a mix of ground beef and ground pork

FOR THE SOUP

3 cups homemade or canned chicken broth

3 cups water

2 large carrots, peeled, trimmed, and cut into ½-inch rounds

2 celery ribs, trimmed and sliced

Half of a 3-pound chicken, cut into 4 pieces

1 cup alphabet, tubettini, or orzo pasta

1 cup diced fresh or canned Italian tomatoes

Grated Romano cheese

1.   To make the meatballs: Beat the parsley, egg, cheese, salt, and pepper together in a mixing bowl until the egg is well beaten. Crumble the ground meat into the bowl and mix everything together until blended. Chill the mixture for 4 hours or as long as overnight.

2.   To make the soup: Heat the broth, water, carrots, and celery in a 5-quart sauce pot over high heat until boiling. Add the chicken pieces and return to a boil. Adjust the heat so the liquid is simmering, and cook, skimming the surface occa-

sionally, until the chicken is cooked through, about 40 minutes. Scoop the chicken pieces onto a plate and let them cool.

3.   Meanwhile, form the meatball mixture into ¾-inch meatballs, rolling them smooth between your palms. Cover with plastic wrap and refrigerate if you're not using them right away.

4.   Pick the meat from the chicken bones and finely shred it. Add as much or as little as you like to the soup. (The soup can be prepared to this point up to 2 days in advance. Bring it back to a simmer before continuing.) Adjust the heat so the soup is at a gentle boil and stir in the pasta, tomatoes, and meatballs. Cook, gently stirring often, until the pasta is tender and the meatballs are cooked through, about 8 minutes. Ladle into warm soup bowls and pass the grated cheese separately.

JEREMIAH TOWER is one of America's foremost authorities on food and restaurant hospitality. He was born in the United States, educated in Australia, at England's King's College, at Harvard College (B.A.), and at the Harvard Graduate School of Design (master's in architecture), and he has an honorary master's degree from the Culinary Institute of America.

Jeremiah
Tower

He began his culinary career as chef and co-owner of Chez Panisse in Berkeley, California. After running several other successful and highly acclaimed restaurants from 1984 to 1998 in San Francisco (Stars, Stars Café, Speedo 690), Hong Kong (The Peak Café), Singapore (Stars), and Seattle (Stars), Jeremiah moved to New York to pursue new projects, including new books, a website, and television shows. Jeremiah has written several cookbooks, including in 1980 the thirty volumes of *The Good Cook* with Richard Olney and Time-Life Books. In 1986 he published the very successful *Jeremiah Tower's New American Classics. Jeremiah Tower Cooks* and *California Dish*—a book on the history of the American dining revolution that started in California—were published in 2002 and 2003, respectively. *America's Best Chefs with Jeremiah Tower*, the companion book for Tower's 26-episode series on PBS, was released in 2003. In addition to his own series, he has appeared in the PBS series *Julia Child's Cooking with Master Chefs* and on *Good Morning America* (ABC) and *CBS This Morning* as well as *The Late Show with David Letterman*.

Awards include the 1993 Regional Best Chef: California by the James Beard Foundation, the prestigious James Beard Foundation's Who's Who of Food and Beverage in America, as well as the 1994 USA Chef of the Year by Chefs in America, and the Outstanding Chef in America by the James Beard Foundation Awards in 1996.

Jeremiah currently lives in Manhattan and Italy.

Three Cods and Three Mothers

MOTHER

Yesterday I found again a little cookbook belonging to my mother, Margaret.

Jeremiah Tower and his aunt just before he started cooking professionally, 1971.

Found again in that I have read it many times before, but it is so thin—only forty-five pages long and less than ¼ inch thick—that it gets lost for years at a time in my cookbooks. It is a book on cod.

La Morue was printed in Paris in 1958 by the Comité de Propagande pour la Consommation de la Morue, which must have been the French equivalent of the American Beef Council.

Flipping through the book I was amazed to see my father's handwriting on one of the recipes. I should not say "amazed," since he was a passionate (rare, weekend, single-dish) cook, as were my mother, sister, brother, and I. There is his written-in translation of *mijoter* as "simmer," of *mouiller* as "moisten." This was all under the recipe for *Bouillabaisse de Morue Fecampoise*, and he took the liberty of adding leeks to the list of ingredients.

But it is the handwriting of my mother on the inside cover that really intrigues me, not just personally and historically but because the recipe includes, along with the title, the note "Sunday Times by ED." I fantasize now that this does not mean my mother is quoting the editor of the *Times* but that it was Elizabeth David who wrote the article on cod. Elizabeth did write for the *Times* when she wasn't furious with it and sending off stuff to the *Observer* or *Vogue* instead. And certainly I made *brandade de morue* for her a couple of times in London while we drank my expensive cache of Condrieu.

Jeremiah Tower's mother, Margaret, in London, sometime in the 1950s.

My mother adored salt cod in all shapes and presentations. The first recipe she wrote down was the Elizabeth David recipe, *Brandade de Morue de Nîmes* (a town my parents were always driving off to from London for the food and the excuse to pass by and stop at La Pyramide in Vienne and the Côte d'Or in Saulieu), and the second was hers.

My Home-style Salt Cod

"Soak fish. Cut in pieces. Put in a marinade of olive oil and wine vinegar, a pinch of pepper and nutmeg, a sliced Brittany [sweet red] onion, and minced parsley. Marinate 12 hours. Drain. Roll each piece in flour, dip in beaten egg, roll in white bread crumbs, and fry lightly in oil. Drain and dust with parsley and serve with creamed potatoes.

"Serve with vin de Langlade."

I have no idea what *vin de Langlade* is, but it is probably not as expensive as Condrieu. Lapping up the white wine would have given my mother an appetite for the second recipe she wrote down: Elizabeth David's salt cod.

ELIZABETH DAVID

I have hardly ever been as happy as when having lunch with Elizabeth David, not so much because of the restaurants of choice, in which anything could go wrong and the hours could be filled with more distressed "oh dears" (when talking about Richard Olney, James Beard, or Alice Waters) than eating, but the conversations—which would come to life after the second bottle of wine and continue until she called it quits in her Chelsea kitchen at around seven in the evening—were spectacular. As was the brandade we fixed one day, taken to new heights by the addition of some fresh black truffles.

Brandade de Morue de Nîmes

Here it is for 2 pounds of salt cod to serve 5 to 7 people:

"Soak salt cod 12 hours. Cut in pieces and bring to a boiling point. Drain. Bring to a boiling point. Drain and pound morue to a paste. As you do this, add, drop by drop, warmed olive oil alternately with the same quantity of warm milk or, better still, cream. Turn constantly until the consistency of potato puree. Pepper to taste, add a squeeze of lemon juice and a mashed clove of garlic. Reheat gently, put in a hot dish, and garnish with small triangles of bread fried in butter and olive oil—or in vol au vents. Serve with pickled black olives and a bottle of vin de Langlade."

Elizabeth would have approved of my aunt (they were both very beautiful when young as well as older) and her cooking, even if she would have thought the Russian emerald parure and huge ring worn at lunch were a bit over the top.

MY AUNT MARY ZAKHARTCHENKO

By the time I was sixteen, my parents felt I could hold down a kitchen of my own, so one summer when my mother left for the United States, my father and I decided to spend that time in our Knightsbridge (London) mews flat. It was my job to cook, so my Washington, D.C., aunt (the one married to the Russian space scientist) wrote constantly with cooking advice: "Take a cut-up bird..." and so on. The most challenging recipe was one for fresh cod, Russian style, meaning French, since that is what those aristocrats spoke and ate. Here is the dish she made for Count Cheremetev, Prince Youssupov's childhood friend and my pal (when I was a teenager)—the crown prince of Poland.

Codfish à la Highlife

"Make a brunoise of the white of 3 leeks, 1 onion, 1 carrot, a small heart of celery, 2 skinned, seeded, and chopped tomatoes, a clove of garlic, salt, and pepper. Moisten with a little water, cover, and let sit on low heat to gently steam for 10 minutes, or until the vegetables start to get soft.

"Put a whole small and trimmed codfish that has been boned through the back à la Colbert into the pan. Pour in ¼ cup Loire dry wine and 1 cup of mussel stock. Cover and poach for 20 minutes, or until the fish is barely cooked through.

"Remove the fish and keep warm. Strain the cooking juices and reduce by half. Add 1 cup of heavy cream and reduce again until syrupy. Drain and set the fish in a bed of very rich mashed potatoes (half butter and cream). Chop fresh black truffles and add to the cream. Spoon the truffles into the cavity of the fish and then the sauce over the fish."

My aunt told me that there were supposed to be crawfish tails with the truffles, which ended up also inside the fish, but she said, "Where would I find those as fresh as the fish and the truffles?"

JOAN NATHAN is the author of award-winning cookbooks and the host of the acclaimed PBS series *Jewish Cooking in America with Joan Nathan*. Joan is an internationally recognized expert on food culture and a recent inductee into the James Beard Foundation's Who's Who of Food and Beverage in America.

Joan
Nathan

With a master's degree in French literature from Michigan, Joan took a job as foreign press officer to Jerusalem mayor Teddy Kollek, a leader who often combined meetings and meals. The experience inspired her to write her first book, *The Flavor of Jerusalem*. In 1994 she published *Jewish Cooking in America*, an instant classic that received numerous accolades from organizations, including a Cookbook of the Year Award from the International Association of Culinary Professionals and the Best American Cookbook of the Year Award given by the James Beard Foundation. Her newest book, *The Foods of Israel Today*, contains recipes from Jewish, Christian, and Muslim traditions.

A founder of New York's Ninth Avenue Food Festival, Nathan has appeared on TV programs ranging from *Today* to *Martha Stewart*. In 1995 she received the Golda Award from the American Jewish Congress for her creative contributions to the quality of life in Washington, D.C., and an honorary doctorate from the Spertus Institute of Jewish Culture in Chicago.

Jewish Cooking in America with Joan Nathan, of which Nathan is both host and executive producer, is her second national television project. The first was the award-winning *Passover: Traditions of Freedom,* which debuted on public television in March 1994.

Joan Nathan and her mom, Pearl.

My mother, Pearl Nathan, learned to cook late in life. When I was growing up in Larchmont, New York, we had a wonderful housekeeper, Susan Marbry, who lived with us and cooked for us. In what my mother refers to as her "prenuptial agreement," cooking was very definitely ruled out.

But even so, Mom had a few things in her repertoire. On the maid's day off she'd make the most delicious beef stew ever, the way her mother taught her. The smell of that stew cooking still brings back taste memories for me. And I remember delicious open-topped plum pies. She always made Thanksgiving dinner, too. (Actually, it was probably the maid who prepared it, but I know my mother's hand was very much in it.) We'd pack the whole thing up in a picnic basket and drive to my grandparents' apartment on Central Park South to watch the Macy's Thanksgiving Parade.

When my mother was around fifty, my father had a business downturn, and we lost our housekeeper. All of a sudden Mom had to learn how to cook, and my mother, being the tough cookie she is, just got down to business. She started out making her mother's roast chicken—simple and good—with lots of garlic and paprika. Then she started experimenting, making such things as chicken cacciatore and cooking her way through the *Settlement Cookbook.*

My mother, like her mother, who was a milliner, was very good with her hands. I think of that still when I prepare the plum tarts we made together when I was young. I get very calm, laying the fruit on one piece at a time. Making things like that is how I still commune with her.

At ninety my mother is still a great cook. She makes her own pickles, grows her own herbs and tomatoes, and cooks almost every day. When she cooks, she celebrates each meal, turning it into an event—something I learned from her. My mother always sits down to each meal, and she has some pretty tough standards.

Joan Nathan and her mom, more recently.

Even for a simple meal the table is beautifully set, the flowers gorgeous.

We're different kinds of cooks, my mother and I. She likes to be completely set up in advance, before she starts to cook. I like the process and don't mind if things get chaotic in the kitchen. My mother always tells me there's too much chaos in my life. Of course, she's right.

I'm spoiled. Here she is, ninety, and we still expect her to cook for us. And she does. She finds "early bird" dinners at restaurants boring and would much rather cook at home. I mean, this is a woman who plays nine holes of golf most days. She doesn't give up and never whines about needing attention. She keeps going with the details of life. And maybe that's the most important thing I've learned from her: to enjoy the "everydayness" of life.

My Mother's Franks and Sauerkraut

My mother doesn't call this cooking—it's assembling! She demonstrated this on one episode of my television show.   MAKES 6 SERVINGS

4 cups sauerkraut

2 cups canned tomatoes

½ cup brown sugar, or to taste

1 pound kosher hot dogs, cut into 1-inch pieces, or cocktail franks

Mix all the ingredients together in a heavy saucepan. Simmer, covered, for 1 hour. Adjust the seasoning and serve.

[Adapted from *Jewish Cooking in America*; Knopf, 1994.]

Joan Nathan poses with her mom.

Roast Chicken

My grandmother Martha Kops Gluck had a millinery store in New York City. Because she was busy during the day, it was my great-grandmother or a maid who did the cooking in their home. Each Friday, however, my grandmother made one dish: roast chicken. Hers is low in calories, delicious, and easy to prepare.   MAKES 6 TO 8 SERVINGS

Two 3½-pound broiler chickens, quartered

Salt

Ground pepper

Garlic, crushed, or garlic powder

Seasoning salt or a mixture of chopped fresh thyme, rosemary, and sage

Paprika

2 small onions

½ cup white wine

1.   Preheat the oven to 350° F.

2.   Season the chicken with salt, pepper, garlic, seasoning salt, and paprika to taste. Lay the pieces, skin side up, in a roasting pan.

3.   Slice the onions and lay them on top and around the chicken.

4.   Roast for 20 minutes. Turn the chicken over and roast 20 minutes more. Add a little water if the pan becomes dry. Turn the chicken over once more and roast for 20 minutes with the skin side up. Baste with the wine.

5.   If you like the skin crisp, place the chicken under the broiler before serving. Otherwise, mere basting from the drippings will add to the flavor.

[Adapted from *The Jewish Holiday Kitchen*; Schocken Books, 1998.]

Aunt Eva's Cookies

The following cookie recipe comes from my great-aunt Eva, whose parents came from Cracow. My mother made them for me as a special after-school treat. It is basically a thin pastry dough spread with jam or cocoa and cinnamon and rolled up jelly-roll or strudel fashion. After it is cooked, finger-sized cookies are cut. This cookie has its origins in the German strudel. Other fillings for this and similar doughs might include apples or cheese.

MAKES ABOUT 4 DOZEN COOKIES

12 tablespoons (1½ sticks) butter or pareve margarine, at room temperature

½ cup sugar

2 eggs

1 teaspoon vanilla extract

2½ cups unbleached all-purpose flour

1 tablespoon baking powder

Pinch of salt

1 cup apricot marmalade or 4 tablespoons cocoa, 1 teaspoon cinnamon, and 1 tablespoon sugar

> **MOM'S TIP**
>
> *The easiest way to form the rolls is to roll out the dough on a pastry cloth and then lift the edge of the cloth so that the dough rolls into a long cylinder.*

1. Using a food processor, electric mixer, or wooden spoon, cream the butter. Add the sugar and mix well. Add the eggs and vanilla. Slowly add the flour, baking powder, and salt. Knead the dough well.

2. Form the dough into 4 balls and place in the refrigerator overnight.

3. Preheat the oven to 350° F.

4. Roll each ball of dough into a flat rectangle about 10 × 6 inches and ⅛ inch thick. Spread with the marmalade or sprinkle with the cocoa mixture, dividing either evenly. Roll jelly-roll fashion, starting at one of the long ends.

5. Place 2 of the rolls on each of 2 large greased cookie sheets, leaving room between them because they will spread and flatten out. Bake about 20–30 minutes, until golden brown. When cool, slice at an angle at 1½-inch intervals, making finger-length slices.

NOTE: **If you have only 1 baking sheet, roll, fill, and bake the cookies in 2 batches.**

[Adapted from *The Jewish Holiday Kitchen*; Schocken Books, 1998.]

MARCUS SAMUELSSON, chef and co-owner of Restaurant Aquavit, was the youngest chef ever to receive a three-star restaurant review from *The New York Times*. In May of 2001, Aquavit was awarded another excellent, three-star review from *The New York Times*. In 2003, Marcus received the great honor of Best Chef: New York City from the James Beard Foundation. In 1999, the James Beard Foundation honored him as best Rising Star Chef.

In 1973, three-year-old Marcus was orphaned when his parents fell victim to a tuberculosis epidemic that raged through his Ethiopian homeland. He and his young sister found refuge at a Swedish field hospital in nearby Addis Ababa, where they were taken in by a nurse who arranged for their adoption by a young couple from Göteborg, Sweden.

Marcus, a graduate of the Culinary Institute in Göteborg, apprenticed in Switzerland and Austria before Håkan Swahn asked him to spend eight months at the newly opened Aquavit restaurant in New York. After that, Marcus spent time in the world-renowned and three-star Michelin restaurant Georges Blanc in Lyon, France.

In 1994 Marcus returned to Aquavit to work under the restaurant's new executive chef, Jan Sendel. Sadly, just eight weeks after they began working together, Sendel died unexpectedly. In May of 1995, Swahn formally appointed Marcus executive chef of Aquavit.

Marcus has been featured in *Gourmet, USA Today, Food & Wine, The New York Times,* and *Bon Appétit,* and has appeared on ABC's *Good Morning America,* Martha Stewart Living Television, CNN, Food Network, the Discovery Channel, UPN's *The Iron Chef USA,* and several New York television programs. He is also the author of two books: *En Smakresa: Middagstips Från Marcus Samuelsson,* which accompanied a series of global food-themed segments that he created for Swedish television; and *Aquavit and the New Scandinavian Cuisine.*

Active in charitable works, Marcus donates his time to the U.S. Fund for UNICEF (which helps provide support for tuberculosis initiatives in developing countries), *Gourmet* UNICEF Trick-or-Treat, and Careers Through Culinary Arts Program (C-CAP), a nonprofit organization that provides inner-city high school students with training, scholarships, and jobs in the restaurant and food service industry.

My grandmother Helga was born in Sweden when it was a very poor country. It's easy to see that those conditions shaped the way she cooked. Nothing was wasted in her kitchen, ever. From one chicken came several meals—a roasted chicken dinner, chicken with dumplings, and, finally, chicken soup. My grandparents ran a bed-and-breakfast on the west coast of Sweden, which meant a lot of hard work—in and out of the kitchen. A lot of what Mormor cooked came from her land. We had an apple tree and a plum tree and grew our own root vegetables—parsnips, carrots, beets, and potatoes. My grandmother was always in action, twelve months a year. Depending on what the season was, we foraged for mushrooms, made aquavit, pickled herring; we were always doing something.

When you're raised around hardworking people, some of that is bound to rub off on you. That kind of hard work and respect for food shaped who I am as a chef. Even though I'm cooking in very different circumstances than my grandmother did, I look at a lobster and wonder how many dishes I can get out of it. When I think about cooking a duck, I think, what can I do with the breast? Should I confit the leg? That kind of cooking not only makes economical sense in a restaurant, I believe it tastes better.

The recipes I've included here remind me very much of Mormor, and of Swedish cooking in general. Some of the things are apparent, and were always close at hand. If you wanted an apple, you went out to the tree and picked it. If you needed mint, you went to the garden and cut some. The other things, like the spices that season the chicken and rice and the cookies, aren't native but came to Sweden through the spice trade of the 1800s.

My menu at Aquavit is largely made up of dishes that spring from the very simple dishes and techniques that would have been familiar to my grandmother—traditional seafood and game dishes and pickling and preserving techniques that I learned firsthand in her kitchen. I always try to find a balance of simple food and complex flavors, like the spiciness of her chewy, flavorful ginger citrus cookies.

My grandmother passed away ten years ago, but part of her is with me every day. I connect with her through my cooking. I'm fortunate—I'm sure that if I were a lawyer or something else other than a cook, I wouldn't feel her presence so strongly with me still.

Swedish Roast Chicken with Spiced Apple Rice

This recipe comes from my grandmother, who roasted a chicken for dinner every Sunday night. The chicken is seasoned with cinnamon, cardamom, star anise, and cloves, spices that have been an important part of Swedish cuisine since the eighteenth century, when the Swedish East India Company first brought them to Sweden from Asia! The spices are used to season the apple-vegetable stuffing as well as the bird. Although some recipes call for roasting chicken at high temperatures, I prefer to cook it at 350° F so that the spices have time to penetrate the flesh inside and out with their flavors. After the chicken is cooked, the stuffing mixture of apples, sweet potato, and onion is added to hot rice, along with a spoonful of yogurt to cool and soften the spicy flavors, and served alongside the chicken.   MAKES 4 SERVINGS

FOR THE CHICKEN

1 medium sweet potato, peeled and cut into ½-inch cubes

1 large onion, cut into ½-inch cubes

2 Granny Smith apples, peeled, cored, and cut into ½-inch cubes

2 shallots, coarsely chopped

1 garlic clove, chopped

1 teaspoon fresh thyme leaves

1 tablespoon finely chopped fresh mint

2 tablespoons water

1 tablespoon olive oil

½ teaspoon ground cinnamon

2 cardamom pods or ¼ teaspoon ground cardamom

2 star anise

2 whole cloves or ⅛ teaspoon ground cloves

2 black peppercorns

4 white peppercorns (or 4 additional black peppercorns)

1 teaspoon kosher salt

One 3½-pound chicken, preferably free-range

FOR THE SPICED APPLE RICE

1 cup long-grain white rice

1 teaspoon kosher salt, or to taste

1½ tablespoons yogurt

Freshly ground black pepper

1. Preheat the oven to 350° F.

2. Blanch the sweet potato in boiling water for 2 minutes. Drain, rinse under cold water, and drain again. In a medium bowl, combine the sweet potato, onion, apples, shallots, garlic, thyme, and mint. Combine the water and olive oil and add to the vegetable mixture, tossing to coat.

3. Using a mortar and pestle, lightly crush the cinnamon, cardamom, star anise, cloves, black peppercorns, and white peppercorns with the salt. (Or combine the spices on a cutting board and crush with the bottom of a heavy pot.) Add half the spice mixture to the vegetables, and reserve the rest.

4. Rinse the chicken inside and out and pat dry with paper towels. Remove all the excess fat. Lightly stuff the bird's cavity with about half the vegetable mixture and tie its legs together with kitchen string. Place the chicken on a rack in a roasting pan and rub it all over with the reserved spice mixture. Scatter the remaining vegetable mixture around the chicken.

5. Roast for about 1½ hours, or until an instant-read thermometer inserted into the thigh reaches 160° F. After the first hour, or when the vegetables in the pan are tender, remove them from the pan and set aside in a bowl. Check the pan occasionally as the chicken roasts, adding a bit of water if it becomes completely dry.

6. When the chicken is cooked, transfer it to a cutting board. Remove the vegetables from the cavity and add to the vegetables in the bowl. Cover the chicken loosely with foil and let rest while you cook the rice.

7. Add ¼ cup hot water to the roasting pan, stirring well to deglaze the pan. Pour the liquid into a measuring cup, skim off the fat, and add enough water to make 2 cups of liquid. Pour this liquid into a medium saucepan. Add the rice and the salt and bring to a boil over high heat. Reduce the heat to low, cover, and cook for about 18 minutes, until the rice is tender and all the liquid is absorbed.

8. Fold the yogurt and reserved vegetables into the rice. Season with salt if necessary and pepper. Carve the chicken and serve with the rice.

[Adapted from *Aquavit and the New Scandinavian Cooking*; Houghton Mifflin, 2003.]

Ginger Citrus Cookies

These cookies are similar to gingersnaps but moister and chewier; the secret ingredient is chopped candied citrus peel. The recipe is another one that was inspired by my grandmother's cooking. We often baked cookies together, and she used to add the zest of bitter oranges to one of her doughs. At Aquavit, we give these cookies as Christmas gifts, but they are delicious year-round. They also keep extremely well.   MAKES ABOUT 5 DOZEN COOKIES

I teaspoon ground ginger

$\frac{1}{2}$ teaspoon ground cinnamon

$\frac{1}{2}$ teaspoon ground cardamom

$\frac{1}{4}$ teaspoon ground cloves

$3\frac{1}{2}$ cups sifted all-purpose flour

I tablespoon baking soda

I teaspoon salt

$\frac{1}{2}$ teaspoon freshly ground white pepper

10 tablespoons ($1\frac{1}{4}$ sticks) unsalted butter, at room temperature

I cup sugar

$\frac{1}{2}$ cup packed light brown sugar

2 large eggs

$\frac{3}{4}$ cup molasses

I cup finely chopped candied citrus peel

1. Preheat the oven to 350° F. Line two baking sheets with parchment paper.

2. Toast the ginger, cinnamon, cardamom, and cloves in a small skillet over medium heat, stirring with a wooden spoon, for 2 to 3 minutes, until fragrant. Remove from the heat. Sift the flour, toasted spices, baking soda, salt, and white pepper into a bowl or onto a sheet of wax paper.

3. In a large bowl, beat the butter and both sugars with an electric mixer until light and fluffy. Add the eggs, one at a time, beating well after each addition and scraping down the sides of the bowl as necessary. Beat in the molasses. Gradually beat in the flour mixture. Stir in the candied citrus peel.

4. Drop rounded tablespoons of the dough onto the prepared baking sheets, spacing the cookies 2 inches apart. Bake for 10 to 12 minutes, until the tops feel firm when lightly touched. Cool on the baking sheets for about 2 minutes, then transfer the cookies to a wire rack to cool completely.

[Adapted from *Aquavit and the New Scandinavian Cooking*; Houghton Mifflin, 2003.]

MARY ANN ESPOSITO is the host of thirteen seasons of *Ciao Italia*, the longest-running cooking show on public television. Past seasons of *Ciao Italia* have taken viewers to Umbria and Tuscany, and next season, airing in the spring of 2004, will take them to Emilia-Romagna. In addition to hosting her own television series, Mary Ann has appeared on many national television shows and networks, including the *Today* show, *Live with Regis and Kathie Lee*, Lifetime, and Food Network.

Mary Ann has written eight cookbooks, the latest of which, *Ciao Italia in Umbria* and *Ciao Italia in Tuscany*, were published in 2002 and 2003, respectively. She has also taught in numerous cooking schools throughout Italy and the United States.

Mary Ann travels to Italy at least twice a year to learn more and to teach in cooking schools in different regions of Italy. Keep up with Mary Ann through her website, *www.ciaoitalia.com*.

Mary Ann
Esposito

When I was growing up, I detested cooking. If anyone ever told me I'd grow up to be a chef, I would have choked on a meatball. You would have thought otherwise, given that I was surrounded by good food my whole life and my maiden name, Saporito, means "tasty."

We lived with my maternal grandmother, Anna Galasso, in Buffalo, New York. Sundays meant a trip to the home of my paternal grandmother, Maria Assunto Saporito, in Fairport, New York. Nonna Saporito was a professional chef and butcher, and ran her own butcher shop. She could wield a butcher's knife like nobody's business, and in no time flat she'd cut a chicken into minute pieces (one chicken would feed twelve of us!) for her famous chicken cooked in wine. Nonna cooked the chicken very slowly in Grandpa's homemade wine until the pieces were dark and sticky. I can still taste that chicken, but I've never been able to duplicate it. You wanted to suck out all the flavor from the bone.

Mary Ann Esposito and her mother,
Chef Luisa Saporito.

Every Fourth of July we'd pile into a car to pick cherries—so many cherries that we'd drive around and give them to friends and neighbors. That's one of the things my family instilled in me: a sense of generosity. My mother, Luisa Saporito, started a pizza stand in front of the house. She made great pizzas with home-grown tomatoes and herbs, and they went like hotcakes. The problem was, she'd give one away for every one she sold.

We were always making homemade pasta, shelling beans, and canning peas and peaches. And because I was the oldest of seven children, I had to help with everything that happened in the kitchen. I learned so much about cooking from Nonna Saporito and Nonna Galasso (who ran a boarding-house) that I knew how to cook well by the time I turned fifteen. But I wanted to get as far away from cooking as I could, so I went to college to be a teacher.

After I got married and had chil-dren, things started to change. We bought an old house, and in the process of reno-vating it, we completely redid the kitchen. I found myself designing a big maple-topped counter with an indentation in one side of it—just like the one my mother had in her kitchen. She'd stand in the cutout so that she was surrounded by counter on all sides and bake. The plum don't fall far from the tree, they say.

Chef Luisa Saporito.

When my mother saw the new kitchen, she bought me a hand-cranked pasta maker. It was like riding a bike, you know—you never really forget it. And I was a little surprised to find that I really enjoyed cooking and making homemade lasagna, fusilli, and cappelletti now that I had my own family. By the time I was in my forties, I started catering. I studied in Italy at various cooking schools and even did a restaurant apprenticeship in Sorrento. That's when I realized that what my grandmother and mother had taught me was so im-portant. They were better cooks than most of the people I studied with!

Now my life has come full circle, back to teaching—in classes and on television. I think of my career as a big minestrone—all the elements go in and contribute to one beautiful result. My mother is still a fabulous cook at eighty-four and my main inspiration. Here are recipes from my mother,

Luisa, and my grandmother Anna, both fabulous cooks and always in the kitchen. The first is simple, just fried fresh ricotta, but it shows how important good ingredients are to Italian cooking.

Fried Ricotta Cheese

When recipes are this simple, you need the best ingredients. Look for someone in your area who makes fresh ricotta and buy it as soon after it's made as you can. MAKES 6 SERVINGS

I pound fresh and firm ricotta cheese, well drained

I large egg

¼ cup finely chopped basil

Salt

Coarsely ground black pepper

¼ cup extra virgin olive oil

MOM'S TIP

Avoid turning the patties until the underside has had a chance to brown and form a smooth surface. They will look prettier and be easier to turn.

1. Mix the ricotta in a bowl with the egg, basil, and salt and pepper to taste. Form the ricotta into small patties, making 6 to 8. Set them aside on a dish.

2. Heat the oil in a large skillet. When it begins to shimmer, add the patties. Cook over medium heat until they begin to brown on the underside. Lift and turn them with a spatula and cook the other side. Serve warm over a bed of lettuce greens.

Cagoots, Potatoes, and Sun-dried Tomatoes

There was never a Saturday lunch, winter or summer, without chicken livers, onion, and zucchini in some form. We called zucchini *cagoots* in dialect and had it with scrambled eggs and lots of pepper. Over the years my mother has come to do more stylized things with zucchini, including this dish to which I add my homemade sun-dried tomatoes. This is a great side for fish or poultry. MAKES 4 SERVINGS

2 tablespoons extra virgin olive oil

1 medium red onion, thinly sliced

2 medium zucchini (about 12 ounces), washed, dried, and cut into ½-inch cubes

1 large Yukon Gold potato (about 12 ounces), peeled and cut into ½-inch cubes

5 or 6 sun-dried tomatoes in olive oil, drained and diced

Salt and black pepper

Heat the oil in a large skillet over medium heat. Stir in the onion, zucchini, and potato, and cook, stirring and turning frequently to brown evenly, until the vegetables are softened and browned, about 30 minutes. Stir in the sun-dried tomatoes and salt and pepper to taste.

Mama's Whiskey Cake

My mother's whiskey cake was served at every holiday meal. This dense cake, soaked liberally with whiskey, filled with a delicious vanilla custard, and covered all over in a cloud of fluffy meringue, won the acclaim of all who were privileged to sample it. Make the filling a day ahead, so you won't have so many steps when you assemble the cake.   MAKES 12 TO 16 SERVINGS

FOR THE CUSTARD FILLING
I cup sugar
¼ cup cornstarch
4 cups milk
4 large egg yolks
I tablespoon vanilla extract

FOR THE CAKE
I½ cups cake flour
I½ cups sugar
6 large eggs, separated, at room temperature
½ cup cold water

I teaspoon vanilla extract
¾ teaspoon cream of tartar
6 tablespoons bourbon whiskey

FOR THE MERINGUE TOPPING
I½ teaspoons cornstarch
¼ cup water
6 large egg whites, at room temperature
I tablespoon bourbon whiskey
½ cup sugar

I.   To make the filling: Mix the sugar and cornstarch together in a small bowl. In the top of a double boiler, bring the milk to just under a boil. Adjust the heat to low. Add ¼ cup of the hot milk to the sugar and cornstarch mixture, and stir to make a paste. Stir the paste into the milk in the double boiler, raise the heat to medium-high, and cook, stirring constantly with a wooden spoon, until the mixture thickens enough to coat the back of the spoon, 10 to 15 minutes. Remove from the heat and let cool slightly.

2.   Beat the egg yolks in a bowl until pale and thick. Beat in ¼ cup of the warm milk mixture and return to the double boiler. Cook, stirring, over medium-

high heat for 5 minutes, or until thickened. Transfer to a bowl and stir in the vanilla. Cover the bowl with a sheet of buttered waxed paper and refrigerate until ready to use.

3.   Preheat the oven to 325° F.

4.   To make the cake: Sift the flour 3 times and set aside. Beat the sugar and egg yolks with an electric mixer in a large bowl until thick and pale yellow. Gradually beat in the water and then the vanilla. With a spatula, fold in the sifted flour, 2 tablespoons at a time.

5.   In another bowl, beat the egg whites with the cream of tartar until stiff peaks form. Fold the whites into the egg yolk mixture and pour the batter into an ungreased 10-inch tube pan. Bake for 40 minutes, or until a wooden skewer inserted in the middle of the cake comes out clean. Invert the cake pan over the neck of a wine or soft drink bottle and let the cake cool completely.

6.   Run a knife around the sides of the pan to release the cake and turn it out onto a plate. With a serrated knife, cut the cake into ¼-inch slices.

7.   Line a 9 × 12-inch ovenproof platter or baking sheet with a layer of cake slices. Fill in any spaces with pieces of cake. Sprinkle 2 tablespoons of the whiskey evenly over the cake slices. Spread the cake slices with half of the custard filling. Place a second layer of cake on top of the custard filling, filling in any gaps with pieces of cake. Sprinkle with another 2 tablespoons of the whiskey. Make a second custard layer and top with a third layer of cake. Sprinkle the top of the cake with the remaining 2 tablespoons of whiskey. Refrigerate the cake while you make the meringue.

8.   Preheat the oven to 325° F.

9.   To make the meringue topping: Dissolve the cornstarch in the water in a small saucepan. Cook over medium-high heat, stirring, until well blended but still liquid. Set aside to cool.

10.   In a large bowl, beat the egg whites with an electric mixer until foamy. Add the whiskey and beat for 1 minute. Beat in the sugar, 1 tablespoon at a time,

until the whites form stiff peaks. Slowly beat in the cornstarch mixture and beat 3 minutes more.

11. Frost the cake with the meringue, making sure to spread the meringue all around the bottom edges of the cake to seal them. Bake until the meringue is golden brown, about 6 to 8 minutes; be careful because it will brown quickly. Let the cake cool for 5 minutes, then refrigerate it for at least 2 hours before serving.

12. To serve, cut into small squares.

NOTE: **This cake will keep for up to a week in the refrigerator.**

ANTHONY BOURDAIN is the executive chef at Brasserie Les Halles in New York. After two misspent years at Vassar College, he attended the Culinary Institute of America in Hyde Park and has followed that with more than two decades of work in professional kitchens. In 2000 his memoir/rant, *Kitchen Confidential*, described in lurid detail his experiences in those kitchens and became a surprise international best-seller. In late 2000, Anthony set out to eat his way across the globe, looking for kicks, thrills, epiphanies, and the ideal of the "perfect meal." The book—along with the companion Food Network series, *A Cook's Tour*—chronicles his adventures and misadventures on that voyage. Anthony is also the author of two satirical thrillers, *Bone in the Throat* and *Gone Bamboo*, the urban historical *Typhoid Mary*, and the recently published crime novel *The Bobby Gold Stories*. He lives in New York City with his wife, Nancy. He is a proud fan of the New York Yankees.

Anthony
Bourdain

The first thing I remember cooking was "toad in the hole," a sunny-side-up egg fried inside the cutout center of a slice of bread. It was the simplest recipe from a cookbook for kids, and I'm sure my mom kept a close eye on me while I massacred her stove top.

Good food and good technique were important in my house long before I ever considered becoming a chef. Among the many things my mother did was encourage us to eat around, to try new things from different cultures. I remember many family trips to Chinese restaurants on Upper Broadway and in Chinatown, smorgasbord at a Scandinavian place, deli on the Lower East Side, southern Italian, Japanese, and, of course, all-important pilgrimages to French restaurants and later to France itself. Needless to say, these experiences resonated powerfully later in my life.

Tony and Gladys Bourdain, at Christopher Bourdain's wedding reception, 1985.

Of my mother's specialties I recall with special fondness her roast beef with amazing Yorkshire pudding (I *still* can't duplicate that pudding, no matter how hard or how often I try), which I always chose for my birthday meal; her date-nut bread, which I loved when afflicted with late-night teenage bouts of the munchies; legendary Christmas butter cookies, which I still shake her down for every year; and her terrific eggnog for a clandestine buzz.

Homemade vegetable-barley soup was another favorite. The smell of good stock, cooked barley, and assorted vegetables still brings back happy memories of childhood. My mother had a good repertoire of family recipes, like pressed jelly sandwiches made in an old cast-iron French press and a meat loaf that is, of course, better than your mom's meat loaf (especially the second day when served cold on a sandwich). She also had a very ahead-of-her-time collection of cookbooks: I remember Craig Claiborne, Julia Child (of course), *The Joy of Cooking*, and numerous volumes on French cookery, including—just for browsing—the *Larousse Gastronomique*.

I was always particularly intrigued, enticed, and fascinated by the smells emanating from our kitchen when company was coming or when my mother cooked for special events. Her coquilles St.-Jacques, served in scallop shells with grated Swiss cheese delicately sprinkled on top, seemed magical with their exotic

Tony, Gladys, and Christopher Bourdain—aboard the Queen Mary *en route to France, 1966.*

scent of white wine, seafood, and mushrooms wafting from under the broiler. Butterflied, marinated, and grilled leg of lamb, roast fillet of beef, a worth-waiting-all-year-for pumpkin chiffon pie—the regular appearance of these dishes, their aromas and flavors, must have inspired me.

But most important, my mother made food special and important for me. Dinner was something in which curiosity, passion, discovery, and pleasure all played a part; the meal was where you got together with the people you loved and enjoyed food made with care, pride, and affection. Whether in a restaurant or at home, food, it was made clear, was not to be taken for granted, shoved into one's face like fuel. It was more than that. I have a lot of things to be grateful to my mom for, but that's a big one.

Coquilles St.-Jacques

I will always associate the smell of this dish with my first imaginings of France—and with the imminent arrival of guests. When I smelled this dish cooking downstairs, I knew company was coming. My mother made it for special occasions only. I remember being terrifically impressed that she served it in scallop shells. I yearned for this dish—knowing it only by smells—and was delighted when I finally turned old enough to sit down to eat with the adults. This was the reward. MAKES 6 SERVINGS

1¾ cups water

¾ cup dry white wine

I small onion, chopped

Bouquet garni (see Mom's Tip)

I teaspoon lemon juice

I pound very fresh scallops

8 ounces mushrooms, washed and chopped

6 tablespoons butter

4 tablespoons flour

½ cup heavy cream

Salt and freshly ground pepper

Bread crumbs

Grated Swiss or Gruyère cheese

1. Heat the water, wine, onion, bouquet garni, and lemon juice to a boil in a saucepan. Add the scallops, cover, and simmer on very low heat until cooked through, about 5 minutes. Remove the scallops with a slotted spoon and set aside.

2. Add the mushrooms to the scallop poaching liquid and simmer uncovered for 10 minutes. Strain, discarding the bouquet garni and reserving the liquid and mushrooms separately.

3. Cut the scallops into ½-inch-thick slices. If too long, cut in half horizontally.

4. Melt the butter in a medium saucepan and whisk in the flour. Do not let it get dark. Add 2 or 3 tablespoons of the scallop liquid and mix until blended. Over very low heat, blend the flour mixture into the scallop liquid. Add the cream and simmer and stir until blended and thickened. Season with salt and pepper to taste. Add the scallops and mushrooms, and stir.

5. Fill 6 scallop shells or shallow 6-inch ramekins almost to the top with the scallop mixture. Dust the top lightly with bread crumbs and sprinkle with the grated cheese. (If you're not ready to serve the scallops, cover them with plastic wrap and refrigerate.)

6. Preheat the broiler. Broil the scallops until the mixture bubbles and the cheese melts and turns golden brown.

> **MOM'S TIP**
>
> *To make a bouquet garni, wrap a sprig or two of parsley, two bay leaves, and a sprig of fresh thyme (or ½ teaspoon of dried thyme leaves) in some cheesecloth. Tie into a neat bundle with thread or clean string.*

Baked Macaroni

Everybody thinks their mom makes the best macaroni and cheese, but my mom actually does. Really. The best in the whole world. You wanna fight about it? Meet you by the flagpole. The crunchy exterior crust

is what really distinguishes this preparation from the rest. Comfort food at its finest.   MAKES 8 TO 10 SERVINGS

1.   Cook 1 pound of macaroni, such as elbows or penne, for 2 or 3 minutes less than the instructions on the box say. Drain the pasta.

2.   Butter a 3-quart Pyrex or other baking dish. Place a layer of macaroni on the bottom and sprinkle with salt and pepper. Cover with diced or shredded Cheddar cheese (see Note) and insert a few dots of butter. Make another layer and repeat, and a third layer. Use cheese liberally. Do not tamp down the pasta; it will make the dish too dense.

3.   Pour milk over the top until it is about 1½ inches deep at the bottom of the dish.

4.   Bake at 400° F for 45 minutes to 1 hour, depending on how crisp you like the top.

NOTE: **One 8-ounce package of shredded Cheddar cheese that is available at the supermarket fills the bill. Choose *sharp* Cheddar, not mild. It is tastier against the blandness of the pasta.**

Crème Renversée

This was a crossover dish—meaning that both family and guests were lucky to get this one. I've made and eaten and served thousands of these over the years, but none has ever touched my mom's. I think the way she takes the sugar a little over the edge—into slight bitterness—is what makes it unique. I often use this recipe myself, but it's better when my mother makes it.

MAKES 8 TO 10 SERVINGS, DEPENDING ON PORTION SIZE

4 cups milk

1 cup sugar, plus 6 tablespoons for the caramel

2 teaspoons vanilla extract

8 eggs

1. Stir the milk and 1 cup of sugar together in a medium saucepan and heat over medium heat until tiny bubbles appear around the edges. Cool to tepid and then stir in the vanilla.

2. Beat the eggs thoroughly in a mixing bowl. Blend the milk mixture and the eggs slowly.

3. Preheat the oven to 325° F.

4. Put the 6 tablespoons of sugar in a 2-quart charlotte mold (see Note) and place over low heat until the sugar liquefies and turns dark brown. Using oven mitts, tilt the mold so that melted sugar coats the entire interior. Let the coating solidify off the heat for a few minutes.

5. Pour the custard mixture into the mold. Place the mold in a roasting pan on a rack in the middle of the oven. Pour enough hot water into the roasting pan to come about halfway up the sides of the mold. Bake about 1½ hours, until a cake tester or thin knife inserted in the center comes out dry. Remove the mold from the oven and let it stand about 30 minutes, then place in the refrigerator.

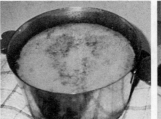

LEFT TO RIGHT: *Baking mold lined with caramelized sugar; custard ready for oven; baked custard ready for refrigerator; unmolded custard.*

6.   When ready to serve, run a knife around the edge of the custard to separate it from the mold. Run about 2 inches of hot water into the sink. Dip the bottom of the mold in the water for a fast count of 10 and remove. Place a serving plate upside down on top of the mold and invert both in a quick move. The custard should drop neatly onto the plate, with liquefied caramel sauce covering it.

NOTE: This may be baked in a 2-quart ring mold with a smooth interior. Increase the sugar for caramelizing by 1 or 2 tablespoons since there is more surface to cover. Reduce the baking time to about 1 hour. After unmolding, it can be sliced as thinly or thickly as desired. Spoon a little sauce over each serving.

ART SMITH, chef, author, and television personality, was a 2002 James Beard Foundation Book Award recipient for his first cookbook, *Back to the Table: The Reunion of Food and Family*. He is also the recipient of the prestigious 2001 Gourmand World Cookbook Award in the category "For Its Human Values." A *New York Times* and national best-selling author, Art has been a keynote speaker for Florida governor Jeb Bush's "Celebration of Reading," sponsored by the Barbara Bush Foundation for Family Literacy.

Art
Smith

A native of Jasper, Florida, Art began his career with two internships at the Greenbrier resort. Art has been the executive chef at the Florida governor's mansion, has run his own restaurant, and has cooked for families all over the globe as a family chef. Once settled in Chicago, he began a career in teaching and has served as personal chef to Oprah Winfrey and Stedman Graham. Currently a contributing editor to *O, the Oprah Magazine*, Art also writes a monthly column for the food page of Oprah.com.

Art has recently created a nonprofit organization, Common Threads, based on his passionate belief that families (whether a family by blood or a family of friends) all share an innate desire to care for one another, regardless of culture, race, or geographic location. Art's mission is to foster a familial environment where children learn to value one another and discover universal understanding and mutual acceptance. He is currently working on his second book, *Kitchen Life.*

⌁⌁⌁

My mom, Addie Mae Smith, was the ultimate southern mother who made the most amazing dinners with ease. Even in the middle of piling the table with fried chicken, biscuits, and vegetables, she'd take the time to kiss me and say, "I love you, sugar!"

Art Smith with his mom, Addie Mae, on Easter Sunday.

My mother and both my grandmothers, Georgia and Mabel, are classic southern cooks. They made chicken and dumplings, pot roast, deviled eggs, Lady Baltimore cakes, and potato salad—and not just for us, but for church suppers and get-togethers. They were used to cooking for crowds. Living on a farm means there's always a lot of hungry people to feed, and they never shied away from the task.

We had our own garden on the farm, where my grandfather grew the most amazing vegetables. All the vegetables on our table were picked that day. (We didn't know about any Green Giant, jolly or otherwise!) Mother and Grandma put up any surplus from the garden. The pantry was always overflowing with preserves, vegetables, pickles, and fruits. It enabled them to get an incredible amount of food on the table in a hurry. We never really considered the table set—no true southerner does—unless there was some kind of "put-up" on it.

The women in my family are such great cooks—without ever having gone to school or worked in a restaurant—and I don't believe they even know it. Great food and sharing it with others is a part of their life.

What's interesting is that so many dishes my mom makes were taught to her by *her* mother. I'm afraid that's not happening too much anymore, and that concern drives me to cook, to teach, and to write. Passing on these recipes and these traditions is my way of honoring the amazing women—superstars, really—

Art Smith and his mom at a book signing in Tallahassee.

who have surrounded me all my life. I didn't realize it when I was younger, but I do what I do today because of the love I've received from the women in my life.

Art Smith, fresh from the bath with his mom, Addie Mae.

The Smith Family's Twelve-Layer Cake

A recipe from my great-great-grandmother, this cake has taken center stage at many Smith family celebrations. It is a stack of twelve thin yellow-cake layers that are held together with a cocoa icing that is just this side of a syrup. If you buy a dozen inexpensive aluminum-foil cake pans (they can be saved for another time), you will be able to knock out the layers in no time. Cakes like these date back to the early eighteenth century, when the layers would have been made in a skillet on the stove top instead of in the oven.

MAKES 16 TO 20 SERVINGS

FOR THE CAKE LAYERS

¾ pound (3 sticks) unsalted butter, at room temperature, plus more for the cake pans

4½ cups all-purpose flour, sifted, plus more for the cake pans

1½ teaspoons baking powder

¼ teaspoon salt

2½ cups sugar

6 large eggs, at room temperature

3 cups milk

1½ teaspoons vanilla extract

FOR THE ICING

3 cups sugar

½ pound (2 sticks) unsalted butter, cut up

One 12-ounce can evaporated milk

½ cup unsweetened cocoa powder, preferably Dutch process

1 tablespoon vanilla extract

Pecan halves

1. Position the racks in the center and bottom third of the oven. Preheat the oven to 375° F. Lightly butter four 8½- to 9-inch cake pans (you will bake the cakes in 3 batches) and line the bottoms with rounds of parchment paper. Flour the pans and tap out the excess.

2. To make the layers: Sift together 4½ cups flour, the baking powder, and salt. Sift the mixture one more time and set aside. Beat the 3 sticks of butter and 2½ cups of sugar on high speed in the bowl of a heavy-duty electric mixer fitted

with the paddle blade or a handheld electric mixer until light in color and texture, about 3 minutes. Beat in the eggs, 1 at a time. Scrape down the bowl and be sure the mixture is well blended. On low speed, add the flour in 3 additions, alternating with 2 additions of the milk, beginning and ending with the flour, and beat until smooth. Scrape down the sides of the bowl often with a rubber spatula. Beat in the vanilla. Using a scant cup for each layer, spread the batter evenly in the pans. It will make a thin layer.

3.   Staggering the pans on the racks so they are at least 2 inches from one another and the sides of the oven and not directly over each other, bake the layers until they feel firm when pressed in the center and are beginning to pull away from the sides of the pans, about 12 minutes. Cool in the pans for 5 minutes. Invert the layers onto cake racks, remove the parchment paper, and cool completely. Wash and prepare the pans. Repeat the procedure until all 12 layers have been baked and cooled.

4.   To make the icing: bring 3 cups sugar, ½ pound butter, the evaporated milk, and cocoa to a full boil in a large saucepan. Adjust the heat to medium-low and cook until the icing has thickened slightly (it will resemble chocolate syrup but will thicken as it cools), about 3 minutes. Stir in the vanilla. Let the icing cool until thick enough to spread but still pourable.

5.   Place a layer of cake on a wire rack set over a jelly-roll pan. Spread with a few tablespoons of the icing, letting the excess run down the sides. Stack the remaining cakes, icing each layer. Pour the remaining icing over the top of the cake. If you wish, smooth the icing on the edges to cover the sides. Place pecan halves around the top perimeter of the cake. Let stand until the glaze sets. The cake is best served the day it is made. To store, cover loosely with plastic wrap and refrigerate for up to 1 day.

[Adapted from *Back to the Table: The Reunion of Food and Family*; Hyperion, 2001.]

Lemon–Sour Cream Pound Cake

My family members are generous people. I remember one time, not long after I had moved to Chicago, I told my mother that I was missing the simple
life back home. A few days later a cake showed up in the mail. (My family has
a practice of freezing cakes, then mailing them. By the time they arrive,
they're perfectly thawed.) Well, the day after that another cake showed up,
then another. It seems my mother told her mother and aunt and everybody
else back home that I was feeling homesick. Finally I had to call her and say,
"Mom, I'm feeling better, really!" Sour cream is the secret ingredient in
many a pound cake. This cake—one of the ones I received in Chicago, if I'm
not mistaken—is based on a lemon pound cake from my family's recipe collection. MAKES 12 SERVINGS

FOR THE CAKE

½ pound (2 sticks) unsalted
butter, at room temperature, plus
more for the cake pan

3 cups all-purpose flour, plus more
for the cake pan

½ teaspoon baking powder

½ teaspoon salt

¼ teaspoon baking soda

3 cups sugar

6 large eggs, at room temperature

1 teaspoon vanilla extract

Grated zest of 2 lemons

1 cup sour cream, at room
temperature

FOR THE LEMON SYRUP

1 cup fresh lemon juice

⅔ cup sugar

¼ cup water

Zest of 1 lemon

1. Position a rack in the center of the oven and preheat the oven to 325° F.
Butter and flour a 10-inch fluted tube pan and tap out the excess flour.

2. To make the cake: Sift 3 cups flour, the baking powder, salt, and baking
soda together, and set aside. Beat ½ pound butter and the sugar in a large bowl with

a handheld electric mixer on high speed until light and fluffy, about 3 minutes. Beat in the eggs, 1 at a time, and then the vanilla and zest. On low speed, add the flour in 3 additions, alternating with 2 additions of the sour cream, beginning and ending with the flour. Beat until smooth, scraping down the sides of the bowl often with a rubber spatula. Spread evenly in the prepared pan.

3. Bake until a wooden skewer inserted in the center of the cake comes out clean, about 1¼ hours.

4. Make the syrup: Bring the lemon juice, ⅔ cup sugar, water, and zest to a boil over high heat and cook until reduced to ½ cup, about 15 minutes. Allow the syrup to cool before drizzling on the cake.

5. Transfer the cake to a wire rack and cool for 10 minutes. Drizzle half of the syrup over the cake. Invert onto the rack and brush with the remaining syrup. Cool completely before serving.

[Adapted from *Back to the Table: The Reunion of Food and Family*; Hyperion, 2001.]

Pear and Cranberry Cobbler

Bakers often disagree about what topping should be used for a cobbler. Should it be pie dough or sweet biscuits? There is another camp that uses cake batter, but that is officially called a buckle. I use biscuits, but I crisscross strips of the dough into an attractive lattice topping. Most big families in the South made cobblers for dessert; they're simple to make, and there is always some kind of fruit in season. Pear was a favorite fruit for cobblers in the fall. The cranberry is my own addition.   MAKES 6 SERVINGS

FOR THE FRUIT

4 firm, ripe Bosc pears, peeled, cored, and cut into ½-inch wedges (about 5 cups)

1 cup fresh or frozen cranberries

½ cup sugar

1 tablespoon cornstarch

1 teaspoon cinnamon

½ teaspoon ginger

FOR THE COBBLER TOPPING

1½ cups all-purpose flour

2¼ teaspoons baking powder

2½ tablespoons sugar

⅛ teaspoon salt

3 tablespoons chilled, unsalted butter, cut up

3 tablespoons vegetable shortening

½ cup buttermilk, or as needed

1.   Position a rack in the center of the oven and preheat the oven to 350° F. Lightly butter an 8-inch square baking dish.

2.   To prepare the fruit: Toss the pears, cranberries, sugar, cornstarch, cinnamon, and ginger in a large bowl. Transfer to the baking dish.

3.   To make the cobbler topping: Combine the flour, baking powder, 1½ tablespoons sugar, and salt in a medium bowl. Add the butter and shortening, and cut in with a pastry blender or 2 knives until the mixture looks like coarse bread crumbs. Stir in enough buttermilk to make a soft dough.

4. Using floured hands, pat out the dough on a floured work surface into an 8-inch square. Using a sharp knife, cut into 3¼-inch-wide ribbons. Crisscross the dough on the filling in a lattice pattern. Sprinkle the remaining 1 tablespoon of sugar over the dough.

5. Bake until the cobbler crust is golden brown and the filling juices are bubbling, about 45 minutes. Serve warm.

[Adapted from *Back to the Table: The Reunion of Food and Family*; Hyperion, 2001.]

MOM'S TIP

To make the simplest, most wonderful fig preserves, start with firm but ripe figs. Fit them snugly in a preserve jar without bruising them. Bring equal parts of water and sugar to a boil and boil until the syrup has thickened slightly. Pour the boiling syrup over the figs. Add a cinnamon stick, a few cloves, and, if you like, a couple of cardamom pods to the jar. Seal the jar and store it in the refrigerator for several weeks before serving. Spread on toast, the preserves become the richest, jammiest fig spread you can imagine.

CHRIS SCHLESINGER was born and raised in Virginia, where he first developed his love for barbecue, spicy food, and live-fire cooking. He entered the food service industry at age eighteen when he left college and became a dishwasher. Fascinated by the intense energy and teamwork that are the heart of any restaurant kitchen, Chris went on to pursue a formal culinary education at the Culinary Institute of America, from which he graduated in 1977.

Chris Schlesinger

In 1986, Chris opened the East Coast Grill; in 1989, Jake and Earl's Dixie BBQ; and in 1990, The Blue Room—all in Cambridge, Massachusetts. All these restaurants received national attention. In 1996, Chris consolidated his restaurant efforts and revamped the East Coast Grill, tripling its size and shifting its focus to seafood. In 1999, Chris opened the Back Eddy in Westport, Massachusetts, overlooking the Westport River. Close relationships with local farmers, fishermen, brewers, vintners, and cheese makers define the menu at the Back Eddy.

Chris is the coauthor with John Willoughby of five cookbooks: *The Thrill of the Grill*; *Salsas, Sambals, Chutneys, and Chowchows*; *Big Flavors of the Hot Sun*; *Lettuce in Your Kitchen*; and *License to Grill*, the James Beard Foundation Book Award winner. They also have a monthly feature in *The New York Times* and have written numerous articles for magazines such as *GQ* and *Food & Wine*. Chris is also a contributing editor for *Saveur* magazine.

An accomplished cooking teacher, Chris has taught culinary students at the Culinary Institute of America at both the New York and Napa Valley campuses. Chris was the winner of the 1996 James Beard Best Chef: Northeast Award. He has appeared on dozens of television shows around the United States to talk about food and cooking, has been a guest speaker at numerous conferences, and has been featured in more than two hundred magazine and newspaper articles. Chris is also a founding member of the national organization Chefs Collaborative and actively works with local farmers to preserve farming in New England.

Growing up in Virginia, I was surrounded by good food—the rich and salty hams from Smithfield, barbecue, and hush puppies, to name a few of my favorites. Another good thing about growing up in Virginia: We were never too far from my grandmother Wetzler's spread in Pennsylvania. I loved those trips, especially the meals. I never really cooked back then—I just ate a lot—but I remember the homemade noodles, the corn relish that Grandma made with corn she grew herself, and the best fresh tomato juice in the world.

Grandma Wetzler's table was always jammed with an incredible variety of dishes: homemade applesauce, pickled eggs, corn pudding, ham salad, homemade baked beans. It always made me think of a picnic. We'd eat hot baked beans with a massive ham at supper, then cold beans the next day at lunch with ham salad. Her common sense, unflagging practicality, and enormous repertoire of German-American dishes resulted from having cooked for her family since the age of sixteen.

Even though I didn't spend a lot of time in the kitchen with Grandma, I must have absorbed a lot about food on those trips. I grew up to be the kind of cook she was. I cook with the seasons, love to put up pickles and tomatoes, and have developed a deep respect for local farmers. A lot of that shows in my restaurants, and some of Grandma's dishes are on our menus—such as her baked beans and pickles. I make fresh tomato juice the way she did and use it as the base for our grilled vegetable gazpacho. Grandma Wetzler passed away a few years ago, but her spirit lives on in my cooking.

Spoon Bread with Smithfield Ham and Cheddar Cheese

This is a variation of a dish from my childhood, a traditional southern spoon bread as found on the Colonial-era menus of Williamsburg taverns, and it is a favorite of my sister. I have added Smithfield ham to the recipe, since it is also a traditional Virginia product, and I think they make a very nice combination. With a simple salad, this dish makes a great brunch for a large group of people. MAKES 12 SIDE-DISH SERVINGS (INGREDIENTS CAN BE HALVED TO MAKE 6 SERVINGS)

4 cups milk

3 cups water

3 cups yellow cornmeal

4 tablespoons unsalted butter, melted

3 tablespoons sugar

2½ teaspoons salt

2 cups finely diced Smithfield ham

I cup grated Cheddar cheese

4 tablespoons very finely chopped sage

10 eggs

2 tablespoons baking powder

1. Preheat the oven to 350° F. Grease two 2-quart casserole dishes or two 10-inch iron skillets.

2. Bring the milk and water to a simmer in a large (6-quart) pot. Add the cornmeal, butter, sugar, and salt, and stir over medium-low heat until the mixture becomes porridge-thick, 5 to 7 minutes.

3. Remove from the heat and blend in the ham, cheese, and sage.

4. Whip the eggs with the baking powder until very frothy. Fold into the corn mixture, mixing lightly but thoroughly.

5.   Divide between the greased casseroles or skillets, and bake for about 45 minutes, or until the top is nicely browned. Serve hot.

[Adapted from *Thrill of the Grill*; Morrow, 1990.]

Grandma Wetzler's Baked Beans

Made from my grandma's Pennsylvania Dutch recipe, these beans just can't be beat. They are filling, satisfying, and slightly sweet, and no picnic or barbecue feast is complete without them.   SERVES 10 AS A SIDE DISH

1¼ pounds navy beans

8 ounces bacon, diced

1 yellow onion, finely diced

1 gallon water

2 cups ketchup

½ cup molasses

½ cup brown sugar

2 tablespoons yellow mustard

Salt and freshly cracked black pepper

1.   Soak the beans overnight in enough cold water to cover.

2.   Sauté the bacon in a large pot over medium heat until browned, about 5 minutes. Add the onions and cook until browned, about 5 minutes.

3.   Add the water, ketchup, molasses, sugar, and mustard, and bring to a boil.

4.   Drain the beans, add them to the pot, and return to a boil. Lower the heat to a slow simmer and cook for 4 to 5 hours, until the beans are soft. Add water from time to time if necessary and stir often to prevent burning. Season with salt and pepper to taste. These beans will keep when covered and refrigerated for about 1 week.

[Adapted from *Thrill of the Grill*; Morrow, 1990.]

Smithfield Ham Hush Puppies with Fresh Corn

Any type of ham can be used in this recipe, but I prefer the salty Smithfield because its homeland is the same as the hush puppy's. Use it raw or cooked, as you wish. You'll find that it tastes much the same either way, but it is slightly saltier when raw, and is less dense and more mealy when cooked.

Hush puppies, basically deep-fried balls of corn bread, originated as a means of keeping hounds quiet around the campfire. Now they are served in the South as an alternative to dinner rolls. The addition of fresh corn here gives the puppies a bit of a fritter look. Serve them with lots of butter.

MAKES A BIG LITTER: ABOUT 2 DOZEN PUPS

¾ cup yellow cornmeal

¼ cup all-purpose flour

1 tablespoon baking powder

1 teaspoon cayenne pepper

½ teaspoon salt

1 egg and enough buttermilk to measure ¾ cup

1 tablespoon melted bacon fat or vegetable oil

½ cup finely diced Smithfield ham

¾ cup fresh or canned and drained corn kernels

½ cup chopped scallions

Vegetable oil for frying

> **MOM'S TIP**
>
> *The amount of oil you use will depend on the size of the skillet. You want to use only enough oil to come halfway up the sides of the puppies.*

1. Sift together the cornmeal, flour, baking powder, cayenne pepper, and salt into a bowl.

2. Whisk the egg and buttermilk in a small bowl until well mixed. Stir in the melted bacon fat.

3. Gently stir the egg-milk mixture into the sifted dry ingredients until completely blended, but do not overmix. Fold in the ham, corn, and scallions.

4. Heat the vegetable oil in a skillet over medium heat until a drop of water crackles when dropped into the oil. Place heaping teaspoons of batter in the hot oil and cook until golden brown on all sides, 2 to 3 minutes. The interior should be dense but not damp. Be careful not to overcook, or they will become dry and slightly bitter. Serve hot with plenty of butter.

[Adapted from *Thrill of the Grill*; Morrow, 1990.]

Grandma Wetzler's Sweet-and-Sour Wilted Chicory

This dish is a variation on hot German potato salad, with its traditional sweet-sour combination. The strong-flavored, slightly bitter chicory is a little too bitter to serve raw, and it needs to be cooked or, as in this dish, wilted.

MAKES 4 SIDE-DISH SERVINGS

I medium-large head chicory
4 slices bacon, finely diced
½ yellow onion, diced
I tablespoon sugar

I tablespoon white vinegar
Salt and freshly cracked black pepper

1. Cut off the root end of the chicory. Since chicory tends to be gritty, soak it in water for a few minutes, then dry it thoroughly in a lettuce spinner or on paper towels. After the chicory is dry, break the leaves in half.

2. In a deep sauce pot, sauté the bacon pieces over medium heat until crisp, about 6 to 8 minutes. Remove the bacon and set aside, leaving the fat in the pan.

3. Add the onion to the fat and cook until clear, about 3 to 4 minutes.

4. Add the chicory and stir well to coat it with the fat. Cook only until the chicory is wilted, I to 2 minutes. Make sure the chicory does not go completely limp.

5. Remove the pot from the heat, add the sugar and vinegar, and toss well. Add the reserved bacon pieces and salt and pepper to taste. Serve immediately.

[Adapted from *Thrill of the Grill;* Morrow, 1990.]

ROCCO'S CULINARY LOVE affair began at age eleven. His parents, who were born in Campagna in southern Italy and emigrated to the United States in the 1950s, instilled in him a deep appreciation for food. When he was sixteen, Rocco entered the Culinary Institute of America. He graduated in 1986 and continued to study classical technique at the prestigious Jardin de Cygne in France, where he trained under Dominique Cecillon. Back in the United States, he learned from some of New York's most prominent master chefs, including Gray Kunz. In 1990, Rocco earned a B.S. in business from Boston University.

In 1997, Rocco opened Union Pacific to widespread critical acclaim and his first three-star review in *The New York Times*. His second came in 2002 from the *New York Observer*. In 1999, Rocco was named *Food & Wine*'s Best New Chef, and in 2000, *Gourmet* magazine dubbed him "America's most exciting young chef." Rocco brought his unique touch to Tuscan restaurant in early 2003 as consulting chef; that restaurant earned a two-star review from *The New York Times* just weeks after relaunching. In June 2003 he opened Rocco's 22nd Street, celebrating the Italian-American cuisine he grew up with. NBC filmed a behind-the-scenes look at the opening of Rocco's on the hugely popular reality show, *The Restaurant*, which aired in July 2003.

Rocco is a frequent guest on television programs such as the *Today show*, *Live with Regis and Kelly*, *The Tonight Show with Jay Leno*, *Late Night with Conan O'Brien*, *Last Call with Carson Daly*, *The View*, and the *Late Show with David Letterman*. In the fall of 2003, Rocco released his first cookbook, *Flavor*. His next book, *Rocco's Italian American*, is expected in the fall of 2004.

〜〜〜

My mother, Nicolina, is one of a disappearing breed of mothers—the ones who had time for everyone and everything. Even though she held two jobs through most of her life, we had fresh, wholesome food on our table every day: *pizza fritta*, spaghetti with oil and garlic or with crab; steak *alla pizzaiola*, and big salads with escarole, tomatoes, and cucumbers. Mom baked fresh bread almost every day and preserved her own tomatoes. No soda, no candy, nothing like that ever made it into our house. If someone smuggled us in some M&M's or a candy bar, my parents made sure it disappeared.

Rocco and "Mamma," Nicolina DiSpirito.

Of all these dishes, the frittata was probably my mother's biggest claim to fame. She donated them to charity events and brought one every time she visited someone's house. Her lasagna was legendary, too. Some of our cousins actually defected from their family get-togethers and showed up at our house when lasagna was on the menu. If I told you what was in it—a thick meat sauce, ricotta, and grated cheese—it would sound like everybody else's mother's lasagna. But it wasn't, and I really don't know why. There was something about the way she made it and let it cool just enough so it wouldn't fall apart when she cut into it. It was an amazing architectural feat, that lasagna.

I can't talk about my mother without talking about my grandmother Anna Maria in the same breath. I know my mother was inspired by her mother in the same way my mother inspires me. My grandmother raised chickens and pigeons, and had something closer to a farm than a garden. My uncle made wine and sausages, and preserved hot and sweet peppers and tomatoes. In short, they lived as they had in Avellino, Italy.

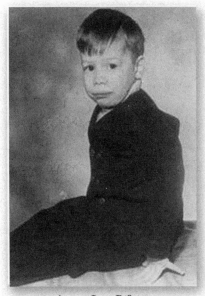

A young Rocco DiSpirito.

With all this food and cooking going on, "restaurant" was a dirty word in our house when I was growing up, but my mom was very supportive when I went off to the Culinary Institute. She was happy that I was doing well and enjoying my work. Working in kitchens gave me a kind of discipline I hadn't had before, and she could see that.

Only in the last five years of my professional life have I given my mother's cooking the respect and deference it deserves. The entire menu at my newest restaurant, Rocco's 22nd Street, is a tribute to the cooking and sense of family I grew up with.

Rocco DiSpirito (second from right) with his sister, Maria; his brother, Michael; and his mother, Nicolina.

Pasta for Breath
Only a Mother Could Love

Spaghettini aglio e olio (or spaghettini with oil and garlic), as this dish is more commonly known, is the perfect dish to serve when friends stop by unannounced. It's an instant party. Even when it seemed as if there was nothing in the house to cook, my mom could make unexpected dinner guests feel that they were part of the family. And there was always enough for seconds.

MAKES 4 TO 6 SERVINGS

Salt

1 pound spaghettini

¼ cup extra virgin olive oil

6 to 8 cloves garlic, smashed

2 tablespoons minced Italian parsley

Pinch of red pepper flakes

Freshly ground black pepper

MOM'S TIP

Time your cooking so that the garlic is done just as the pasta is al dente.

1.   Bring a 6-quart pot of water to a boil over high heat. Add 2 tablespoons of salt and the pasta, and stir well. Cook, stirring occasionally, until the pasta is *al dente*, about 8 minutes.

2.   While the pasta cooks, heat the oil in a 10-inch skillet over medium heat. Add the garlic and cook until golden brown, taking care not to let the garlic get too dark, about 2 minutes. When the garlic is light brown, add the parsley and red pepper flakes.

3.   Drain the pasta and add it to the skillet. Toss, season with salt and pepper, and serve right away in warm bowls.

Potato and Green Pepper Frittata

I love this recipe because it exemplifies everything that is great about Italian home cooking: The ingredients are inexpensive and readily available, the frittata is easy to make but really delicious, and the finished dish can be whipped up in less than twenty minutes to feed a hungry crowd. My mom made this all the time when I was growing up. MAKES 8 SERVINGS

2 tablespoons extra virgin olive oil

1 green bell pepper, chopped

1 sweet onion, chopped

1 clove garlic, minced

2 Idaho potatoes, peeled and finely diced

1 teaspoon salt

4 cranks fresh ground pepper

12 eggs

¼ cup grated Parmigiano-Reggiano cheese

1. Heat the oil in a large omelet pan over medium heat. Add the pepper, onion, and garlic, and cook until slightly softened. Add the potatoes and season with salt and pepper. Cook until the potatoes are soft, about 10 minutes.

2. Beat the eggs with the cheese, salt, and pepper in a mixing bowl. Pour the egg mixture over the vegetables in the omelet pan. Stirring constantly, cook the frittata about 5 minutes on one side, until the eggs are firm around the sides and just slightly loose in the middle. The edges and bottom of the frittata should be golden brown. Using a plate if necessary, flip the frittata and return it to the pan. Cook until the eggs on the second side are cooked through, about 10 minutes. Transfer the frittata to a platter and serve warm or at room temperature, cut into wedges.

> **MOM'S TIP**
>
> Using a large omelet pan with sloped sides instead of a skillet makes it easier to flip the frittata. If you need a little help flipping the half-cooked frittata, slide it out onto a plate. Then hold the pan upside down over the frittata and in one quick move invert the frittata and pan so the frittata lands cooked side up back in the pan.

Porterhouse and Potatoes alla Mamma

I don't know why this steak is so good, but it never fails to amaze me! Maybe it's the simplicity of it, maybe it's because I grew up eating it, maybe it's because my mother had a special way of making everything she touched taste delicious. MAKES 4 TO 6 SERVINGS

FOR THE POTATOES

1½ cups plain dry bread crumbs

½ cup olive oil

Salt and freshly ground pepper

4 pounds Idaho potatoes

2 cups shredded mozzarella cheese

¼ cup grated Parmigiano-Reggiano cheese

FOR THE STEAKS

2 tablespoons dried oregano

2 tablespoons onion powder

2 tablespoons garlic powder

Four 1-inch-thick porterhouse steaks

4 tablespoons olive oil

Salt and freshly ground pepper

2 lemons, halved

1. Preheat the oven to 350° F.

2. To make the potatoes: Mix together the bread crumbs, oil, and a pinch of salt and pepper in a small bowl. Peel the potatoes, quarter them lengthwise, and season them with salt and pepper. Coat the potato pieces generously with the bread crumb mixture. Place the seasoned potatoes crumb side up on a baking sheet or in a lasagna pan in which they fit snugly. Bake until tender, 45 minutes to 1 hour. Remove and sprinkle the cheeses on top.

3. To make the steaks: Preheat the broiler. Mix together the oregano, onion powder, and garlic powder. Coat the steaks on both sides with the oil and this mixture. Season generously with salt and pepper, and place in the broiler pan.

4. Broil the steaks for 5 minutes, then turn and cook the second side for an additional 3 to 5 minutes for medium-rare steaks. Adjust the timing if you like

your steaks more or less done. Remove the steaks from the broiler and let them rest while you finish the potatoes.

5. Adjust the oven temperature to 400° F and put the potatoes back in. Cook until the cheese has melted and is beginning to brown, about 3 to 6 minutes. Squeeze half a lemon on each steak and serve with the potatoes.

ROZANNE GOLD, award-winning chef and author, is one of the most prominent women in the food world today. She is chef-director of the renowned Joseph Baum & Michael Whiteman Co., the international food and restaurant consulting firm, best known for recreating New York's magical Rainbow Room (where Rozanne was co-owner and consulting chef for fifteen years), Windows on the World, and five of New York's three-star restaurants.

Rozanne began her career at the age of twenty-four as first chef to New York's mayor Ed Koch. As chef to Mayor Koch, she cooked for presidents, prime ministers, and dignitaries from all walks of life.

As the author of eight books, Rozanne is a three-time winner of the prestigious James Beard Foundation Book Award and winner of the IACP/Julia Child Cookbook Award. Her books include *Little Meals: A Great New Way to Eat and Cook*; *Recipes 1-2-3: Fabulous Food Using Only Three Ingredients*; *Recipes 1-2-3 Menu Cookbook*; *Entertaining 1-2-3*; *Healthy 1-2-3*; *Desserts 1-2-3*; *Christmas 1-2-3*; and *Cooking 1-2-3: 500 Fabulous Three-Ingredient Recipes*. The original *Recipes 1-2-3* has been published in four countries.

Rozanne is the entertaining columnist for *Bon Appétit* magazine, where her "Entertaining Made Easy" column is read by 5 million fans.

She has written for *The New York Times* (her articles can be found on the op-ed page and in the Dining In section), *Gourmet, Cooking Light, FoodArts, More,* and *Modern Maturity.*

A frequent guest on national television, Rozanne has appeared on the *Today* show; *B. Smith with Style; Everyday Elegance with Colin Cowie; Good Morning America; Home Cooking* on PBS; Discovery Channel's *Home Matters;* Lifetime's *Our Home;* and Food Network.

Rozanne is currently writing a screenplay about a woman chef who runs for president. She is past president of Les Dames d'Escoffier and lives in Park Slope, Brooklyn, with her husband, Michael Whiteman.

Rozanne and Marion Gold.

My mother, Marion, and I express our deep connection by cooking special things for each other all the time. We rarely cook together anymore, except on an occasional holiday, but we derive the greatest pleasure by surprising the other with her favorite dish.

In my case, my mother makes me cabbage and noodles—a homey Hungarian standard that she, too, ate in her childhood. It is our comfort food that connects us to a previous generation and also to each other. I never know exactly when a steamy, buttery bowl will make an appearance on her dining room table, but at age forty-nine, I still delight in its random offering and in the joy she shows in preparing it. My mother often says, "It's not as good as last time," but it always is.

I have learned that some recipes, even more than photographs, provide the most intimate transfer of information from mother to daughter. As victims of a horrendous time in history, most of our Hungarian relatives never made it through World War II. This simple dish is a witness to my past. It is a poignant conduit of things unspoken.

From the time I was a child my daytime fantasies were filled with food and travel. My mother recalls that my first cookbook was worn to tatters because I carried it everywhere like a security blanket. I knew that I wanted to be a cook (despite a serious academic background), but what I didn't acknowledge was that the desire was in my blood. Sometime in 1930, somewhere in Astoria, Queens,

Rozanne Gold and her mom, Marion, at the Rainbow Room.

my maternal grandfather and great-grandmother (whose wedding ring I wear) opened a Hungarian restaurant that featured cabbage and noodles!

The cooking at my parents' home was simple and robust: paprika-scented flavors from my mother; mammoth steamed lobsters, popovers, and blueberry muffins from a quasi-Yankee father whose roots ran from Boston directly back to Russia and Poland. My parents' divergent pasts met in the center of the table.

My mother cooked her heart out when she made her now-famous pot roast. The motivation behind her laborious browning (well, actually, burning) of the onions was that my father and brother loved their deep caramelized taste and the almost black gravy. I must admit I did, too.

And like most women who cook their hearts out for others, she rarely sat down to eat what she made. "Why?" I recently asked my beautiful seventy-six-year-old mother. "I don't like pot roast," she replied. That's just how women are.

Rozanne Gold and her mom, Marion.

In 1999, *Gourmet* magazine ran a cover story about how my family celebrates Hanukkah. My mother came from her gracious apartment in Queens to my 120-year-old Brooklyn brownstone to help out. Her arrival prompted a flood of reminiscences as we worked together. "I think I just grated my finger into the latkes," she said. We parboil our potatoes before shredding them, which means they never turn black the way some raw potatoes do, but cooking the potatoes makes them slippery. We laughed and admitted that a little grated knuckle was indeed another tradition we shared.

My mother has visited me in other people's kitchens, too. The largest one was the kitchen of Gracie Mansion when I became the chef, at the age of twenty-four, to the mayor of New York, Ed Koch. The year was 1978, and I had dropped out of graduate school to become a cook. My mother was quite helpful as she walked me through the construction of the perfect matzo ball for the mayor's first seder. And her recipe for pot roast proved to be a blessing in disguise.

I feel incredibly blessed to have the kind of relationship that I do with my mother. We continue to surprise each other with edible gifts of love and cherish the things unspoken.

Hungarian Cabbage and Noodles

This was my comfort dish growing up, thanks to my beautiful Hungarian mother. The goal in making it is to squeeze the water from shredded cabbage after it is salted and left to wilt and then to "melt" it in sweet butter until it is transformed into dark golden strands. Once it was then tossed with curly egg noodles, I considered this the ultimate dinner when I was a child. Today my mother still prepares it as a special treat when I come to visit, which is very often! Cabbage and noodles can be served as a first course or as a felicitous side dish with pot roast or braised chicken; or it can be eaten all by itself on wistful days.

Years later, when "interviewing" my mother about how she made the dish (I eventually stood by her side to watch her technique), I realized that this was the three-ingredient recipe that gave birth to my series of 1-2-3 cookbooks. (I don't count salt and pepper as ingredients.) My mother once tried to improve the recipe by adding a fourth ingredient, sautéed onions, but it took away from the clarity and authenticity of the dish that she, too, ate as a child.   MAKES 4 SERVINGS

I very large head green cabbage

Kosher salt

¼ pound (I stick) unsalted butter

12 ounces medium-wide egg noodles

Freshly ground black pepper

I.   Cut the cabbage in half and remove the core. With a sharp knife, shred the cabbage into ¼-inch-wide slices. Place in a large colander and sprinkle heavily with salt, using your hands to coat it. Cover with a plate and put a heavy object on top to weight it down (a water-filled tea kettle is perfect). Put the colander in a pan to collect any liquid or set it in the sink. Let sit for 3 to 4 hours. Press down hard and squeeze the cabbage with your hands to extract as much water as possible.

2. Melt the butter in a very large nonstick skillet and add the cabbage. Cook over medium heat, stirring frequently, for 30 to 40 minutes, until the cabbage is deep golden brown. It will shrink considerably. Lower the heat if necessary so that the cabbage does not burn.

3. Cook the noodles in a large pot of boiling water until just tender, about 5 minutes.

4. Drain the noodles thoroughly and place in a warm bowl. Add the hot cabbage and toss together so that the noodles are completely integrated with the cabbage. Add salt, if needed, and lots of pepper.

Palacsintas with Apricot Jam

When I told my mother I wanted to include her recipe for my beloved treat in this book, she said, "Oh, they're not that special. They're made in every *language.*" I loved that! But in fact these ultra-thin crepes are a specialty of Hungary, where they are filled with chocolate and walnuts or rolled around a thick ribbon of *lekvar* (prune butter) or best-quality apricot jam. While the idea of preparing crepes can be daunting, my mother's recipe is effortless. She whips up the batter in her blender and then refrigerates it (in the blender) until she's ready to make them. The batter pours easily from the blender's tapered spout.

I have lovely visions of her swirling the batter around in her pan. "For some reason," she said, "the first one is always too thick," so she gave it to me to eat out of hand, a ritual that continued for decades. My favorite version is the simplest: palacsintas filled with thick apricot jam, at once sweet and tart, and showered with powdery sugar.

This exceptional old-world dessert can be served with a glass of chilled sweet Hungarian Tokay wine.   MAKES 4 SERVINGS

I cup milk

I cup plus 2 tablespoons flour

2 tablespoons granulated sugar

2 extra-large eggs

I tablespoon melted butter

Pinch of salt

3 tablespoons cold butter

¾ cup best-quality apricot jam

⅓ cup confectioners' sugar

I.   Preheat the oven to 350° F.

2.   Put the milk, flour, granulated sugar, eggs, melted butter, and salt in a blender or in the bowl of a food processor. Blend or process until very smooth. (You can refrigerate, covered, at this point. When ready to use, blend again briefly.)

3.   Melt I teaspoon of butter in an 8-inch nonstick skillet until it sizzles. Coat the bottom of the pan with a very thin layer of batter, swirling a bit so that the batter spreads evenly. Cook over medium-low heat until bubbles form on top and the crepe browns lightly on the bottom. Turn over and cook for 30 seconds on the second side.

4.   While it's still in the pan, put a heaping tablespoon of jam down the center of the crepe and fold it like a jelly roll, pressing down as you roll. Remove to a baking sheet, cover with aluminum foil, and keep warm in the oven. Repeat the process, adding more butter to the pan each time you make a crepe.

5.   Sprinkle liberally with the confectioners' sugar pushed through a sieve. Serve 2 per person on warm plates.

"Tunk-a-lee"

Soft Scrambled Eggs with Tomato, Pepper, and Onion

My mother has no idea why she called this dish this funny name. She supposes it sounded like something she heard growing up when her parents spoke Hungarian at home. This lovely egg dish, perfect for breakfast or lunch, is based on *lecso*, the Hungarian trilogy of sautéed onions, green pepper, and tomatoes. "Be careful not to embellish this," counsels my mother, who values its pure taste and simple goodness.   MAKES 4 SERVINGS

3 tablespoons butter

1 large onion, cut into ¼-inch dice

2 medium green peppers

3 large ripe tomatoes

Salt and freshly ground black pepper

9 extra-large eggs

1.   Melt the butter in a large nonstick skillet over very low heat. Add the onions and cook until soft and translucent, about 5 minutes.

2.   Meanwhile, wash the peppers and dry them. Cut in half and discard the seeds. Cut the peppers into ¼-inch dice and add to the onions. Continue to cook over medium heat for 10 minutes, or until softened.

3.   Wash the tomatoes and cut in half. Squeeze out the seeds. Cut the tomatoes into small dice, add to the pan, and stir. Add the salt and pepper to taste. Continue to cook over medium heat for 10 minutes, or until softened.

4.   Beat the eggs very well and add a large pinch of salt. Stir the beaten eggs into the vegetables, cook over medium-high heat, and use a flexible rubber spatula to scramble the eggs. Continue to cook until the eggs are softly scrambled and just set. Serve immediately with toast.

Marion Gold's Pot Roast

If there is one dish my mother is known for, it is her luscious pot roast—served every holiday and in between. The secret is lots and lots of onions, sautéed in sweet butter until burnished. "The meat must be browned well along with the onions, which should become 'this side' of burnt," she says with a laugh. The meat cooks slowly in a covered pot until done. It is then chilled so that it slices easily and can better absorb the flavorful juices when reheated. Sometimes my mother slices the meat herself; other times she brings the cooked meat to her butcher so he can slice it very thin on his electric slicer. More secrets: She cooks potatoes with the oniony gravy while the meat is chilling. Not only do the potatoes absorb the delicious juices, but they help thicken the sauce a bit. MAKES 8 SERVINGS

4 tablespoons unsalted butter	One 4½-pound rump roast
3 large onions	3 large bay leaves
Salt	½ cup dry vermouth
4 cloves garlic	4 large waxy potatoes
Freshly ground pepper	

1. Melt the butter in a large, heavy casserole with a cover. Cut the onions into small pieces and add to the butter. Cook over high heat, stirring occasionally, until very well browned or, as my mother put it, "just this side of burnt." Add salt to taste.

2. Push the garlic through a garlic press and rub all over the roast. Season liberally with salt and pepper. Push the onions to the sides of the pan and add the meat. Brown the beef well on all sides while continuing to stir the onions to prevent them from burning further. Cover the pot and simmer on low heat until the beef is

tender, about 3 hours. Turn the meat every 30 minutes. There should be plenty of gravy produced from the onions and meat.

3. Remove the beef from the pot. Taste the gravy and add more garlic if necessary. Add the bay leaves and vermouth, and bring to a boil. Lower the heat to medium and cook for 5 minutes. (You can cook the potatoes and serve the pot roast at this point, or refrigerate the beef in the liquid overnight. If you refrigerate the beef, lift off the solidified fat from the surface, remove the chilled beef from the gravy, and proceed as follows.)

4. Peel the potatoes and cut them into large chunks. Bring the gravy back to a boil, if necessary, and cook the potatoes in the gravy until just tender, about 30 minutes. Scoop the potatoes into a bowl and cover them with aluminum foil to keep them warm.

5. Carve the meat into thin slices, salt lightly, and return them to the pot to warm through. Serve the meat and potatoes side by side and spoon some of the gravy over both.

BORN IN HEMINGWAY, South Carolina—where she met Herbert Woods—Sylvia moved to New York in the 1940s. Sylvia and Herbert established Sylvia's Restaurant of Harlem in 1962 with a seating capacity of thirty-five people. Today, Sylvia's occupies most of a New York City block.

Sylvia Woods

Sylvia and three of her children, Bedelia, Kenneth, and Crizette, and their family friend Clarence Cooper manage the restaurant, catering, and banquet facilities. Sylvia's son Van has led the family on an aggressive expansion of the restaurant since the early 1980s with the acquisition and development of real estate. In 1992, Sylvia launched a line of Sylvia's soul food products. She and her family opened their second restaurant in Atlanta, Georgia, across the street from City Hall in 1997. She has written two cookbooks, *Sylvia's Soul Food Cookbook* and *Sylvia's Family Soul Food Cookbook*.

When Sylvia is asked about the secret of her success, she is quick to answer: love of God, love of family, love of friends and customers, and love of work. Sylvia, her children and grandchildren, and a great group of employees have worked together to make Sylvia's a world-famous African-American-owned business where on any given day you can meet people of many nationalities and cultures from around the world.

My grandmother raised me for the first several years of my life. My father passed away the week I was born, and my mother, Julia Pressely, left Hemingway, South Carolina, a couple of years after that to go to New York to find work. That was the Depression, and work anywhere was hard to find, but it was really tough in the rural South.

My mother made it back to Hemingway in 1936 with enough money to buy the farm adjoining my grandmother's. She built a four-room A-frame house on the land, and we started farming. My mother prepared me well for all the hard work in the restaurant business. When it was raining too hard to work outdoors, I had inside chores—mending socks, sewing clothes, and things like that. If I ever asked why the neighbors' children could play and nap when it was raining, my mother's response was always the same: "Do they have a car, Sylvia? We do."

My husband, Herbert Woods, and I met in a bean field when we were young. We were married in 1943, and I moved with him to New York after he left the service in 1945. I had a plan when I went looking for work in the city. That was something else my mother taught me—always have a plan. I knew I wanted to work close enough to the house to save car or bus fare, and I knew I wanted to work in a restaurant so I would have at least one meal a day taken care of. I found a job in a luncheonette on 126th Street and Lenox (we lived at 131st at the time) and started working there during the day.

Seven and a half years later I had an opportunity to buy the luncheonette. With help from my mother—who mortgaged her farm—I bought the restaurant, and our family has been running Sylvia's ever since, expanding from a 35-seat luncheonette to a 250-seat restaurant and catering hall, plus a restaurant in Atlanta, two franchised restaurants, and a line of packaged soul food products.

We don't farm on the land in Hemingway anymore, but we go there religiously twice a year, once for Labor Day and once around Christmas. With four children and seventeen grandchildren, it's quite a houseful.

The recipes I'm sharing with you here make up a meal my grandmother and mother prepared every Sunday morning when I was a girl on the farm in Hemingway. We hold a big family reunion every Labor Day when we get to see all of our cousins who still live in the area. We still have this meal before the kids head off to Sunday school and the adults go to church. I hope your family enjoys this breakfast as much as mine does.

Fried Virginia Spots

Virginia spots are a type of small, sweet fish known as drum. They run along the South Carolina coast in September. I remember going to the docks in Merrill's Inlet to buy them right off the dock in big wooden crates. We'd take them home, clean them up, and load up the freezer. If you can't find spots, any small (about 1 pound), white-fleshed, sweet fish will do.

If we have a large crowd around the table, we fry up a bunch of spots before we say prayers, then let people get started while we cook up the rest.

MAKES 8 SERVINGS

8 Virginia spots, cleaned and heads removed

Salt

Pepper

Garlic powder

$\frac{1}{3}$ cup all-purpose flour

$\frac{1}{3}$ cup fine cornmeal

Vegetable oil

> **MOM'S TIPS**
>
> *You can keep the fried fish warm on a baking sheet in a 200° F oven while you finish the frying. You can use two frying pans, cutting the frying time in half.*

1. Cut through the belly side of the fish so you can open them up and lay them flat, but don't cut through the backbone to separate the fish into 2 fillets. Season the fish generously with salt, pepper, and garlic powder, preferably the night before you cook them. Refrigerate until you plan to cook them.

2. Mix the flour and cornmeal together on a baking sheet. Pour enough oil into a deep, heavy skillet to fill about ½ inch. Heat until the flour-cornmeal mix gives off a sizzle when you sprinkle a little of it on the oil. Coat the spots lightly with the mix and fry them, 2 at a time, until the underside is crispy brown. Flip them over and fry until the second side is crispy brown and the fish are cooked through, about 3 minutes. Remove and drain them on paper towels. Fry the remaining fish, replacing the oil if necessary.

Tomato and Okra Gumbo

Some people like to spoon this over their grits and eat them together along with Fried Virginia Spots (previous recipe). Some skip the gumbo and pour cane syrup over the grits and mop up the extra with biscuits. MAKES 8 SERVINGS

1 quart water

1 smoked turkey neck

½ cup diced onion

⅓ cup diced green pepper

¼ cup diced celery

2 tablespoons chopped fresh parsley

2 teaspoons gumbo filé

1 teaspoon seasoned salt or salt to taste

1⅓ cups canned chopped tomatoes in puree

1 pound sliced fresh okra or one 1-pound bag frozen okra

1 to 2 teaspoons cornstarch (more for a thicker gumbo) dissolved in 2 tablespoons water

One 1-pound bag frozen corn

1.   Bring the water, turkey neck, onion, green pepper, and celery to a boil in a large (about 5 quarts), heavy pot. Add the parsley, filé, and seasoning. Bring to a boil and boil for 5 minutes.

2.   Add the tomatoes and okra, and boil gently until the okra is very tender and the gumbo is thickened, about 30 minutes.

3.   Add the cornstarch mixture and stir until thickened. Stir in the corn. Serve immediately.

Grits

Figure ¼ cup of white (not instant) grits per person. Heat twice the amount of water as you have of grits and season it generously with salt. Pour in the grits very gradually, stirring the whole time to prevent lumps from forming. When all the grits are added, adjust the heat so only 1 or 2 bubbles rise to the top at a time. Cook, stirring constantly, until the grits are tender, about 10 minutes. Grits should be as thick as oatmeal, not runny or stiff. If the grits are too thick toward the end of cooking, stir in a little hot water. Check the seasoning, add more salt if necessary, and serve hot.

Biscuits

It shouldn't take you more than a few practice batches to make biscuits just as light and fluffy as the ones we serve at Sylvia's. MAKES ABOUT 2 DOZEN

½ cup solid vegetable shortening, plus more for the pan

5 cups all-purpose flour, or as needed

½ cup sugar

4 teaspoons baking powder

2 teaspoons salt

1¼ cups milk

4 large eggs

1. Preheat the oven to 400° F. Grease two 13 × 9-inch baking pans with shortening.

2. Stir together 5 cups flour, sugar, baking powder, and salt in a large mixing bowl until blended. Make a well in the center and add the milk, ½ cup of shortening, and the eggs. Mix the wet ingredients with your hands until the eggs and

milk are blended. (There will still be some lumps of shortening.) Slowly work the dry ingredients into the wet ingredients with your fingertips. The finished dough should be soft but not sticky, so you may have to add a little more flour if it seems too wet or stop mixing before all the flour is added if it seems too dry.

3. Turn the dough out onto a lightly floured surface. Roll the dough out to ½ inch thick. Cut into 3½-inch rounds and place side by side on the prepared pan. (The rounds should be touching but not overlapping.) Reroll the dough as many times as necessary to cut all the rounds possible. Let them rest in a warm place for 10 to 15 minutes (on top of the warm oven is a good place).

4. Bake until the biscuits are deep golden brown and light to the touch when you pick one up, about 20 minutes. If some of the biscuits are browning more quickly than others, rotate the pan after about 10 minutes. Break the biscuits apart and serve.

[Adapted from *Sylvia's Soul Food*; Hearst Books, 1992.]

MING TSAI was born in Dayton, Ohio, where he spent countless hours cooking alongside his mother and father at their family-owned restaurant, Mandarin Kitchen. He was graduated from Yale University with a degree in mechanical engineering and from Cornell University with a master's degree in hotel administration and hospitality marketing. During his university years Ming never strayed far from the kitchen; his sophomore summer was spent at Le Cordon Bleu cooking school in Paris. After graduating, Ming traveled to kitchens around the globe, training in Paris under renowned pastry chef Pierre Herme and in Osaka with sushi master Kobayashi.

> # Ming
> # Tsai

In February 1998, Ming and his wife, Polly, opened the doors to Blue Ginger, a bistro-style restaurant dedicated to East-West cuisine. Located in Wellesley, just outside Boston, Massachusetts, Blue Ginger brings urban dining and sophistication to the Boston suburbs.

Esquire magazine honored Ming as Chef of the Year 1998, and the James Beard Foundation named him 2002 Best Chef: Northeast. Ming is the 1998 Emmy Award–winning host of *East Meets West with Ming Tsai* and *Ming's Quest*. *Blue Ginger: East Meets West Cooking with Ming Tsai*, now in its fifth edition, was selected by *Food & Wine* magazine as one of 1999's twenty-five best cookbooks. *Simply Ming*, his second book, was published in 2003.

My mom, Iris, was born in Beijing, China, and came to America in 1946 with her parents. The family settled in New Haven, Connecticut, where both her parents taught Mandarin Chinese at Yale University. Mom graduated from New York University in 1958 with a degree in mathematics and met my dad, Stephen Tsai, at Yale, where he was an engineering student.

Ming and Iris Tsai frying egg rolls, c. 1980.

My mother has always been an accomplished cook. She taught cooking classes at the local high school in Dayton, Ohio, for years. In 1980, when she found herself with an empty nest—both boys left home to attend school on the East Coast—Mom took the advice of her students and opened a restaurant called Mandarin Kitchen. She ran the restaurant successfully for eight years. It was a family affair. I worked there during the summers, at jobs that ranged from janitor to cook to manager. That's where I caught the restaurant bug, hanging around the kitchens.

My mother has always been very supportive of everything I've done. She and Dad always told me, "You can be whatever you want as long as it's a doctor, lawyer, or engineer." But after I graduated Yale with a degree in engineering and told them I wanted to be a chef, they backed me one hundred percent. My mother even said, "I saw your grade in fluid dynamics. Maybe you *should* become a chef."

So many of the dishes on the menu at Blue Ginger draw their inspiration from my early days in the kitchen with my mother. Shrimp 3-2-1 uses a classic Mandarin marinade of three parts vinegar to two parts sugar to one part soy sauce. I've updated it by using three types of vinegar, but the base is pure tradition. I have built a career on the lessons I learned all those years ago in Dayton.

Ming and Iris Tsai cooking together in 2001.

Chinese Fire Pot

Almost every culture has a special dish that is cooked and eaten communally, whether it is Swiss fondue, Korean barbecue, Japanese shabu-shabu, or French raclette. Here is the Chinese version, named after the traditional cooking vessel, a kind of chafing dish fueled originally by charcoal. When I was growing up, it was always a treat when we had this dish, and it was especially welcome on cold winter nights. The steam from the large vat of boiling chicken stock was very good for the skin, my mom would remind us as she set it on the table. MAKES 8 TO 12 SERVINGS

CONDIMENTS

2 cups creamy peanut butter

2 cups Chinese sesame paste

1 cup toasted sesame oil

1 cup oyster sauce

1 cup rice wine vinegar

1 cup shaoxing wine

1 cup soy sauce

2 cups chopped scallions

2 cups chopped fresh cilantro

1 egg per diner (optional)

½ cup sambal oelek (see Notes)

FOR COOKING

2 pounds soft tofu, cut into ¼-inch slices

2 Shanghai cabbages or bok choy, roughly chopped

2 bok choy, roughly chopped

4 packages (4 ounces each) bean threads, soaked in warm water to cover until soft, about 30 minutes

1 pound shiitake mushrooms, stems removed

2 pounds flank steak, cut across the grain into ⅛-inch slices

2 pounds boneless and skinless chicken breasts, sliced across the grain into ¼ × 2-inch strips

1 pound large shrimp, peeled and deveined

2 pounds bay scallops

2 quarts chicken stock or low-sodium canned broth

1. Place the condiments in individual bowls or plates and bring them to the table with spoons for serving. Arrange the tofu, cabbages, bok choy, bean threads,

mushrooms, steak, chicken, shrimp, and scallops attractively on platters and bring these to the table as well.

2.   Heat the stock in a large pot on the stove and, when boiling, carefully transfer it to the wok(s) or casserole(s). Bring to the table and place on your heat source (see Notes). Return to a boil. Before the guests begin to cook, put a few large handfuls of the vegetables, some bean threads, mushrooms, and tofu into the stock. Allow the vegetables to cook until softened, about 6 minutes.

3.   Invite your guests to take whatever condiments they wish with spoons and prepare their own dipping sauces in their bowls. They should then select whatever they want from the meat, chicken, and seafood platters, and cook it in the boiling stock. Nothing requires more than 3 minutes' cooking time. As the diners retrieve their cooked meat and seafood, they should also help themselves to the cooked vegetables, bean threads, mushrooms, and tofu. After everyone has been served, replenish the wok or casserole with vegetables, tofu, and bean threads as necessary. The stock must be kept boiling throughout the meal, so don't add too much of any of these ingredients at one time. Allow the stock to return to a boil after each addition. If the stock level becomes low, replenish it with boiling water.

4.   When all the ingredients have been cooked and eaten, or whenever the guests are ready, ladle the cooking broth into soup bowls and serve.

NOTES: Sambal oelek is the most common and most popular hot chili pepper paste used as a table condiment in China and Southeast Asia. It contains chilies, salt, vinegar, and sometimes garlic and tamarind.

A portable butane burner works well as the heat source. Make sure it is set in a level position.

[Adapted from *Blue Ginger: East Meets West Cooking with Ming Tsai*; Clarkson Potter, 1999.]

Pork and Ginger Pot Stickers

The recipe for these fried dumplings was passed down to me by my mom, Iris Tsai, and I wouldn't think of changing it. Some things are perfect as they are. MAKES 20 TO 25 POT STICKERS

FOR THE FILLING

4 cups finely chopped napa cabbage

1 tablespoon kosher salt

8 ounces ground pork (not too lean)

2 tablespoons finely chopped fresh ginger

1½ tablespoons finely chopped garlic

2 tablespoons soy sauce

3 tablespoons toasted sesame oil

1 egg, lightly beaten

FOR THE DOUGH

2 cups water

4 cups all-purpose flour

½ teaspoon kosher salt

2 tablespoons canola oil

1. To make the filling: Combine the cabbage and 1½ teaspoons of salt in a large bowl and toss together. Set aside for 30 minutes. Transfer the cabbage to a clean dish towel or cheesecloth, gather the ends of the cloth together, and twist to squeeze as much water as possible from the cabbage (this will make the filling more cohesive). In a second large bowl, combine the cabbage with the pork, ginger, garlic, soy sauce, sesame oil, the remaining 1½ teaspoons of salt, and egg.

2. To make the dough: Bring the water to a boil. In a large stainless-steel bowl, combine the flour and salt. Slowly add the boiling water in ¼-cup increments, mixing until a ball is formed and the dough is no longer too hot to handle. All the water may not be needed. Knead the dough on a floured work surface until it becomes smooth and elastic, 15 to 20 minutes. Form the dough into a ball, return it to the bowl, and cover with a damp cloth. Allow the dough to rest for 1 hour.

3. To form the wrappers: Add more flour to the work surface. Divide the dough in half. Shape one portion into a log and roll it back and forth under your

palms to make a thin sausage shape measuring about 1 inch in diameter. Cut into ½-inch pieces. One by one, stand each piece on end, flatten it with your palm, and roll it out to form a circular wrapper about 3 inches in diameter and ¹⁄₁₆ inch thick. Repeat with the remaining dough.

4. To fill the pot stickers: Place about ½ tablespoon of the filling in the center of each wrapper. Avoid getting filling on the edges of the wrapper, which would prevent proper sealing. Fold each wrapper in half to form a half-moon shape. Seal the top center of each dumpling by pressing between the fingers and, starting at the center, make 3 pleats, working toward the bottom right. Repeat, working toward the bottom left corner. Press the dumplings down gently on the work surface to flatten the bottoms.

5. Heat a large nonstick skillet over high heat. Add the oil and swirl to coat. When the oil shimmers, add the pot stickers, flattened bottoms down, in rows of 5. Cook in batches without disturbing until brown, about 6 minutes. Add about ½ cup of water and immediately cover to avoid splattering. Lift the cover and make sure about ⅛ inch of water remains in the pan; if not, add a bit more. Steam until the pot stickers are puffy yet firm and the water has evaporated, 8 to 10 minutes. If the water evaporates before the pot stickers are done, add more in ¼-cup increments. If the pot stickers seem done but water remains in the pan, drain it and return the pan to the stove top.

6. Continue to cook over high heat to allow the pot stickers to recrisp on the bottom, 2 to 3 minutes. Transfer them to a platter and serve with a dipping sauce.

[Adapted from *Blue Ginger: East Meets West Cooking with Ming Tsai*; Clarkson Potter, 1999.]

Hoisin Pork Tenderloin Sandwiches

I grew up enjoying hoisin-roasted pork. My mom would pack it into a thermos and send it with me to school. At first I was embarrassed by my "different" lunch, but I soon found myself fielding many requests for a taste. This led to bartering and, usually, more food than I'd begun with. Thanks, Mom!

MAKES 4 SERVINGS

I cup hoisin sauce

2 tablespoons sambal oelek (see Note on p. 157)

2 tablespoons finely chopped garlic

2 tablespoons finely chopped fresh ginger

½ cup red wine

¼ cup chopped scallions, white parts only

2 pork tenderloins (about 8 ounces each)

Kosher salt and freshly ground black pepper

2 tablespoons canola oil

4 large sesame seed buns

Napa Slaw (recipe follows)

I. In a nonreactive baking dish large enough to hold the pork, combine the hoisin sauce, sambal oelek, garlic, ginger, wine, and scallions. Add the pork and turn to coat. Cover and refrigerate for at least 3 hours, preferably overnight.

2. Preheat the oven to 350° F. Season the pork with salt and pepper. Heat a large ovenproof skillet over high heat, add the oil, and swirl to coat the pan. When the oil shimmers, add the pork and brown, turning once, about 5 minutes. Transfer the pork to the oven and roast until just done, 150° F inside, about 12 to 15 minutes. The interior of the pork should remain pink. Allow the pork to rest for 5 minutes, then cut into ¼-inch slices.

3. Halve the buns and toast lightly, if you wish. Top the bottoms with half of the slaw. Add 6 to 8 slices of pork per sandwich and top with the remaining slaw and bun halves. Cut the sandwiches in half and serve.

[Adapted from *Blue Ginger: East Meets West Cooking with Ming Tsai*; Clarkson Potter, 1999.]

Napa Slaw

SERVES 4

½ cup Thai fish sauce

½ cup rice wine vinegar

1½ teaspoons red pepper flakes

8 large basil leaves, cut lengthwise into ¼-inch ribbons

1½ teaspoons sugar

1 medium head napa cabbage, cut into ⅛-inch ribbons (3 cups)

1 cup shredded carrots

1 cup bean sprouts

½ cup scallions (green part only), sliced ⅛ inch thick

Kosher salt and freshly ground black pepper

1. In a large bowl, combine the fish sauce, vinegar, pepper flakes, basil, and sugar, and whisk to blend.

2. Add the cabbage, carrots, bean sprouts, and scallions and toss well. Season with salt and pepper to taste and let rest to allow the flavors to mingle, about 3 minutes.

[Adapted from *Blue Ginger: East Meets West Cooking with Ming Tsai*; Clarkson Potter, 1999.]

BORN IN MAY 1975, Jamie took an early interest in all things culinary. He grew up in Essex, England, where his parents run their own highly respected pub/restaurant, the Cricketers, in the small village of Clavering. At the age of eight, Jamie would help the chefs in the pub kitchen by peeling potatoes and shelling peas. With his fascination for food and cooking clearly not merely a teenage fad, sixteen-year-old Jamie left school and completed his training at Westminster Catering College. He spent time cooking in France before moving on to work at Antonio Carluccio's restaurant in London as head pastry chef. From there Jamie graduated to the acclaimed River Café, where he worked for three and a half years.

> Jamie
> Oliver

Over the last six years Jamie has become one of Britain's and America's best-loved television personalities, with three hugely successful series of *The Naked Chef* and *Oliver's Twist* seen on Food Network. Jamie's books, which include *The Naked Chef, The Naked Chef Takes Off*, and *Happy Days with the Naked Chef*, have been translated into eleven languages. His latest book, *Jamie's Kitchen*, was published in 2003.

In November 2002, Jamie Oliver opened Fifteen, a restaurant in London's Hoxton district, with a unique staff: The majority of the chefs were picked from more than one thousand hopefuls who turned up to "audition" and who, by and large, couldn't really cook! In six months

Jamie and his friends and contacts had not only renovated an old gallery building but also turned these fifteen hopefuls into decent chefs. The reviews have been exceptional. The whole Fifteen saga was caught on film by a documentary TV crew. The results, *Jamie's Kitchen*, aired on Food Network.

Jamie has cooked for Prime Minister Tony Blair at 10 Downing Street. In 2000, Jamie married his childhood sweetheart, Jools. They have two daughters, Poppy Honey and Daisy Boo.

[Sally Oliver, Jamie's mum, gave her take on Jamie's culinary roots in a phone conversation from the Olivers' pub, the Cricketers.—Editor]

Jamie grew up in the kitchen, really. His dad (my husband), Trevor, is a trained chef. Even as a little boy Jamie worked right alongside the chefs in our pub, the Cricketers.

Jamie Oliver and his "Nan."

On Sundays we closed the pub around two o'clock in the afternoon. It took us a bit to clear up, then we'd sit down to dinner around three. Sunday dinner was always a roast of some sort—beef, pork, lamb, or chicken, always served with gravy. Jamie's nan and grandpa were always there, and there were other people—aunts, uncles, and the like—coming round. It was a big chaotic scene with a big roast, lots and lots of vegetables, wine being poured, and quite a bit of noise being made. Trevor always carved, and people would just sort of tuck into the big platters of sliced meat and roasted vegetables. Usually the younger ones would take care of the older folks—making sure they had what they needed before they got started. Those dinners were a lot of fun. The kids would always prod my husband to make some sort of speech or toast. You know, "Lovely to have you all here, gathered around the table." That sort of thing. Well, the kids would egg him on, he'd start to get all emotional, and then the kids would laugh and laugh.

We always did a pudding of some sort for Sunday dinner—steamed puddings were Jamie's favorites—with lots of custard, what you in the States would call crème anglaise.

I see that these pud-dings turn up a lot in Jamie's cookery books, and I see that on his shows there are big plates of stuff in the middle of the table, with everybody diving in. And I hear him on the telly talking about simple roasts and how little you have to do to make fresh vegeta-bles taste good. Just like our Sunday dinners.

Jamie Oliver (left) with his sister, Anna-Marie, and grandparents, at teatime.

Not that I'm taking credit, mind you. Jamie has always had a knack for cooking, and there are other women in his life who have influenced him. Ruth Rogers and Rose Gray from the River Café in London, where Jamie worked when he was younger, really got him into getting the best ingredients and poking and prodding dishes until he got them just right.

Now that Jamie and his wife have two little girls and his sister, Anna-Marie, has three little boys, Sunday dinners can be a complete madhouse—even more chaotic than they used to be. But Jamie loves the hectic thing of everyone chatting and talking. He wouldn't have it any other way, and neither would I.

Sunday at Cricketers: Roast Beef, Best Spuds, and Huge Yorkies
(Yorkshire Puddings)

Roasting is easy, but timing is important. Before you start, get all your vegetables prepped and have your Yorkshire pudding batter made. With this done, you can get your Yorkies on while the beef is resting out of the oven.

MAKES 8 SERVINGS

FOR THE YORKIES

I cup milk

I cup all-purpose flour

Pinch of salt

3 eggs

FOR THE BEEF AND SPUDS

Olive oil

One 5½-pound standing rib roast or sirloin of beef

Sea salt

Freshly ground pepper

3 red onions, halved

7 pounds roasting potatoes, peeled

4 large parsnips, peeled and quartered

3 sprigs rosemary

4 cloves garlic, peeled

2 thumb-sized pieces fresh ginger, peeled and diced

Flour

½ bottle robust red wine

I. Beat together all the Yorkie ingredients and put to the side.

2. Preheat the oven to 450° F. Heat a large thick-bottomed roasting pan on the stove top over high heat and add a little olive oil to the pan. Rub your beef generously with salt and pepper, and lightly color the meat on all sides. Lay your onions in the pan with the beef on top of them. Cook in the oven for a total of 1½ hours.

3. While the beef is cooking, parboil your potatoes in boiling salted water for around 10 minutes, then drain in a colander. Toss about to chuff them up—this will make them really crispy.

4. After 30 minutes, take the pan out and toss in your potatoes, parsnips, and rosemary. With a garlic press or grater, squeeze or grate the garlic and ginger over everything in the pan, which will taste fantastic. Shake the pan and whack it back in the oven for the final hour.

5. Remove the potatoes and parsnips to a dish to keep warm. Place the beef on a plate to rest, covered with aluminum foil, and get your Yorkshire puddings on: Pour about ½ inch of oil into each section of a Yorkshire pudding tray or a heavy 6-cup muffin pan. Preheat the pan for 10 minutes, then divide the batter among the cups. Cook for about 30 minutes, until crisp. Don't open the oven door before then, or they won't rise.

6. Remove most of the fat from your roasting pan, and you should be left with caramelized onions and sticky beef goodness. Pick out the onions and add them to the bowl with the parsnips and potatoes. Add 1 teaspoon of flour to the pan and mash everything together. Heat the pan over a burner, and when hot, add your red wine. Simmer for 5 to 10 minutes, stirring every couple of minutes, until the gravy is really tasty and coats the back of a spoon. Add any juice from the beef and feel free to add some water or stock to thin the gravy if you like. Pour through a coarse sieve, pushing it through with a spoon, and serve in a warmed gravy jug.

P.S. Just so you know, beef needs about 15 minutes per pound to cook, plus an extra 20 minutes at the end, no matter how big it is. This will cook it medium, so give it a bit more or less depending on your preference.

[Adapted from *Happy Days with the Naked Chef*; Hyperion, 2002.]

Pound Pudding

This is a traditional pudding that I think makes a wicked change from Christmas pud, which is sometimes a bit heavy. It's one of the classic old English desserts. It is great served with some brandy butter, crème fraîche, whipped cream, or custard.   MAKES 8 SERVINGS

1 pound mixed dried fruit (apricots, raisins, prunes)	1 cup all-purpose flour
4 ounces dried pitted dates, chopped	½ cup sugar
One ½-inch piece preserved ginger or 1 teaspoon dried ginger	2 cups fresh bread crumbs
4 ounces suet or butter	2 tablespoons brandy
Grated zest of 1 orange	Pinch of salt
	1 medium egg, beaten
	⅔ cup milk

1.   Grease a 1½-quart soufflé dish. Mix together the mixed fruit, dates, ginger, suet, zest, flour, sugar, bread crumbs, brandy, and salt. Add the beaten egg and milk, and mix well. Put the mixture into the dish and cover with aluminum foil or a cloth. Place in a large saucepan with water halfway up the sides of the dish. Bring the water to a boil, put on a tight-fitting lid, and simmer for 3 hours. Check occasionally, remembering to carefully top up with boiling water to prevent dryness. When serving, remove the foil or cloth and turn out onto a plate.

2.   Feel free to flame the pudding safely! First, make sure the pudding is piping hot. Place it on a plate with a wide rim in the center of the table. Heat a little rum and brandy in a small pan—ideally one with a lip—on the stove. When the alcohol is warm, carry the pan carefully to the pudding and pour the alcohol over the pudding. Stand back and carefully put a lit match next to the pudding—no need to touch it—and the fumes will ignite. The flames will go out in a few seconds, and then you can tuck in!

Rhubarb Daisy Cake

This dish was created by my mum, Sally Oliver, on the occasion of the birth of her second granddaughter, Daisy Boo Oliver. Be sure the rhubarb you use is nice and juicy, and lay it, pretty side down, over the syrup so it looks nice when you take the cake out of the pan. MAKES 8 SERVINGS

I vanilla bean

¼ pound (I stick) butter, plus more for greasing the pan

½ cup golden syrup (see Notes)

Teeny bit of finely chopped ginger in syrup, plus some of the syrup from the jar, if you like

Grated zest of 2 lemons

1½ pounds rhubarb (the nice thin pink bits, not the tough ends)

½ cup plus 2 tablespoons vanilla sugar (made by adding vanilla beans to superfine sugar) or granulated sugar

I cup self-rising flour

2 eggs

Milk, if needed (see Notes)

Crème fraîche or *fromage frais* (see Notes)

1. Preheat the oven to 375° F. Split the vanilla bean in half lengthwise and scrape out the seeds.

2. Grease a 12-inch, high-sided, ovenproof, nonstick frying pan with butter. Spoon the golden syrup (and about I tablespoon of the syrup from the ginger if you like) into the bottom. Stir in the chopped ginger, lemon zest, and vanilla seeds.

3. Cut the rhubarb into 3-inch pieces. Take one-third of the slices and cut them into small pieces, then make a circle with them in the center of the pan over the syrup. Arrange the rest of the rhubarb slices on the syrup like the petals in a daisy. Lay the fruit on the syrup nice side down (think how it will look upside down). Sprinkle with the 2 tablespoons of sugar.

4. Mix together the butter, ½ cup of sugar, flour, eggs, and milk if you want. Spoon the mixture over the fruit and level the top as best you can. It doesn't

matter if there is some fruit showing through, although do try to get it as evenly distributed as possible. It is important to use really juicy fruit.

5. Cook for 40 minutes. It goes a lovely color. Let sit for 10 minutes before turning out. (I have cooked mine 1 or 2 hours in advance and stuck it in the warming oven just before serving.) Serve with whatever you like. (I use crème fraîche and *fromage frais* mixed with the zest of an orange.)

NOTES: **If you can't find golden syrup, combine two parts light corn syrup with one part molasses *or* equal parts of honey and corn syrup.**

You don't really need any milk, and I try not to use any. But it can be a bit tricky to spread the mixture over the juicy fruit. If you add 1 to 2 tablespoons of milk to the batter, it will be easier to pour, although I think the finished cake is nicer without any milk.

***Fromage frais* is a fresh, cow's milk cheese. It is imported from France and is available in specialty grocery stores.**

MOLLIE KATZEN, with more than 5 million books in print, is listed by *The New York Times* as one of the best-selling cookbook authors of all time. Named by *Health* magazine as one of the five "Women Who Changed the Way We Eat" and personally selected by the dean as a founding member of the new Harvard School of Public Health Leadership Council, Mollie holds a charter seat at the Harvard School of Public Health Nutrition Roundtable and was an inaugural inductee to the new Natural Health Hall of Fame. Largely credited with moving healthful gourmet food from the fringe to the center of American dinner plates, Mollie has now formed a partnership with Harvard University as both a consultant to Harvard University dining and the architect of their new, groundbreaking Food Literacy Initiative.

Born in Rochester, New York, Mollie studied at the Eastman School of Music, Cornell University, and the San Francisco Art Institute, where she received a bachelor of fine arts degree with honors in painting. Her classic *Moosewood Cookbook*, first published in 1972 and completely revised in 1992 and 2000, has been enthusiastically embraced by several generations. Mollie has shared more of her favorite recipes and unique artwork in *The Enchanted Broccoli Forest* and *Still Life with Menu*. Both have become perennial best-sellers, as has the award-winning *Mollie Katzen's Vegetable Heaven*, a finalist for the IACP/Julia Child Cookbook Awards.

Mollie Katzen

To inspire young cooks to explore the wonders of the kitchen, Mollie illustrated and coauthored the award-winning, best-selling children's cookbook *Pretend Soup*, which was followed by a cookbook for school-age kids, *Honest Pretzels*. Mollie's newest work is a comprehensive twelve-chapter, four-hundred-recipe book about breakfast, *Mollie Katzen's Sunlight Café*.

My grandmother Minnie wasn't your typical Jewish grandmother; she had long red nails and loved a good poker game. But she was brilliant and amazingly skilled at everything she put her mind to, including sewing, crocheting, and cooking. She had hands that just *knew*.

Grandma made her own dough for strudel, starting at eight in the morning and working all day long. She didn't roll the dough, she worked it with her hands—*nudging* it, she called it—until it was paper-thin. I was transfixed watching her. It seemed like an act of such incredible devotion. In fact, *all* acts of devotion in our household seemed to take place around food. It was as if Grandma was saying, "I will make there be something where there was nothing." And that is a feeling I carry with me today just about every time I cook.

Mollie Katzen and her mom, Betty, with a cake Mollie baked for her.

My mother, Betty, is a different kind of cook. Grandma went to the fish store and ground her own fish for gefilte fish. Mom opened a jar. Mom learned to cook after her marriage—from women's magazines and from the backs of boxes. She was a real 1950s' housewife. (Regardless, I still thought her food was delicious!) The fact is, Grandma had been so skilled around the house, she never turned to anyone for help, and so my mother never really spent any time in the kitchen during her childhood.

It was different with my mom and me. I was always in the kitchen, watching, touching, and helping, from when I was three years old. Eating my favorite snack (brown sugar right out of a measuring cup), I'd sit and watch her cook. Watching her cook with the sweet brown sugar melting on my tongue was a kind of high, a magic state. (The brown sugar probably didn't hurt, either.)

If I wasn't in her kitchen, I was in the backyard in my "mud kitchen," making concoctions of dirt, water, grass, and violet leaves using hand-me-down, chipped bowls and discarded spoons. Even before the kitchen there was kitchen play. Mom used to pour bubble bath in the tub and hand me an egg beater to whip up some bubbles.

Watching my mother cook wasn't less of an experience than sitting in my grandmother's kitchen, it was just different—a clean, crisp kind of cooking. My mother's goal was to come up with meals in which everything went in the oven and came out of the oven at the same time. But it was different on the Sabbath. On Fridays my mother cooked all day long. I may not have tasted fresh vegetables until I was twelve, but I never tasted store-bought challah, either. I remember putting my three-year-old hand on the warm ball of dough. The bread rising was for me the holy part of the Sabbath.

My grandmother's sense of devotion influences everything I do. And today a lot of the teaching I do is with children. In a sense, I'm letting those children into my kitchen exactly as my mother let me into hers.

Matzo Brei

Matzo brei is similar in concept to French toast, but instead of soaking bread in eggs and milk, you soften matzo in a little water and then drain it off, mix it with beaten egg, and fry it in butter. It's actually very easy!

It was impossible to extract a precise recipe for matzo brei from my grandmother because she never measured anything. She owned no cookbooks (not even recipes on scraps of paper) and had never heard of measuring cups or spoons. Both cooking and baking were done by "feel" or by sight—judging things in relationship to the size of her hand, for example. That said, this is a close approximation of our family recipe for matzo brei. It might not be your family's recipe, but that's okay. If you are Jewish and you remember your grandmother making it differently (for instance, going a savory route with sautéed onions and leaving off the sweet toppings), please, by all means, improvise in that direction. There is neither a right nor a wrong way to make it! MAKES 1 LARGE OR 2 SMALL SERVINGS (EASILY MULTIPLIED)

2 matzos

2 large eggs

Salt

1 tablespoon butter, or a little more

OPTIONAL TOPPINGS

Fresh fruit

Preserves

Honey

Cinnamon sugar

1. Break the matzo into 3-inch pieces (approximate, of course!) and place them in a bowl. Add tap water (any temperature) to cover and let stand for 3 to 5 minutes.

2. Drain off the water. You don't need to press it out, just get rid of any that is in the bowl.

3. Break the eggs into a second, smaller bowl and beat with a fork until smooth. Pour the eggs over the matzo, add a few dashes of salt, and mix until the matzo is completely coated. It's okay if the matzo breaks further into smaller pieces.

4. Place a 10-inch skillet over medium heat and wait for a few minutes. When it is hot, add the butter, wait a few seconds longer, and then swirl the butter around so it coats the pan as it melts. Add the matzo-egg mixture to the hot pan, distributing it evenly to the edges of the pan. Let it cook undisturbed over medium heat for 5 to 8 minutes, and possibly a little longer, or until golden on the bottom. You can peek!

5. Lift the matzo brei gently with a spatula, add a little more butter to the pan, and wait a few seconds for it to melt. Flip the matzo brei over to cook on the second side until golden. (If it breaks during the flipping process, don't worry about it. You need to break it up to serve it anyway.) Break into pieces and serve hot or warm with your chosen toppings.

> **MOM'S TIP**
>
> *If you have any matzo brei left over, it reheats well in an oven or toaster oven. Line the tray with aluminum foil and spread out the matzo brei in a thin layer. Reheat at 200° F for about 10 minutes.*

Tsimmes

Tsimmes is a festive Jewish dish that combines vegetables and fruit, savory with tart and sweet. There is no official recipe; each family seems to have its own traditional version, handed down by word of mouth from generation to generation. One thing all versions have in common is the technique: Just throw everything together and bake it for a long time.   MAKES 6 SERVINGS

3½ pounds sweet potatoes or yams, or a combination

2 large carrots, sliced

I large (3- to 4-inch diameter) apple, cored and sliced (peeling optional)

I heaping cup chopped onion

2 cups chopped dried apricots

3 to 4 tablespoons fresh lemon juice

I teaspoon salt

½ teaspoon cinnamon

⅔ cup orange juice

I cup apple juice

¼ cup fine bread crumbs or matzo meal

I. Preheat the oven to 350° F.

2. Peel the sweet potatoes and cut them into I-inch pieces. Place them in a large bowl and add the carrots, apple, onion, apricots, lemon juice, salt, cinnamon, orange juice, and apple juice. Toss until nicely combined. Don't worry if it's not perfectly uniform.

3. Transfer to a 2-quart casserole or equivalent baking pan. Sprinkle with the bread crumbs and cover with aluminum foil. Bake for I½ to 2 hours, or until everything is very tender and indistinguishable from everything else.

[Adapted from *The Enchanted Broccoli Forest*; Ten Speed Press, 2000.]

Mushroom-Barley Soup

Mushroom-barley soup was a specialty of my grandmother. She liked it because mushrooms and barley can be cooked into the next century but will never overcook. They will keep their spunk no matter what, through thick or thin (and this soup is relentlessly thick)! That spunkiness could describe my grandmother as well—in a good way.   MAKES 8 SERVINGS

½ cup uncooked pearl barley

6½ cups water

1 to 2 tablespoons butter

1 medium onion, chopped (about 1½ cups)

2 medium cloves garlic, minced

1 pound mushrooms, sliced

½ to 1 teaspoon salt

3 to 4 tablespoons soy sauce

3 to 4 tablespoons dry sherry

Freshly ground black pepper

1.   Place the barley and 1½ cups of water in a large saucepan or a Dutch oven. Bring to a boil, cover, and simmer until the barley is tender, 20 to 30 minutes.

2.   Meanwhile, melt the butter in a skillet. Add the onions and sauté over medium heat about 5 minutes. Add the garlic, mushrooms, and salt. Cover and cook, stirring occasionally, until everything is very tender, about 10 to 12 minutes. Stir in the soy sauce and sherry.

3.   Add this mixture to the cooked barley along with the remaining 5 cups of water. Grind in a generous amount of pepper and simmer over very low heat, partially covered, for another 20 minutes. Taste to correct the seasonings and serve.

[Adapted from *Moosewood Cookbook*; Ten Speed Press, 2000.]

Noodle Kugel

Noodle Kugel, a dairy version, was one of our eight or ten "alternative" dinner entrées on the one night each week when my mother didn't serve meat in our kosher home. She fortified the kugel with umpteen rich ingredients to "keep body and soul together" in the absence of brisket or chicken. By the way, usually four or five of those "alternative" entrées were served at a single meal to compensate for the meat. You can make this recipe richer or lighter. Options for both persuasions are listed below.   MAKES 8 SERVINGS

One 1-pound or 12-ounce package wide egg noodles

2 to 3 tablespoons butter or margarine (optional)

3 eggs (yolks can be omitted)

2 cups (1 pound) cottage cheese (low-fat okay)

¾ cup sour cream or yogurt

8 ounces cream cheese (low-fat okay) (optional)

1 teaspoon vanilla extract

1 to 2 teaspoons cinnamon

¼ to ½ cup sugar (to taste)

½ to 1 teaspoon salt (to taste)

ADDITIONS (OPTIONAL)

1 to 2 tablespoons lemon juice (to taste)

½ cup packed raisins

1 tart apple, peeled and sliced

2 ripe peaches, peeled and sliced

TOPPING (OPTIONAL)

1 cup bread crumbs and/or wheat germ

1½ teaspoons cinnamon

¼ cup packed brown sugar

1.   Preheat the oven to 375° F. Lightly grease a 9 × 13-inch baking dish.

2.   Cook the noodles until about half done. Drain and toss with butter or rinse in cold water and drain again. Transfer to a large bowl.

3.   Combine the eggs, cottage cheese, sour cream, cream cheese, vanilla, cinnamon, sugar, and salt in a blender or food processor and whip until smooth. Do

this in several batches, if necessary. Stir this into the noodles along with whatever optional additions you choose. Transfer to the prepared baking dish.

4. Combine the topping ingredients and sprinkle them over the top. Bake, uncovered, for about 40 minutes. Serve hot, warm, or at room temperature.

[Adapted from *Moosewood Cookbook*; Ten Speed Press, 2000.]

ARTHUR SCHWARTZ, also known as "the Schwartz Who Ate New York," was one of the first male newspaper food editors in the country and is now a cookbook author, cooking teacher, and host of *Arthur Schwartz with Food Talk*, a daily program heard on WOR radio, New York's number one talk station.

Arthur's career started thirty years ago as assistant food editor and food feature writer at Long Island's *Newsday*. Nine years later he created the *New York Daily News'* s Good Living section and became executive food editor as well as food and restaurant critic. All four of his cookbooks were nominated for national awards: *Cooking in a Small Kitchen*, *What to Cook When You Think There's Nothing in the House to Eat*, *Soup Suppers*, and his latest work, *Naples at Table: Cooking in Campania*.

You might say Arthur was born with a wooden spoon in his mouth. His paternal grandfather was first a professional chef, then a food manufacturer, then a curmudgeonly waiter in a Jewish dairy restaurant. His maternal grandmother's home cooking was the envy and despair of the neighbors. His father could spend an entire day shopping for just the right ingredients for one dinner. In short, he grew up in a food-obsessed Brooklyn family that went, and still goes, to any length for a good meal.

He is the author of numerous articles for a wide range of magazines, including *Saveur, Food & Wine, Cuisine, Vintage, French Vogue, German Lui, Playbill,* and *Great Recipes.* Arthur has been the New York restaurant critic for *Travel-Holiday* magazine and *Good Day New York.* He has also appeared several times on *Good Morning America* and *Live with Regis and Kathie Lee,* and continues to make frequent TV appearances on Food Network, Learning Channel, Discovery Channel, Lifetime Network, and New York's MetroGuide.

Arthur teaches to sold-out classes at all the major cooking schools in the metropolitan New York area and has lectured and conducted seminars at many institutions of higher education.

In 1999, Arthur received the IACP Award of Excellence in Electronic Media for his radio show, which was also nominated for the 1999 James Beard Foundation Broadcast Media Award for the best radio show on food. He is also listed in *Who's Who in America.*

M y mother, Sydell Bedona Sonkin Schwartz, was a very good cook, but she didn't like cooking. Every day we had simple meals of mostly fresh food. Broiled meat, poultry, and fish were standard. She made a great meat loaf—but didn't every mother in America? Every once in a while she would do a long-cooked dish, such as potted meatballs or sweet-and-sour calf's tongue or a beef stew. For my father's delectation, and eventually mine, she'd occasionally sauté kidneys with mushrooms or broil lamb chops, which she detested. She'd even, on occasion, take a day to simmer a big pot of the Neapolitan-style meat sauce (*ragú*) that she'd learned to make from our Italian neighbors. She'd serve the meat sauce on fresh cheese ravioli bought at the Italian market or over macaroni and spaghetti, of course. That's probably why I always say I want ricotta ravioli with *ragú* for my final meal.

True, canned tomato soup, canned peas, and canned sweet potatoes were in her repertoire. This was, after all, the 1950s, when the slogan and the national attitude was "less work for Mother" (a real-life advertising slogan that sold millions of dollars' worth of Horn & Hardart prepared foods).

Still, my friends all thought we were weird because we ate whatever fresh vegetables were in season—even brussels sprouts and asparagus—and had salad with every dinner. Most revolutionary, we had fruit, not sweets, for everyday dessert. A huge treat was chocolate pudding with liquid heavy cream seeping into the cracks of the skin that formed on the surface of the pudding as it cooled. Cakes and pastries from our great neighborhood bakery (who needed to bake?) were for company and my mother's mahjong game, although the day after these events, my sister, father, and I indulged on the leftovers.

Come the Jewish holidays, my mother joined my grandmother Elsie Sonkin, who lived downstairs, in the kitchen. Not only did Elsie love to cook, but she may have been the best cook in the neighborhood. (My mother's friends went to my grandmother for cooking advice before they went to their own mothers.)

It was Elsie who enlisted me to do my first kitchen chores: shelling nuts—which would have destroyed Elsie's manicure—for cakes and confections; the arm-breaking chore of chopping the fish for gefilte fish until the proteins in the fish became sticky and formed a natural thickener that made starch filler unnecessary; manning the crank on the meat grinder; peeling onions or potatoes—you get the picture.

Years later when my grandmother was too infirm to honcho the holiday preparations and after she died, my mother proved herself a master of all the special dishes we had inherited from her parents and grandparents (and, I had always assumed, *their* parents and *their* parents before them).

My mother had stopped cooking daily meals by then. Once my sister and I had left home, my parents went out to dinner every night. I'll never forget when my father came to visit me at my country house one May. I cooked, of course. He said—and this was no joke, although he was a big jokester—"I haven't had a home-cooked meal since Thanksgiving."

I may have learned to appreciate fresh, simple, well-cooked food from my mother, and even how to shop for it, but Elsie was my big influence. It was from her that I learned cooking could be fun. Eventually she gave me considerable responsibility in her kitchen. When she allowed me to make the crepes for her famous blintzes—"They have to be so thin you can see your hand through them"—I knew I had arrived.

I've had many Italian influences in my cooking, including Caesar Benvenuto, my father's best friend who lived down the block from us. But it wasn't until many years later, when I hired Iris Carulli as a personal assistant, that I got to live (well, practically) with a great Italian cook. Iris, whose father was Sicilian, married a Sicilian she met in graduate school in Venice. For fourteen years she lived in Italy, part of the time with her mother-in-law in Siracusa, from whom she picked up many of the wonderful Italian housewifey ways. Iris loved pretending she was a little old Sicilian lady when in fact she was an elegantly turned out, highly educated, and very sophisticated New Yorker. I have always believed that old-fashioned ways of cooking are aesthetically more pleasing and nurturing than the high-tech ways. So does Iris. I knew how to put myself in touch with my past and perpetuate it through cooking and eating, just as my mother did when she prepared our family's holiday foods. Iris showed me how I could experience a bit of other people's pasts in the same way.

My Family's Passover Walnut Cake

This is the reason I spent so many spring days of my childhood shelling walnuts. It is a true torte. Except for a couple of tablespoons of matzo meal, its structure comes from only ground nuts and egg yolks. Its leavening is beaten egg whites. MAKES 8 SERVINGS

9 eggs, separated	1 teaspoon vanilla extract
1 cup sugar	⅛ teaspoon salt
2 tablespoons matzo cake meal (see Notes)	2 cups ground walnuts

1.   Preheat the oven to 350° F.

2.   Beat the egg yolks in a large bowl with a handheld or stand-up mixer until foamy. Beat in ¾ cup of sugar, 2 tablespoons at a time, beating well after each addition. Beat in the matzo cake meal, stir in the vanilla and salt, and blend thoroughly. Stir in the walnuts.

3.   Beat the egg whites in a separate medium bowl until foamy. Add the remaining ¼ cup of sugar, 1 tablespoon at a time, and continue beating until the whites are stiff but not dry. Fold the egg whites carefully into the batter with a rubber spatula.

4.   Scrape the batter into a 2-piece 10-inch tube pan and smooth the top. Bake until the cake shrinks away from the sides of the pan, 45 to 50 minutes. Turn the pan upside down and cool completely (see Notes).

5.   When the cake is cool, run a knife around the edges of the cake and around the tube. Grab the center tube and gently lift the cake from the sides of the pan.

> **MOM'S TIP**
>
> *Cooling a delicate cake like this upside down prevents it from falling and becoming dense. If your pan does not have "legs" that allow you to turn the pan upside down without the cake touching the surface of the table, slip the neck of a bottle into the center and tube, and cool the cake like that.*

Slip a knife underneath the cake to separate it from the bottom. Gently slide the cake off the tube and onto a cake platter. My grandmother actually just left the cake on its tube bottom. She felt it was too delicate to remove.

NOTES: **We never frosted or decorated this cake, but if you do not follow Passover dietary laws, it wouldn't hurt to dust the top with some confectioners' sugar—just enough to dress it up.**

Matzo cake meal is very finely ground matzo. It is available in some supermarkets, or you can make your own by passing regular matzo meal through a fine sieve until you have the right amount of fine meal.

Spaghetti with Tomatoes, Basil, and Green Peppercorns

Iris's and my favorite lunch together was spaghetti with nothing but the best olive oil we had in the house, extended with a few spoons of the salty-starchy pasta cooking water. Not even cheese. Not even an herb. Sometimes we added a bit of minced raw garlic. Not even heated.

This sauce isn't quite so straightforward, but it is very simple and takes no more time than it takes to boil the pasta. Its fineness, even genius, is in the choice of butter over olive oil, in merely heating the tomatoes and not cooking them, and in the slightly eccentric seasoning combination of basil and green peppercorns, which was very trendy in the 1970s, when Iris lived in Italy. The green peppercorns pop in your mouth, which adds another dimension. The following formula suited our taste, but the proportions are adjustable. Add more garlic, green peppercorns, basil, and/or cheese if you wish. It's unlikely you'll want less. If you don't have or don't want to buy green peppercorns—which are juicy beads of pepper that come packed in vinegar brine in a can or jar—use plenty of freshly ground black pepper instead. (By the way, when green peppercorns are cured and aged, they become black peppercorns. So you might say green peppercorns are pickled raw peppercorns.) MAKES 4 TO 6 SERVINGS

I pound spaghetti

3 tablespoons butter

3 large cloves garlic, finely chopped

I pound ripe fresh "salad" type tomatoes, cut in half, juice and seeds squeezed out, and diced (about 2 cups)

2 cups loosely packed basil leaves, finely shredded

½ teaspoon salt

I rounded tablespoon well-drained green peppercorns

1½ cups freshly grated Parmigiano-Reggiano cheese

I.   Bring at least 4 quarts of well-salted water to a boil and cook the spaghetti.

2.   Meanwhile, melt the butter in a saucepan or skillet over medium heat. Add the garlic and cook until soft but not colored.

3.   Add the tomatoes and stir well. Increase the heat to high. When the tomatoes are heated through and just beginning to look saucy, about I minute, stir in the basil. Heat another 30 seconds. Add the salt and green peppercorns, and stir well again. Remove the sauce from the heat.

> **MOM'S TIP**
>
> *Adding the cheese gradually helps prevent it from becoming gummy.*

4.   When the spaghetti is done, drain well, place in a serving bowl, and toss it together with the hot sauce. Add the cheese, about one-third at a time, tossing between additions. Serve immediately.

Salt-Seared Swordfish with Garlic and Mint

You have to love salt and raw garlic as much as Iris and I do to love this dish. You can make it with herbs other than dried mint. Finely chopped fresh sage is my second choice. Very coarse sea salt is essential. It goes without saying that you should use condiment-quality extra virgin olive oil—it never gets heated, so it will retain all its flavor and antioxidants. When a dish has so few ingredients, each one must be the absolute best quality you can afford. That I learned from my grandmother, who could drive a fishmonger crazy until she found the right live fish to point out with her well-manicured finger.

MAKES 2 SERVINGS

6 to 8 tablespoons extra virgin olive oil

2 tablespoons red wine vinegar

6 to 8 large cloves garlic, finely minced

1 tablespoon sieved dried mint (see Note)

Two ¼-inch-thick swordfish steaks

2 tablespoons coarse sea salt

1. Choose a platter that will hold the fish in 1 layer or with very little overlapping. Combine the oil, vinegar, garlic, and mint on the platter and crush the garlic as you blend the sauce ingredients together with a fork.

2. Cut the skin off the swordfish and discard it. Sprinkle the salt evenly over the bottom of a heavy skillet and place the pan over high heat. Don't worry if the salt pops a bit. That's actually an indication that the pan and salt are hot enough.

3. When the pan is very hot, place the swordfish on top of the salt and cook until the fish has firmed up, about 3 minutes. Turn the fish and cook another 2 or possibly 3 minutes, until cooked through but still moist.

4.   When the fish is cooked, transfer it with tongs or a fork to the platter. If desired, brush off any large pieces of salt that still cling to the fish. Turn the steaks to coat them with the raw sauce. Spoon some of the sauce on top of the fish and serve immediately.

NOTE: Rub dried mint leaves through a fine sieve to get 1 tablespoon of mint powder.

NIGELLA LAWSON is one of England's most influential food writers. She has a growing international reputation and several best-selling books to her name, as well as the Style Network's hit shows *Forever Summer* and *Nigella Bites*, which was honored with a Gold Ladle for best television show at the 2001 World Food Media Awards.

Born in 1960, Nigella read medieval and modern languages at Oxford and went on to pursue a successful career in journalism, becoming deputy literary editor of *The Sunday Times*. This was followed by a successful freelance career writing for a range of publications including *Gourmet* and *Bon Appétit*.

Nigella's love of cooking and food started at home and became part of her working life when she started the restaurant column in *The Spectator* and later wrote the food column for *Vogue*. Her first book, *How to Eat: The Pleasures and Principles of Good Food*, was published to critical acclaim in 1998. It established Nigella's relaxed attitude toward food and eating, and won her a wide and dedicated audience. In 2000, Nigella introduced a whole new generation to the art of baking with another best-seller, ironically titled *How to Be a Domestic Goddess: Baking and the Art of Comfort Cooking*. In 2001, Nigella was voted author of the year at the British Book Awards, and her *Nigella Bites Christmas Special* appeared in December that year.

Nigella's most recent book, *Forever Summer,* was released in 2002. She has been awarded the British Book Award twice, for illustrated book of the year (*How to Eat,* 1998) and author of the year (2000).

In 1992, Nigella married fellow journalist and broadcaster John Diamond. John was diagnosed with throat cancer in 1997 and died in 2001. Nigella lives in London with her two children, and has recently remarried.

I must have been about fifteen before I realized that people cooked from cookbooks. That isn't to say that I hadn't known of their existence—my mother had a battered *Larousse Gastronomique* and a few other titles high up on a kitchen shelf—but I thought they were like dictionaries or atlases, books that you knew you could refer to but didn't actually read as part of everyday life.

My mother cooked entirely instinctively, and these instincts of hers were always right. She taught us to cook in exactly the same way—though when I say "taught," I can't ever remember an actual instruction. She believed in child labor and was naturally impatient with her workforce, so she didn't really explain what needed to be done, but just asked us to do it. We'd make mayonnaise together: She'd get us to mix together yolks and a drop of Dijon mustard, and she'd drip-drip in the oil while we whisked and whisked until we had a primrose emollient goo in front of us. We learned that you sat the as-yet-uncracked eggs in a bowlful of warm water first, thus warming the eggs and the bowl so that the mayonnaise was less likely to split, and we saw how the final squeeze of lemon juice into the mixture, once enough oil had gone in, added not just requisite sharpness but bleached the mayonnaise to the "right" pale yellow. And what we learned, too, was that "enough" oil was never a specific amount: She didn't measure; she watched, she felt, she tasted. When I cook with my children now—getting them to help top and tail beans with a pair of kitchen scissors, say—I remember my early start and hope that they, too, will learn, by osmosis practically, how to go about the unchallenging business of preparing something to eat. If cooking is turned into the stressful following of a recipe, all barked orders, and no room for the personal or the unforeseen, everything that matters about food is lost.

This is what I learned, not just in my mother's kitchen, but in her mother's, too. My grandmother and I used to cook together on Fridays. I don't know whether this meant it was a preschool exercise or whether we spent these days together during vacations, but I remember being deposited at her house in the morning, walking to the local butcher's—dropping into the library to renew or return her books on the way—and buying strange delicacies we'd cook together in her big, airy kitchen with its black-and-white checkerboard floor. None of the women in my family baked, and they were not conventional types, so my early memories of food and cooking seem almost comically outlandish now. I'd make calves' brains with black butter with my granny, and snails with garlic butter with my mother. I just didn't know these were odd things for a child to be cooking.

I can't honestly say that my childhood memories of kitchen life are perfect ones: Neither my mother nor my grandmother was a homey, relaxed type. But I did learn what cooking was about. Both had their ways in the kitchen, as they did outside of it. The relationship between a person and the food that person cooks was evident right from the start. I still follow some of my grandmother's recipes—she didn't use books much, either, but kept a file of recipes that she'd received from friends or torn out of a newspaper— but most of all I cook in the way my mother cooked, squeezing a lemon into a chicken before roasting it, impatiently rummaging through the fridge to scrape together supper, feeling and tasting my way to make what *I* want to cook, what *I* want to eat. I've just learned to measure a little more and to write recipes even if I didn't grow up reading them.

Italian Sausages with Lentils

My mother used English sausages mostly and those flat, sludgy lentils (Puy lentils weren't so easily available then), but this is at its best made with highly flavored Italian sausages and either French Puy lentils or the similar Italian ones from Umbria.

This isn't about fancifying a down-home dish; it's about doing what feels right and responding to what's available. In short, it's about cooking. This, incidentally, is what Italians serve traditionally on New Year's Day; the coin-shaped lentils symbolize the prosperity that is hoped for over the coming year, much as Jewish tradition uses honey richly for the Rosh Hashanah meal to represent the wish for a sweet and happy life in the year ahead.

MAKES 4 SERVINGS

3 to 4 tablespoons olive oil (not extra virgin)

I onion, finely chopped

Sprinkling of salt

18 ounces dried Puy lentils (about 2¾ cups)

I fat clove garlic, skin removed and squished with the flat side of a knife

8 Italian sausage links

⅓ cup plus I tablespoon red wine

¼ cup water

Flat-leaf parsley for sprinkling

I. To cook the lentils, put 2 to 3 tablespoons of oil into a good-sized saucepan (one that has a lid that fits) on the heat, and when it's warm, add the onion. Sprinkle with salt (which helps prevent it from browning) and cook over a low to medium heat until soft, about 5 minutes. Add the lentils, stir well, and cover generously with cold water. Bring to a boil, cover, and simmer gently for 30 minutes or so, until cooked and most if not all of the liquid has been absorbed. I don't add salt at this stage since the sauce provided by the sausages later (which will be poured over the lentils) will be pretty salty itself. So wait and taste. And remember: You can of course cook the lentils in advance.

2. Anyway, when the lentils are nearly ready or when you're about to reheat them, put a heavy frying pan over medium heat, cover with a film of oil, and add the bruised garlic. Cook for a few minutes, then add the sausages and brown them on both sides, which won't take more than 5 minutes or so—throw in the wine and water, and let bubble up. Cover the pan with a lid or aluminum foil and cook about 15 minutes. Using a fork, mash the now-soft garlic into the sauce and taste for seasoning. Add a little more water if it's too strong.

3. Remove the lentils to a shallowish bowl or dish. (I evacuate the sausages from their cooking pan, plonk the lentils in, and then proceed). Cover with the sausages and their garlicky, winey gravy. Sprinkle on some flat-leaf parsley.

[Adapted from *Nigella Bites*; Hyperion, 2002.]

Liptauer

If we're talking about family favorites, I couldn't leave *liptauer* out. It was *the* deli counter delicacy of my childhood and another eating item I'd all but forgotten about. But something made me remember it, and from taste-memory and some notes from the kitchen book inherited by my friend Olivia from her mother, I tried my hand at making it myself. I can confidently and categorically state that it's not some sentimental yearning that makes me want to see its comeback. You don't need to go in for the retro-molding here, just mix the ingredients and plonk them in a bowl if you like; but whatever, this glorious cream cheese, caper, caraway seed, and paprika combination, spread over sour black bread or—if you don't have the genetic taste for it—over slices of any dark or brown bread that you can get from the supermarket, is rhapsodically unbeatable. MAKES ABOUT 4 CUPS

18 ounces cream cheese

2¼ cups cottage cheese

4 to 5 tablespoons capers

8 cornichons, chopped

3 teaspoons paprika

Pinch of salt

Good grating of black pepper

2 teaspoons caraway seeds

2 teaspoons French mustard

1 to 2 tablespoons flavorless vegetable oil

Fat pinch of paprika

1. Beat the cream cheese and cottage cheese together until they are very smooth. Add the capers, cornichons, paprika, salt, pepper, caraway seeds, and mustard. Mix together well and turn into a 1-quart bowl lined with plastic wrap for easier unmolding later. Smooth the top with a spatula and cover with the overhanging plastic wrap. Place it in the refrigerator to set.

2. When it has become cold enough to turn out—a few hours should do it—unwrap the folded-over plastic wrap on top, place a plate over the now uncovered bowl, turn it over, and unmold. Pull the plastic wrap off and drizzle over a rust-red ooze made by mixing the oil with the paprika.

3. Serve this with bread or poppy-seed bagels, gherkins, and, if you like, some chopped red onions.

[Adapted from *Nigella Bites;* Hyperion, 2002.]

MOM'S TIP

I put a couple of cans on top of the liptauer to press it down while it's chilling. I don't feel it's crucial; I think I do this because my mother was always putting pâtés and such in the refrigerator with weights on.

My Grandmother's Ginger-Jam Bread and Butter Pudding

This recipe comes from my maternal grandmother's recipe folder, a wonderfully retro piece of design, circa late sixties, early seventies. Bread and butter pudding has gone, I know, from stodgy disparagement to fashionable rehabilitation and back to not-that-again clichédom, but I am not prepared to let any of that bother me. My grandmother, more austerely, used milk; I go for mostly cream. Nothing creates so well that tender-bellied swell of softly set custard.   MAKES 6 SERVINGS

6 tablespoons unsalted butter	1 egg
⅓ cup golden raisins	3 tablespoons sugar
3 tablespoons dark rum	2¼ cups heavy cream
10 slices whole wheat bread	¾ cup plus 2 tablespoons milk
10 tablespoons (approximately) ginger conserve or marmalade	1 teaspoon ginger
4 egg yolks	2 tablespoons Demerara or granulated brown sugar

1.   Preheat the oven to 350° F. Grease a 1½-quart pudding dish or shallow baking dish with some of the butter.

2.   Put the raisins in a small bowl, pour the rum over them, microwave on high for 1 minute, then leave them to stand. This is a good way to soak them quickly but juicily.

3.   Make sandwiches with the bread, butter, and ginger conserve (2 tablespoons of conserve for each one); leave yourself some butter to smear on the top later. Cut the sandwiches in half into triangles and arrange them evenly along the middle of the dish. (I put one in the dish with the point of the sandwich upward, one with the flat side uppermost, one with the point side uppermost, and so on,

198   MOM'S SECRET RECIPE FILE

and then squeeze a triangle down each side, but do as you please.) Sprinkle on the raisins and the rum that remains in the bowl.

4. Whisk the egg yolks and egg together with the sugar and stir in the cream and milk. Pour this over the triangles of bread and leave them to soak up the liquid for about 10 minutes, by which time the pudding will be ready to go into the oven. Smear the bread crusts that are poking out of the custard with soft butter. Mix the ginger and Demerara sugar together and sprinkle on the buttered crusts and then lightly over the rest of the pudding.

5. Sit the pudding dish on a baking sheet and put in the oven to cook for about 45 minutes, or until the custard has set and puffed up slightly. Remove, let sit for 10 minutes—by which time the puffiness will have deflated somewhat—and spoon into bowls. If you wish, place a pitcher of custard (see recipe, p. 202) on the table to be served alongside.

[Adapted from *Nigella Bites;* Hyperion, 2002.]

Coffee and Walnut Layer Cake

Neither my grandmothers nor, indeed, my mother, was a baker, but this cake is nevertheless *the* cake of my childhood. When I was little, I used to make it for my younger sister's birthday every year, beating away vigorously with my bowl and wooden spoon. This, however, is a simplified version: Everything just goes into the processor.

Although this is a coffee cake, the coffee flavor is subtle, muted—not too strong for a child and sweetly comforting for an adult.   MAKES 8 TO 12 SERVINGS

FOR THE CAKE LAYERS
½ cup walnut pieces
I cup plus 2 tablespoons sugar
½ pound (2 sticks) unsalted butter
2 scant cups flour
I tablespoon baking powder
4 eggs
2 tablespoons milk, or as needed
I tablespoon instant coffee dissolved in I tablespoon boiling water

FOR THE BUTTERCREAM FROSTING
2½ cups confectioners' sugar
12 tablespoons (I½ sticks) unsalted butter, softened
I tablespoon instant coffee dissolved in I tablespoon boiling water
¼ cup walnut halves to decorate

I.   Preheat the oven to 350° F. Butter two 8-inch round cake pans and line the base of each with baking parchment.

2.   Make the cake layers: Put the walnut pieces and sugar in a food processor and blitz to a fine nutty powder. Add the butter, flour, baking powder, and eggs, and process to a smooth batter. Add the milk to the coffee dissolved in water and pour this mixture down the funnel, with the motor on or just pulsing, to loosen the cake mixture; it should have a soft, dropping consistency, so add more milk if you

need to. Divide between the 2 lined pans and bake for 25 minutes, or until the cake has risen and feels springy to the touch.

3.   Cool the layers on a rack for about 10 minutes before turning them out onto a wire rack and peeling off the baking parchment.

4.   To make the buttercream frosting: When the layers are cool pulse the sugar in the food processor until it is lump free. Add the butter and process until smooth. Add the instant coffee dissolved in water while it is still hot. Pulse to blend.

5.   Place 1 layer upside down on your cake stand or serving plate. Spread with about half of the frosting and then place the second layer, right side up (so the 2 flat sides meet in the middle), on top. Cover the top of the cake with the remaining frosting in a ramshackle swirly pattern. This cake is all about old-fashioned, rustic charm, so don't worry about this unduly. However the frosting goes on is fine. Similarly, don't fret about some of the buttercream oozing out around the middle; that's what makes it look so inviting. Gently press the walnut halves about ½ inch apart all around the edge on top of the icing. Finish the cake decoration with a walnut half in the middle.

Custard

MAKES ABOUT 3 CUPS

I vanilla bean or I teaspoon vanilla extract	5 large egg yolks
2½ cups light cream or half-and-half	I generous tablespoon sugar

I. If you've got a vanilla bean, cut it lengthwise so that the seeds are released and heat the bean in a pan with the cream until nearly boiling. Take off the heat, cover, and leave to steep for 20 minutes. If you're using vanilla extract, place in a pan with the cream on the heat. Beat the egg yolks and sugar together in a bowl. When the cream is warm, pour it over the yolks, beating all the while. Pour the uncooked custard back into the rinsed-out and dried pan and cook over medium heat, stirring constantly, until the custard has thickened. Ten minutes should do it unless you're being very timorous and leaving the flame too low.

2. Fill the sink with enough cold water to come about halfway up the sides of the pan.

3. When the custard has thickened, plunge the pan into the cold water in the sink and whisk it for a minute or so. You can eat it straightaway, or if you want to make it in advance, reheat later in a bowl over a pan of simmering water.

[Adapted from *Nigella Bites*; Hyperion, 2002.]

JIM PERDUE, chairman of the board of Perdue Farms Incorporated, grew up in the family poultry business, working side by side with his grandfather Arthur, the company founder, and his father, Frank.

After high school, Jim left Salisbury, Maryland, to attend college and pursue his interest in biology. He received his undergraduate degree from Wake Forest University, a master's degree in marine biology from the University of Massachusetts at Dartmouth, and a doctorate in fisheries from the University of Washington in Seattle.

In 1983, Jim accepted his father's invitation to return to the family business. He started as an entry-level plant management trainee at the company's Salisbury processing plant and worked a variety of management jobs before being named vice president of quality improvement. During this time he earned an MBA from Salisbury State University in Maryland.

In 1991 he was named chairman of the board, becoming the third-generation Perdue to lead the company. As chief executive officer, Jim heads the company's executive team and is responsible for developing the company's vision and growth strategies. Jim guides the company with a people-first management style and a commitment to quality and integrity. Jim is active in poultry-industry organizations, is a member of the World President's Organization, and is on the board of directors of Leadership Maryland. In his hometown he is a member of the Greater Salisbury Committee, an organization of business leaders dedicated to solving community problems. He is also a member of the board of Salisbury Urban Ministries and has chaired the city's Salvation Army Christmas Kettle Drive Campaign since 1994.

My mother, Madeline Godfrey, was a farm girl and the youngest of eight children. As a young girl she worked hard to help her family make ends meet. Even with all the children pitching in, they eventually lost the farm, but she never lost her spirit.

As a young woman she married Frank Perdue, who at the time was working for his father, Arthur, and trying to grow their fledgling chicken company, Perdue Farms. Frank and Madeline had four children—me and my three sisters. Since Dad worked long hours, Mom was the disciplinarian. She taught us that hard work and frugality were important. We children worked for what we wanted, and like most kids, we had daily chores. The chore I dreaded most was pulling weeds because before Mom let us go play, she inspected each pulled weed to make sure we got the root. (To this day, she still pulls weeds—always getting the root.) Even though I disliked my chores, they instilled a strong work ethic in me that would later help me manage the family business.

Jim Perdue with his mother, Madeline, and two sisters.

My mother influenced not only my work ethic but also my passion for chicken. One of my favorite pastimes as a child was watching my mother dress chickens in the backyard as she prepared them for Sunday dinner. Madeline's kids thought her Sunday night special, fried chicken, was probably the best in the state! I'm happy to share that recipe with you here. Behind the CEO and president of Perdue Farms is a kind and loving mother who taught me the importance of hard work. Madeline's fried chicken dinners and discipline certainly made me the passionate chicken expert I am today, dedicated to the highest quality standards.

Of course, I wouldn't consider making any of the following recipes with anything other than PERDUE® products.

Jim Perdue with his mother and sisters.

Madeline's Fried Chicken

MAKES 4 SERVINGS

2 cups all-purpose flour

2 teaspoons salt

1 teaspoon freshly ground pepper

1/2 teaspoon poultry seasoning

1/2 teaspoon garlic powder

1/2 teaspoon ground red pepper

1 cup buttermilk

1 cup solid vegetable shortening

One (1 1/4-pound) package Perdue fresh chicken drumsticks

1 (2-pound) package Perdue fresh chicken thighs

1. Combine the flour, salt, pepper, poultry seasoning, garlic powder, and red pepper in a medium-sized shallow bowl. Pour the buttermilk into a second medium-sized shallow bowl. Heat the vegetable shortening in a large skillet with sides 2 1/2 to 4 inches high over medium heat until it reaches 350° F. While the oil is heating, dip the chicken pieces, 1 at a time, in the buttermilk and then roll in the flour mixture to coat them evenly. When the shortening reaches the proper temperature, add the chicken pieces, arranging larger pieces toward the center. Fry, uncovered, until the chicken is golden brown, about 15 minutes, turning to brown the pieces evenly.

2. Turn the heat to low and cook, covered, for 5 minutes. Uncover again and cook 5 to 10 minutes more, turning once or twice, until the juices run clear and a meat thermometer inserted in the thickest part of a thigh registers 180° F. Drain on paper towels or on a metal rack. Serve hot or refrigerate and serve cold.

Sweet 'n' Smoky Chicken

My wife, Jan Perdue, says that when I was courting her, I invited her over for dinner and served her Sweet 'n' Smoky Chicken for two. Jan was enchanted with my culinary skill and thought that this would be a sample of what marriage would be like. She learned later that this is just about the only thing I cook. Fortunately, Jan enjoys cooking and doesn't mind my limited repertoire. MAKES 4 SERVINGS

1 large onion, sliced

1 whole Perdue fresh young chicken (about 4 pounds), cut into serving pieces, or 4 pounds of your preferred chicken part

2 teaspoons hickory-smoked salt

¼ teaspoon pepper

½ cup ketchup

½ cup maple syrup

¼ cup red wine vinegar

2 tablespoons prepared mustard

1. Preheat the oven to 350° F.

2. Scatter the onion slices over the bottom of a shallow baking pan. Place the chicken in a single layer, skin side up, on top of the onion. Sprinkle with the salt and pepper. Stir the ketchup, maple syrup, vinegar, and mustard together in a small bowl and pour over chicken. Bake, uncovered, until a meat thermometer inserted in the thickest part of thigh registers 180° F, about 1 hour.

Harvest Turkey

With its meat infused with orange, onion, and cranberry flavors, and with a brandied fruit compote instead of traditional gravy, Harvest Turkey is one of the Perdue family's Thanksgiving favorites. MAKES 12 TO 16 SERVINGS

FOR THE TURKEY

1 Perdue fresh turkey (12 to 16 pounds)

4 whole navel oranges

1 tablespoon chopped fresh thyme leaves

Salt and freshly ground pepper

1 cup fresh or frozen cranberries

2 medium onions, peeled and quartered

FOR THE DRIED FRUIT STEW

2 cups peeled and diced apple (approximately 2 apples)

½ cup raisins

½ cup chopped dried apricots

2 bay leaves

1 cup chicken broth, either homemade or canned

2 tablespoons brandy, water, or chicken broth

3 navel oranges, sliced or cut into wedges

Fresh thyme sprigs

1. Preheat the oven to 325° F. Slide your hand between the turkey's skin and breast meat to loosen the skin. Work gently to avoid tearing the skin. Thinly slice 1 of the oranges and slide the slices along with the thyme under the skin. Season the turkey with salt and pepper.

2. Quarter the 3 remaining oranges and toss together with the cranberries and onions. Stuff the turkey with this mixture. Tie the turkey's legs together with kitchen twine. Pour 1 cup of water into a large roasting pan. Set the turkey in the pan, cover with aluminum foil, and roast for 2½ hours.

3. Remove the foil and continue to roast, basting with the pan juices every 20 minutes, until the Bird-Watcher® thermometer pops and a meat thermometer inserted in the thickest part of the thigh registers 180° F, 10 minutes

to 1½ hours. Remove from the oven, cover with aluminum foil, and let stand at least 20 minutes.

4. Remove the stuffing and discard. Combine all the dried fruit stew ingredients in a medium saucepan and bring to a boil. Adjust the heat and simmer the liquid until it is absorbed and the fruit is tender, about 15 minutes.

5. Transfer the turkey to a platter. Garnish with the remaining oranges and thyme sprigs. Serve with dried fruit stew on the side.

Ginger Brew–Glazed Roaster

For years southerners have glazed ham with cola for a sticky sweet, caramelized coating. This practice has seen a resurgence with the return of "retro" and comfort cuisine. With this recipe I offer a new way to glaze chicken, with reduced nonalcoholic ginger brew. The result of this method is a shiny, sticky, gingery sweet glaze that is absolutely tasty. We think it's a new classic. MAKES 4 SERVINGS

One 12-ounce bottle nonalcoholic ginger beer (see Note)

One 5- to 7-pound Perdue Fresh Whole Oven-Stuffer Roaster

I tablespoon vegetable oil

½ teaspoon salt

¼ teaspoon pepper

I lemon, sliced

I. Pour the ginger beer into a small saucepan and bring to a boil. Continue boiling for 10 to 15 minutes, or until the ginger brew has reduced in volume by at least half. Meanwhile, preheat the oven to 350° F. Remove the giblets from the roaster and place it, breast up, in a roasting pan.

2. Whisk the oil, salt, and pepper into the reduced ginger brew. Brush half of the mixture over the roaster. Stuff the lemon slices into the cavity. Cover the roaster with aluminum foil and roast for 45 minutes.

3. Remove the foil. Brush the remaining half of the ginger beer mixture over the roaster. Continue roasting, uncovered, basting with the sticky pan juices every 20 minutes. Remove when the Bird-Watcher® thermometer pops up and a meat thermometer inserted in the thickest part of the thigh registers 180° F, about 1¼ hours. Remove the Bird-Watcher® thermometer. Remove the roaster from the pan and let stand for 10 to 15 minutes. Carve the bird, transfer to a serving platter, and moisten with more sticky pan juices.

Baked Chicken Thighs with Port and Fresh Mushroom Sauce

This is one of our family's favorite recipes as well as one of the most requested recipes on Perdue's website. It is an elegant and easy entertaining dish that's a classic combination of ingredients.   MAKES 4 SERVINGS

I package (about 2 pounds) Perdue fresh chicken thighs

8 ounces wide egg noodles

I cup port wine

One 8-ounce package cleaned and presliced fresh mushrooms

One 14½-ounce can chicken broth

I to 1½ tablespoons cornstarch

1. Preheat the oven to 350° F.

2. Arrange the chicken thighs, skin side up, in an 8 × 8-inch baking pan. Bake for 30 minutes, or until a meat thermometer inserted in the thickest part of the thigh measures 180° F. About 10 minutes before the thighs are done, prepare the noodles according to the package directions.

3. Meanwhile, simmer the port in a large skillet over medium heat about 5 minutes. Add the mushrooms and simmer, stirring occasionally, 5 minutes more. Stir together 3 tablespoons of the chicken broth and the cornstarch (using the larger amount for a thicker sauce) in a small bowl until the cornstarch is dissolved. Pour the remaining broth into the pan and bring to a simmer. Slowly stir in the cornstarch mixture, bring to a boil, and continue boiling, stirring frequently, until the sauce thickens, about 1 minute. Serve the chicken and sauce over the hot cooked noodles.

PINO LUONGO, cookbook author, chef, and restaurateur, has a love for food that extends back to childhood afternoons spent in his mother's kitchen and summers working at his uncle's restaurant in Porto Santo Stefano, Italy. Although he originally trained to become an actor, Pino ended up following his initial passion, pursuing a career as a chef/restaurateur, when he moved to New York City from Florence in 1980. In 1983 he opened Il Cantinori, which became an instant hit. In 1988 he introduced regional Italian cuisine with Sapore di Mare (Taste of the Sea) in East Hampton, and again in 1989 with Le Madri (The Mothers), for which he flew in Italian mothers to ensure the utmost authenticity. Pino opened his first Coco Pazzo (The Crazy Chef) in 1990 on Manhattan's Upper East Side. Since then he has opened several more in New York and Chicago.

Pino Luongo

Pino realized his dream of bringing the Tuscan lifestyle to America in the form of a ten-thousand-square-foot location in Rockefeller Center, the aptly named Tuscan Square, which features a restaurant and bar upstairs, and espresso bar, bakery, and marketplace with prepared foods downstairs. In March 2001, Pino opened Centolire, which means one hundred lire and is the name of an old song that stated "with one hundred lire you can go to America."

In addition to his prodigious activities as a restaurateur, Pino has also written three cookbooks: *A Tuscan in the Kitchen, Fish Talking,* and *Simply Tuscan,* a best-seller. A fourth book, *La Mia Cucina Toscana,* was published in 2003.

Pino's own line of Coco Pazzo foods can be found in many fine food stores. He travels home to Tuscany several times a year with his wife and children, with whom he resides in Westchester, New York.

⁓

Everything I learned about taste came from my mother, Mafalda. Her passion for food and the way she carried on her life were and are an inspiration to me.

My mother was dedicated to making lunch and dinner every day for all six of us kids. We each had our own favorite dishes. We'd show up for lunch—which was just as big a deal in our house as dinner—not knowing whose favorite meal was waiting for us.

Pino Luongo (second from left) holding his son, Lorenzo, with Pino's mother, father, and sister, Rita.

I didn't realize it then, but that was my mother's way of keeping tabs on us. We were so into her cooking that we'd never stray far and always return on time for meals. I remember one of my favorite dishes from those days—penne with fresh ricotta, cinnamon, and sugar, served warm, moistened with a few tablespoons of water from the pasta pot. There were two rabbit dishes I loved: *coniglio in padella*—rabbit that was browned with garlic and olive oil and then simmered with white wine, rosemary, and sage before it was finished up in the oven; and fried rabbit with artichokes. My mother cut the rabbit into small pieces and then marinated them in milk overnight. The batter, a blend of flours, was always a little different, but it was always light and flavorful. The artichokes were tiny and tender and coated with the same batter, then fried together with the rabbit pieces in butter.

I've adapted many of the dishes from those meals somewhat and used them in my restaurants and books over the years. But there is one dish that I never changed at all: *rostinciana*—my mother's "secret weapon" dish that she made in the summer when we roamed farther than usual from the house and needed extra coaxing to return home. She prepared *rostinciana* by coating one side of a rack of pork ribs with very coarse sea salt and roasting them in a pan that collected the fat.

Pino Luongo's mother and father, with Pino's son, Lorenzo.

When they were done on one side, she'd flip them over, salt the other side, and cook them until they were browned and crispy. Then she cut them into two-rib pieces with her big butcher knife and drizzled extra virgin olive oil over them. Those ribs and a side of *panzanella*, a simple bread and tomato salad, made a perfect meal.

Every restaurant I've opened came from a specific inspiration. I opened Il Cantinori to celebrate the food of Tuscany. (Nobody was doing regional Italian cuisine back then.) Sapore di Mare was modeled on the little places I used to go to near the beach in Italy for a plate of clams or mussels. With Le Madri—"the mothers"—the model was much more personal. I grew up influenced by the way my mother stood up for me, took care of me, loved me, and cooked for me. I wanted to have that kind of heritage represented. I want to maintain that kind of commitment, not just to my Italian mother but to the spirit of all Italian women, and the kind of cooking that formed my personality, me as an individual.

Lasagne di Pane e Cavolfiore

LASAGNE OF BREAD AND CAULIFLOWER

The following recipe reminds me of my mother's Wednesday night dinners in the fall. Pecorino Toscano—a sheep's milk cheese very common in Tuscany—is much softer and younger than pecorino Romano. MAKES 6 TO 8 SERVINGS

2 tablespoons salt

I medium head (about 2 pounds) cauliflower, separated into florets and thick stalks discarded

¼ cup plus 2 tablespoons extra virgin olive oil

One ¾-pound loaf Tuscan country bread, ends trimmed and discarded, sliced crosswise ½ inch thick, and toasted

10 ounces 3- to 6-month-old pecorino Toscano cheese, grated

Freshly ground black pepper

1. Preheat the oven to 325° F.

2. Fill a medium pot with water and add the salt. Bring to a boil over high heat. Add the cauliflower and cook until soft, 4 to 6 minutes. Strain the cauliflower liquid through a fine-mesh strainer placed over a bowl. Set aside the florets and reserve the cooking liquid.

3. Pour ¼ cup of oil into a baking pan measuring about 11 × 8 inches, tipping the pan from side to side and using your fingers to coat the bottom and sides evenly.

4. Lightly soak half of the toasted bread slices, a few at a time, in the cauliflower cooking liquid and arrange in a single layer on the bottom of the baking pan. Sprinkle half of the cauliflower evenly over the bread, top with half of the cheese, season generously with pepper, and drizzle with 1 tablespoon of the remaining oil. Add another layer of bread, top with the remaining cauliflower and cheese, season generously with pepper, and drizzle on the remaining oil.

5. Cover with aluminum foil and bake for 10 minutes. Remove the foil and continue to bake for 20 minutes, or until golden on top. Cut into portions and serve at once.

Fettuccine di Biete Rosse al Sugo D'Agnello BEET FETTUCCINE WITH LAMB SAUCE

This is an old recipe of my mother's. My personal enhancement was adding the beets to the recipe. MAKES 6 SERVINGS

FOR THE PASTA

2 cups peeled and diced (½ inch) beets

Olive oil

1½ cups flour, or as needed

2 eggs

½ teaspoon freshly grated nutmeg

½ cup freshly grated Parmigiano-Reggiano cheese

Semolina flour

FOR THE SAUCE

Olive oil

½ cup chopped shallot

¼ cup chopped carrot

¼ cup chopped celery

2 cups diced (½ inch) boneless lamb from the shoulder or leg

Fine sea salt

Freshly ground black pepper

2 tablespoons red wine vinegar

1 cup dry red wine

1 cup veal or chicken stock

Herb sachet: 2 garlic cloves, 1 bay leaf, 4 crushed juniper berries, and 5 peppercorns tied in a cheesecloth bundle

1 cup frozen peeled chestnuts or canned chestnuts in natural juice

FOR THE ROASTED SQUASH

2 cups peeled and diced (½ inch) butternut squash

1 sprig fresh rosemary

3 sprigs fresh thyme

1 clove garlic

2 teaspoons light brown sugar

1 tablespoon olive oil

Fine sea salt

Freshly ground black pepper

¼ cup freshly grated Parmigiano-Reggiano or pecorino Romano cheese

1.   To make the pasta: Preheat the oven to 375° F. Toss the beets with enough oil to coat them lightly. Spread them out on a baking sheet and roast until tender, about 20 minutes. Cool completely. Place the cooled beets in the work bowl of a food processor and process until very smooth. Scrape the beet puree into a double thickness of cheesecloth. Twist the cheesecloth to squeeze as much liquid from the beets as possible.

2.   Place 1½ cups of flour on a smooth, clean surface and make a well in the middle. Place the eggs, beet puree, nutmeg, and ½ cup cheese in the middle and mix them into the flour, a little at a time, with the help of a fork. Knead until the dough has a smooth, even consistency, adding flour as necessary to prevent the dough from sticking to your hands and the surface.

3.   Roll the dough through a pasta machine to make thin sheets about ⅛ inch thick. Dust a rimmed cookie sheet with semolina flour, then pass the dough sheets through the pasta machine attachment for fettuccine and spread them out on the pan.

4.   To make the sauce: Pour enough oil into a flameproof casserole to cover the bottom and warm it over medium heat. Add the shallot, carrot, and celery, and turn the heat to low. Sauté until the shallot is translucent, about 20 minutes.

5.   In the meantime, pour enough oil into a wide, deep skillet to cover the bottom and set over medium-high heat. Add the lamb, season with salt and pepper, and sear it for 3 to 5 minutes.

6.   Add the meat to the vegetables and mix well. Cook for 5 minutes, then deglaze first with the vinegar and then with the wine. Let evaporate, then add the stock and herb sachet, stirring well. Season with salt and pepper, and simmer until the meat is soft and the sauce has reduced, about 30 to 40 minutes. After 20 minutes, add the chestnuts and let them simmer as well. If the sauce dries up, add a little water.

7.   Meanwhile, roast the squash: Place the squash in a mixing bowl and add the rosemary, thyme, garlic, brown sugar, and oil. Season with salt and pepper, place

on a baking sheet, and roast in the oven for about 25 minutes, until soft but still firm.

8. Add the squash to the sauce and cook together for 5 minutes.

9. Set a large pot of salted water over high heat and bring to a boil. Add the fettuccine and cook, stirring, until *al dente*, 2 to 3 minutes.

10. Drain the pasta in a colander, add to the sauce, and mix thoroughly. Serve in warm bowls or on a warm platter with the cheese sprinkled over the top.

Insalata di Cozze e Zucchini

SALAD OF MUSSELS AND ZUCCHINI

MAKES 6 SERVINGS

6 tablespoons olive oil

2 pounds mussels, shells rinsed
and scraped clean

¼ cup white wine

2 pounds zucchini, trimmed and
cut into matchstick-size pieces

Salt

Juice of ½ lemon

Freshly ground pepper

8 fresh mint leaves, shredded

1. Heat 4 tablespoons of oil in a large skillet over high heat. Add the mussels and cook until the shells open. Discard any mussels that don't open. Add the wine and simmer over medium heat until the wine evaporates. Remove the mussels from their shells, reserve the cooking liquid, and set aside.

2. Cook the zucchini in a large saucepan of salted water just until it turns bright green, about 30 seconds. Drain and set aside.

3. In a small bowl, whisk together the remaining 2 tablespoons of oil, the lemon juice, and 2 tablespoons of the reserved cooking liquid. Add salt and pepper to taste.

4. Make a ring of zucchini around the edge of a serving platter. Pile the mussels in the center, sprinkle with mint, and drizzle with the dressing.

STEVEN RAICHLEN is a multi-award-winning author; journalist; cooking teacher; and TV host. His best-selling *Barbecue Bible* cookbook series (more than 2 million copies in print) and *Barbecue University* TV show on PBS have reinvented American barbecue.

Raichlen's adventure with barbecue began with *The Barbecue Bible*, an encyclopedic study of global grilling chronicling his four-year, 200,000-mile odyssey on the world's barbecue trail.

In 2000, he published *How to Grill*, the world's first step-by-step guide to live fire cooking, with more than one thousand color photographs, hailed by *The New York Times* as "astute, approachable, and eminently appealing." *How to Grill* won an IACP/Julia Child Cookbook Award, as well as a Jacob's Creek Silver Ladle Award in Australia. Raichlen's most recent book, *BBQ USA*, is a 780-page, 650-photograph, 425-recipe love song to regional American barbecue.

Raichlen's twenty-five books also include *Barbecue Bible Sauces, Rubs, and Marinades*; *Beer Can Chicken*; the perennially popular *Miami Spice*; the James Beard Award–winning *Healthy Latin Cooking*; and the new *Big Flavor Cookbook*. In all, Raichlen has won four James Beard Foundation Book Awards and three IACP Awards, and his books have been translated into French, Italian, Spanish, Dutch, Danish, German, Polish, Hungarian, Japanese, and Chinese.

Steven Raichlen

Raichlen's TV show, *Barbecue University with Steven Raichlen*, debuted on public television in Spring 2003. Taped on location at the luxurious Greenbrier resort in White Sulfur Springs, West Virginia, the twenty-six-part series focuses on the techniques of live fire cooking.

In 2000, Raichlen launched Barbecue University at the Greenbrier, and it has been profiled on Food Network (which ranked it the "Best BBQ Experience in the U.S.") and in *Bon Appétit*, *Travel & Leisure*, and *Esquire*. In 2003, *Bon Appétit* named Raichlen "Cooking Teacher of the Year."

In August 2003, Raichlen defeated Iron Chef Rokusaburo Michiba in a barbecue battle on Japanese television. Oprah Winfrey called him the "Gladiator of Grilling," and Howard Stern hailed him as the "Michael Jordan of Barbecue."

In 1975, Raichlen received a Thomas J. Watson Foundation Fellowship to study medieval cooking in Europe, as well as a Fulbright Scholarship to study comparative literature. He holds a degree in French literature from Reed College and trained at Le Cordon Bleu and La Varenne cooking schools in Paris. Raichlen lives with his wife, Barbara, in Coconut Grove, Florida, and Martha's Vineyard, Massachusetts.

M y mother was a ballet dancer. She was also a lousy cook. While other moms were baking cookies for classroom parties, her life was a frenzied sequence of classes, practicing, rehearsals, and performances. This simple truth, as much as any subsequent culinary training, shaped my career as a food writer.

Even if my mother had enjoyed cooking, her devotion to ballet would have nixed it. Like most dancers, she had conflicted attitudes about food. Despite her petite size (five feet tall; ninety pounds), she was always on some sort of diet. (She once lived on roast veal breast for a month straight.) She "scooped" bagels (scraped out the doughy interior) long before the advent of Dr. Atkins.

Our meals were adult and impromptu, thrown together at the last minute and served at the then unfashionably late hour of 8:00 or 9:00 P.M. (How I envied my friends, who sat down for dinner with their families at 5:30 P.M.) I was often served a new phenomenon that was supposed to revolutionize American eating habits in the 1950s: the TV dinner. So I taught myself to cook at an early age; it was a matter of self-defense.

That's not to say that my childhood was completely devoid of food memories—on the contrary. For starters, my aunts, Annette Farber and Rosa Miller, were fabulous cooks, the former in the Jewish Ashkenazi tradition, the latter in the Greek Sephardic. I remember our boisterous extended family holiday meals with wistful pleasure. My paternal grandmother, Ethel Raichlen, made legendary fudge and cookies. Even my mother's mother, Sarah Goldman, who had a natural distrust of any meat that was not overcooked to the toughness of shoe leather, could turn out superior salmon croquettes.

Steven Raichlen and his mother, Frances.

Of the little cooking my mother did, I chiefly remember its robustness—extreme cuisine before it was fashionable. Steaks charred as black as coal on the outside, served rare, almost raw within. Prime rib with plate-burying bones seared crusty and dark for gnawing. (Curiously or perhaps prophetically, my mother was the family grill master.) She never made a sauce I can remember, and her idea of the ideal condiment was an astringent relish of raw cranberries and kumquats.

Appropriately for a noncook, my mother loved raw foods. Back in the fifties, you could eat uncooked hamburger without running the risk of salmonella poisoning, and we would devour it greedily—decades before I heard of steak tartare. When fresh peas were in season, we'd shuck and eat them raw, too. Even my mother's take on milk—that staple for kids in growth spurts—had a curiously adult twist: She'd add a splash of black coffee.

Frances Raichlen.

No, I didn't get my passion for food from my mother. I learned something far more important: a passion for and unwavering dedication to one's craft.

My mother died young (at the age of thirty-eight), long before I became a food writer. I suspect she would have regarded my career with no small amazement (the apple fell very far from the tree in our family) and a twinge of alarm. I mean, if she were to sample the fruits of my food writing, would she still look good in a leotard?

My Mother's "Pittsburgh Rare" Steak

Fearless. Impetuous. Passionate. Impatient. Extreme. These may be odd words to use to describe a steak, but they certainly described my mother. Whatever she did, she did boldly, even recklessly. Whether executing a complicated ballet routine or the simple task of grilling a steak, she did so with grand gestures and a blithe disregard for convention. No politically correct chimney starters for my mother, no. She doused the charcoal with gasoline and lit it with a Vesuvian vwoomp! (Do not try this at home.) No handsome crosshatch of grill marks. No carefully monitored cooking times or instant-read meat thermometers. She'd throw the meat on the grill, char it until the outside was just a little paler than the color of coal and the inside was just shy of still mooing, and slap it onto a plate. The name for this style of steak in the 1950s was "Pittsburgh rare"—the black evoking the smoke or perhaps coal from the Pittsburgh steel mills—and if you love the sanguine flavor of beef, there is no better way to grill it, carcinogens be damned. Of course, Mom used nothing more than salt and pepper for seasoning, but I think she would have approved of the brash Roquefort butter in this recipe.   MAKES 2 SERVINGS

1 ounce Roquefort cheese

2 tablespoons unsalted butter, at room temperature

2 T-bone steaks, each 10 to 12 ounces

Coarse sea salt and cracked black pepper

1. Place the cheese in a bowl and mash to a paste with the back of a fork. Add the butter and stir to mix.

2. Set up your grill for direct grilling and preheat to high. Ideally, you'll be using a charcoal grill and you'll bank the coals thickly on one side (a sort of ex-

treme three-zone fire). Brush and oil the grill grate, although Mom would never have done it.

3. Very generously season the steaks on both sides with salt and pepper. Arrange the steaks on the grate over the hottest part of the fire and grill until darkly browned, even charred black, on the outside but still very rare in the center. You'll want to cook a 1-inch-thick steak about 3 minutes per side.

4. Transfer the steaks to plates or a platter and let rest for 2 minutes. Place a dollop of Roquefort butter in the center of each and serve at once.

Smoked Veal Breast

Being a ballet dancer, my mother was always obsessed with her weight. I don't think she ever topped one hundred pounds, but she was convinced she was fat and more often than not was on a diet. Being the creative person she was, she concocted her own diets. One in particular I recall was her veal breast diet, in which this tough, ornery cut of meat was her main source of nutrition for several weeks. She'd thickly crust the veal breast with paprika and garlic powder and bake it in the oven. It looked fabulous, crusty and brown, but tasted about as tender and appetizing as shoe leather. It wasn't until half a lifetime later that I came to realize she was on to a very good idea but had used the wrong cooking technique. The secret was to barbecue the veal breast—that is, cook it "low and slow" (at a low heat for a long time)—preferably in a smoker. The prolonged cooking melted the tough connective tissue, while the low heat and smoke kept the meat moist and incredibly flavorful. I wish my mother could have tasted this veal breast; it certainly would have given her pleasure and possibly might have given her a more positive attitude about food. MAKES 8 SERVINGS

FOR THE RUB

2 tablespoons kosher salt

2 tablespoons paprika

2 tablespoons brown sugar

1 tablespoon black pepper

1 tablespoon garlic powder

1 large or 2 small veal breasts (3½ to 4 pounds)

3 cups hickory or other wood chips, soaked in water to cover for 1 hour and then drained

1. To make the rub: Combine the salt, paprika, sugar, pepper, and garlic powder in a small bowl and stir to mix. Wash the veal breast, blot dry, and place it on a large baking sheet. Sprinkle the rub over the veal breast on all sides and rub it into the meat with your fingers.

2. If using a charcoal grill, set it up for indirect grilling and preheat to medium-low (300° F). Place the veal breast, fat side up, in the center of the grate over the drip pan. Toss ¾ cup of wood chips on each of the 2 mounds of coals. If using a smoker, set it up according to the manufacturer's instructions and preheat to 275° F. Add half of the wood chips. If using a gas grill, set it up for indirect grilling and put the wood chips in the smoker box or in a smoker pouch. Preheat the grill on high until you see smoke, then adjust the heat to medium-low. Just know that you won't get much smoke flavor on the gas grill.

3. Smoke-roast the veal until darkly browned and very tender. (You should be able to pull it apart with your fingers.) The internal temperature will be about 195° F. If using a charcoal grill or smoker, replenish the coals and wood chips after 1 hour. After 2 hours, or when the veal breast is dark brown, wrap it tightly in heavy-duty aluminum foil and continue cooking until very tender, 1 to 1½ hours more. The total cooking time will be 3 to 3½ hours in a charcoal or gas grill and a little longer in a smoker. Unwrap, thinly slice, and serve with your favorite barbecue sauce. And think of all the ballet dancers who starve themselves on the altar of beauty.

Frances Raichlen's Cranberry-Kumquat Relish

This was the perfect recipe for someone like my mother, a woman who hated to cook. It requires no cooking for the simple reason that the cranberries and kumquats are served raw in all their astringent glory. Lest fears of their mouth-puckering tartness deter you from trying it, know that the fruit is mellowed by the addition of brown sugar, honey, and port wine. It's pretty amazing with turkey, and it's not half bad eaten straight off a spoon by itself. MAKES ABOUT 2 CUPS

One 12-ounce bag fresh cranberries

6 to 8 kumquats or 1 small orange

½ cup shelled pecans or walnuts

⅓ cup light brown sugar, or to taste

½ teaspoon cinnamon

3 tablespoons port wine or red wine

2 tablespoons honey

Pick through the cranberries, removing any with blemishes or any stems. Cut the kumquats in quarters and remove the seeds. Place the kumquats and pecans in a food processor and chop them coarsely, running the machine in short bursts. (See Note.) Add the cranberries, sugar, and cinnamon, and chop coarsely. Add the port and honey, and pulse the processor just to mix. The relish should have some chew to it. Correct the seasoning, adding additional honey or cinnamon to taste.

NOTE: For an unconventional but electrifying touch, add 1 to 2 seeded jalapeño chilies when you chop the cranberries and kumquats.

Grilled Ham Steaks with Grilled Pineapple and Pineapple Glaze

My mother wasn't much of a cook (that's putting it mildly), but she knew her way around a grill. Steaks would come off our rickety old charcoal grill the perfect Pittsburgh rare (coal black outside; red, almost mooing, inside). Her ham steaks bore the surface caramelization that makes sweet-cured meats such a thrill to grill. Ham steak has fallen somewhat out of fashion in these days of uptown pork T-bones and tenderloins. I say it's time to bring it back, especially if you've never enjoyed the pleasure of a ham steak served sizzling hot off the grill. Mom wouldn't have grilled pineapple, of course (this *was* the 1950s), but she was just wacky enough to appreciate how the burnt sugar sweetness of the pineapple could counterpoint the salty tang of the ham. MAKES 4 SERVINGS

FOR THE GLAZE

4 tablespoons unsalted butter

I clove garlic, finely chopped

1/4 cup pineapple juice

1/4 cup dark rum

1/4 cup brown sugar

I tablespoon ketchup

1/4 teaspoon ground cloves or 4 whole cloves

Salt and freshly ground black pepper

4 ham steaks, each 6 to 8 ounces and 1/2 inch thick (see Note)

Four 1/2-inch-thick slices fresh pineapple

I. To make the glaze: Place the butter and garlic in a heavy saucepan. Cook over medium heat until the butter has melted and the garlic begins to brown, about 3 minutes. Stir in the pineapple juice, rum, brown sugar, ketchup, and cloves. Boil until thick and syrupy, about 5 minutes, adding salt and pepper to taste. The glaze can be prepared several hours ahead and stored in the refrigerator.

2. Set up a grill for direct grilling and heat to high. Brush and oil the grill grate. Arrange the ham steaks and pineapple slices on the grate and grill until nicely browned, 3 to 6 minutes per side, basting with the glaze. Transfer the ham steaks to plates or a platter, top with the grilled pineapple, and drizzle any remaining glaze on top.

> NOTE: This recipe calls for the supermarket variety of ham steak—cut from a cooked ham. If you want to get fancy, you could grill slices of Smithfield, Virginia, or honey-baked ham. Look for them in gourmet shops or Asian markets (the Chinese love Smithfield ham). Smithfield steaks are quite salty, so you may need to soak them in water first to remove some of the excess salt before grilling.

[Adapted from *BBQ USA*; Workman Publishing, 2003.]

TOM COLICCHIO, born in Elizabeth, New Jersey, spent his childhood immersed in food, cooking with his mother and grandmother. He made his kitchen debut in his hometown at Evelyn's Seafood Restaurant.

Tom continued to cook at prominent New York restaurants such as the Quilted Giraffe, Gotham Bar & Grill, Rakel, and Mondrian. During Tom's tenure as executive chef of Mondrian, *Food & Wine* magazine selected him as one of the top ten "Best New Chefs" in the United States and *The New York Times* awarded the restaurant three stars.

In July 1994, Tom, along with partner Danny Meyer, opened Gramercy Tavern in Manhattan's Gramercy Park neighborhood. After a three-time nomination for the James Beard Foundation's Best Chef: New York Award, he won it in 2000. One year later, in March 2001, and one block south of Gramercy Tavern, Tom opened Craft, which in 2002 was awarded the James Beard Foundation's Best New Restaurant Award.

Tom's first cookbook, *Think Like a Chef*, won a James Beard Foundation Book Award in May 2001. In October 2002, Tom received the Chef of the Year Award from *Bon Appétit* and Food Network in their American food and entertaining categories.

Tom opened Craftsteak at the MGM Grand in Las Vegas in July

Tom Colicchio

2002. With the opening of Craftbar (a more casual restaurant next door to Craft) in January of that year, Tom introduced Craftkitchen, a line of olive oils and condiments he imports from Calabria, Italy.

Tom's latest projects are 'wichcraft, a take-out sandwich shop that opened in May 2003, and a second cookbook, *Craft of Cooking*.

Tom and his restaurants are involved with many of the community's charities, including Share Our Strength, Children of Bellevue, The College Fund, and Kids for Kids. Tom serves on the board of directors of Avero Inc., a provider of Web-based software applications for operations of the hospitality industry.

I spent time in the kitchen with my mother and grandmother starting at a pretty early age. I loved cooking with them, especially around the holidays. My grandmother Esther Corvelli cooked Christmas Eve dinner every year. As in most Italian homes, we'd have some fish dishes, like fried smelts, salt cod salad, and shrimp scampi. But we'd have other things, too, like linguini with parsley and garlic and a great beet salad. Easter was my mother's holiday. Easter dinner started out with a big assortment of antipasti, followed by cannelloni—crepes filled with ricotta cheese and eggs, covered with tomato sauce, and baked. Then we'd have a roast fresh ham.

Some of the dishes we ate for the holidays have evolved into dishes I've put on my restaurants' menus. At Gramercy Tavern I combined a version of my grandmother's beet salad and her flaked salt cod salad with a roasted cod fillet. And when I wanted to add a cannelloni dish to

Tom Colicchio in his Sunday best with his mom, Beverly.

Gramercy's menu, I called my mom. I used her exact recipe for the crepes but added a Swiss chard filling and chanterelle sauce of my own.

But more than any specific recipes, I use the flavor memories from my mother and grandmother's kitchen from time to time. Food and cooking are mostly memory. The more you're exposed to, the more you're influenced. I don't consciously think of "what my grandmother did with eggplant," for example. It's more ingrained in me than that.

Tom Colicchio and his mom.

When I opened Craft in Manhattan, it was the memories of those family and holiday meals, with everyone sharing food around the table, that influenced my thinking. Most New Yorkers don't eat at home. That experience of passing food around the table was missing from their lives. I wanted the kind of restaurant that felt like eating at home, with all the memories, smells, and flavors that I grew up with. I wanted to put that back in the average New Yorker's life. I'm one of those New Yorkers who miss that. But all I need is a Sunday dinner with my family, and it all comes back to me.

Swiss Chard Cannelloni with Chanterelle Sauce

This recipe idea comes from a manicotti recipe my mom makes for Easter. The recipe for the crepe batter is the exact one she makes, but instead of her ricotta filling and tomato sauce, I fill the crepes with Swiss chard and make a chanterelle sauce.   MAKES 4 SERVINGS

FOR THE CHANTERELLE SAUCE

1 tablespoon peanut oil

1 shallot, peeled and minced

1 clove garlic, peeled and minced

8 ounces chanterelle mushrooms, cleaned and trimmed

Kosher salt and freshly ground black pepper

1½ to 2 cups chicken stock or canned reduced-sodium chicken broth

1 sprig fresh thyme

FOR THE CANNELLONI

2 pounds Swiss chard

3 tablespoons peanut oil

1 leek, white part only, trimmed and chopped

1 clove garlic, peeled and chopped

Kosher salt and freshly ground black pepper

Eight 8½-inch crepes (recipe follows)

1 tablespoon unsalted butter

8 spring onions, white parts only, halved lengthwise

1. To make the sauce: Heat the oil in a deep skillet over medium heat until it slides easily across the pan. Add the shallot and garlic, and cook, stirring frequently, until the shallot begins to soften, about 3 minutes.

2. Reserve 8 small chanterelles for garnish. Add the remaining mushrooms to the skillet. Season with salt and pepper, and cook, stirring frequently, until the mushrooms soften slightly, about 5 minutes. Add 1½ cups of stock and the thyme, and simmer until the mushrooms are very tender, 5 to 10 minutes.

3. Puree the mushroom mixture in a blender until smooth. Add up to ½

cup of stock if the sauce is too thick; the sauce should be just thick enough to nap a wooden spoon. Adjust the seasoning if necessary and set the sauce aside.

4.   To make the cannelloni: Cut the Swiss chard leaves from the stalks, discarding all but 4 of the stalks. Heat I tablespoon of oil in a large skillet over medium heat until it slides easily across the pan. Add the leek and garlic, and cook until the leek begins to soften, about 3 minutes. Add the Swiss chard leaves, a handful at a time, and season with salt and pepper. Let the chard wilt a bit before adding the next handful. Cook, stirring frequently, until the chard is wilted and tender, about 10 minutes. Transfer the chard to a colander, drain thoroughly, squeeze dry, and then chop.

5.   Prepare the crepes and trim them into even circles. Fill with chard and roll tightly.

6.   To assemble the dish: Preheat the oven to 250° F. Heat I tablespoon of oil in a large skillet over medium heat until it slides easily across the pan. Place the cannelloni in the skillet, seam side down. Add the butter and cook, turning to brown on all sides, about 3 minutes. Keep the cannelloni warm in the oven.

7.   Cut the reserved chard stalks into 2-inch matchsticks. Heat the remaining tablespoon of oil in a small skillet over medium heat until it slides easily across the pan. Add the chard stalks, onions, salt, and pepper, and cook, turning once or twice, until the stalks begin to soften, I to 3 minutes. Add the reserved chanterelles and cook until the vegetables are tender and golden, about 10 minutes.

8.   Meanwhile, warm the chanterelle sauce over low heat. Divide the sauce among 4 plates. Place 2 cannelloni on each plate and garnish with the onions, chanterelles, and chard mixture.

Crepes

MAKES ABOUT EIGHT 8½-INCH CREPES

½ cup flour

½ cup milk

¼ cup lukewarm water

2 eggs, beaten

2 tablespoons unsalted butter, melted and cooled

½ teaspoon kosher salt

3 tablespoons peanut oil

1. Combine the flour, milk, water, eggs, butter, and salt in a blender and mix until smooth. Cover the batter and refrigerate it for at least 30 minutes.

2. Heat a crepe pan or small nonstick skillet over medium heat. Add just enough oil to barely coat the surface, about ½ tablespoon. Stir the batter and pour about 2 tablespoons into the skillet. Cook until the top of the crepe is set and the bottom is golden. Turn the crepe over and cook a few seconds more, then transfer it to a plate. Repeat, adding oil as necessary and stacking the finished crepes separated by layers of parchment or waxed paper. Cover the crepes with a clean dish towel to keep warm.

Polenta Gratin with Mushroom Bolognese

My grandmother used to make a polenta gratin. She layered it with a simple tomato sauce, and we'd have it as a side dish. I make it now with a mushroom Bolognese for a heartier dish that can be the center of the meal. MAKES 4 SERVINGS

FOR THE BOLOGNESE SAUCE

2 tablespoons peanut oil

I onion, peeled and diced

I carrot, peeled and diced

I stalk celery, peeled and diced

Kosher salt and freshly ground black pepper

I clove garlic, peeled and minced

8 to 12 ounces mixed wild and cultivated mushrooms, cleaned, trimmed, and diced

I tablespoon fresh thyme leaves

I tomato, seeded and diced

I cup brown chicken stock or canned reduced-sodium chicken broth

FOR THE POLENTA

Kosher salt

I cup polenta (coarse yellow cornmeal)

¼ cup extra virgin olive oil

4 tablespoons freshly grated Parmigiano-Reggiano cheese

1. To prepare the Bolognese sauce: Heat the oil in a large skillet over medium heat until it moves easily across the pan. Add the onion, carrot, celery, salt, and pepper, and cook, stirring occasionally, until the vegetables begin to soften, about 5 minutes. Add the garlic, cook for 1 minute, then add the mushrooms and thyme leaves. Cook, stirring frequently, until the mushrooms are almost tender, about 3 minutes. Add the tomato, cook about 2 minutes more, then add the stock, 2 tablespoons at a time, bringing the pan to a simmer before each addition. Simmer the Bolognese until it is concentrated but not yet dry, about 30 minutes. Set aside to cool.

2. To make the polenta: Bring 4 cups of water to a boil in a saucepan over high heat. Add a pinch of salt and gradually whisk in the polenta. Stirring con-

stantly, bring the polenta to a boil, then adjust the heat to low. Cook the polenta, stirring occasionally, until it is no longer grainy, about 30 minutes. Whisk the oil and salt to taste into the polenta and remove it from the heat.

3. Assemble the gratin: Preheat the oven to 350° F. Spoon half the polenta into a medium baking dish (an 11-inch oval dish works fine) and cover with half of the sauce. Spoon in the remaining polenta, spread it evenly, then sprinkle with the cheese. Transfer the remaining sauce to a small saucepan and reserve.

4. Bake the gratin until the top is golden, about 40 minutes. Just before serving, warm the reserved sauce over low heat. Divide the gratin and sauce among 4 plates, top each serving with sauce, and serve.

Beet Salad

My grandmother used to make this side salad on Christmas Eve to accompany salted cod. I use this dish as a garnish for a roasted cod and brandade dish. When I make this salad at Gramercy Tavern, I roast the beets and prepare my own marinated artichokes. You can do the same or go with the boiled beets and bottled artichokes called for here. This is a rustic salad, so the slices do not have to be perfect.   MAKES 4 SIDE-DISH SERVINGS

FOR THE SALAD

6 medium beets, stems and leaves removed

4 anchovy fillets, chopped

2 celery stalks, peeled and sliced

6 bottled hot cherry peppers, chopped

1 small jar (about 8 ounces) marinated artichokes, drained and sliced

1 small red onion, sliced

¼ cup oil-cured pitted black olives, halved

Half a bunch of Italian parsley, chopped

FOR THE DRESSING

¼ cup red wine vinegar

1 cup extra virgin olive oil

Kosher salt and freshly ground black pepper

1. To prepare the beets: Place the beets in a medium pot. Cover with water by 2 inches and generously salt the water. Bring to a boil over medium-high heat, lower to a simmer, and cook until there is no resistance when the beets are pierced with a sharp knife, about 20 to 25 minutes.

2. Once the beets are cooked and just slightly cooled, use a clean dish towel to rub off the skins and slice off the remaining root or rough tops. Slice them in half and then cut 6 to 8 wedges from each half, depending on the size. Place the beets in a small stainless-steel bowl and add the anchovies, celery, cherry peppers, artichokes, onion, olives, and parsley. Toss together. If making ahead, cover and refrigerate until ready to use.

3. Just before serving, whisk the dressing ingredients together in a bowl. Pour the dressing over the salad and toss well. Serve at room temperature.

SUSAN FENIGER AND MARY SUE MILLIKEN are two of America's most beloved chefs. The duo have been business partners for more than twenty years, beginning with the opening of City Café in 1981. Now they are hands-on owner-operators of the popular and critically acclaimed Border Grill restaurants in Santa Monica, Pasadena, and Las Vegas, as well as Ciudad in downtown Los Angeles. Natural teachers, the partners are prolific in many media: authors of five cookbooks (four dedicated to the Latin kitchen); veterans of 396 episodes of the popular *Too Hot Tamales* and *Tamales' World Tour* programs on Food Network; and radio hosts of "Hot Dish" features heard daily on KFWB (980 AM in southern California). The chefs have also created a line of prepared foods under their Border Girls brand at Whole Foods Markets, as well as a line of pepper mills. In 2001 their foods "starred" in the Samuel Goldwyn feature film *Tortilla Soup*.

Susan Feniger and Mary Sue Milliken

[ED. NOTE: All recipes in Susan Feniger's and Mary Sue Milliken's chapters are adapted from *City Cuisine*; William Morrow, 1989.]

SUSAN FENIGER was drawn into food at an early age by a mother who loved to cook and entertain. But she got her start in the food business while attending high school and working in the kitchen of a cafeteria in a local shopping center. Although thoughts of a career in the restaurant industry were still years away, Susan fell in love with the camaraderie she experienced with her fellow workers.

Susan
Feniger

Even after leaving college in Vermont, while finishing furniture for a living and residing in a tepee, Susan was never far from good food. Her stove was a Coleman camper stove and her refrigerator was the stream that ran nearby the tepee, but that was all she needed. Breakfast consisted of fresh berries from a local farm with fresh cream scooped from the tops of the glass jars of milk she'd chilled in the stream.

After transferring to Pitzer College in Claremont, California, to study economics, Susan began working in the college's cafeteria. The chef, Perry, who ran the cafeteria and was a former Army cook, opened Susan's eyes to the restaurant business and encouraged her to attend the Culinary Institute of America in Hyde Park, New York.

Once accepted to the CIA, Susan convinced her economics professor, Harvey Botwin, to let her complete her degree requirements by doing an independent study at the CIA. She fell in love with the school, studied constantly, and took on after-school jobs that included working in a local fish market (with midnight trips to New York's Fulton Fish Market) and in the kitchens of an excellent nearby French restaurant, Harrolds, in Brewster, New York.

Fresh out of the CIA and relocated to Kansas City, Susan found another mentor at La Bonne Auberge restaurant and pastry shop. Swiss Chef Gus Reidi did it all: He built his own lobster and trout tanks and did all the restaurant's butchering and bread making. La Bonne Auberge served soufflés and tableside Caesar salads—heady stuff for the late seventies. Kansas City was Susan's last stop before heading to Chicago and the kitchen of Le Perroquet restaurant, where she encountered Mary Sue Milliken—a meeting that shaped the next twenty-five years of her career.

—————

My mom, Ruthie, was a great cook. As far back as I can remember, she was always in the kitchen. Of course, there were family meals

Susan Feniger cooking with her mom, Ruthie, c. 1973.

like artichoke and chicken casseroles, brisket, and pickled tongue; Sunday morning meant chicken livers with caramelized onions and scrambled eggs. But there were little treats and big meals for friends and family, too. And the parties! I have a picture from the fifties of my mother and father and a bunch of their friends at one of their get-togethers. They would decide on a theme—Filipino, Hawaiian, Chinese, or whatever—and decorate, cook, and dress accordingly.

For a woman who taught herself to cook, my mom was a pretty professional kind of cook. She may have spent days in the kitchen before one of their parties, but during the party she was hardly ever in the kitchen. She had it all together.

Mom had her "prep" together, too. Our big chest freezer was always stocked for times when my parents were out of town and we kids had to fend for ourselves, or for when surprise guests showed up. And show up they did. We had an open-door kind of house. If you were in the house anywhere near dinnertime, you were probably staying.

That freezer was full of steaks, chops, and fully cooked brisket that, with a little planning, became a meal. There was a stock of items for spur-of-the-minute gatherings, too, things like appetizers that could be taken from the freezer and popped under the broiler. I loved her "cheese dreams"—bread dipped in a sauce made with Velveeta and rolled up tightly. Those and frozen canapés topped with peanut butter, jarred chutney, and bacon were pulled from the freezer and out of the broiler in about 10 minutes. Whenever my mother made a batch of fudge, some of it ended up in the tin she kept on the counter, and some of it ended up in the freezer. And there was always at least one icebox cake in there, too, made with ladyfingers and mocha, lemon, or coffee filling.

She also had a chef's sensibility when it came to seasoning—even the way she marinated a steak, with not just a sprinkling of salt and pepper but with a mix of dry mustard, Worcestershire, garlic, and soy sauce. If she made a chocolate chip cookie, it was loaded with chocolate chips; vegetable soup was loaded with vegetables. When it came to cooking and flavor, she definitely got it. She had a preference for strong flavors that I see in my own cooking.

My mother continued to inspire me after I started to cook professionally. When Mary Sue Milliken and I opened our first restaurant, City Café in Los Angeles, you could see a lot of influence from my mother. The roast duck and goose my mother made around Christmas took on a honey, orange, and chipotle glaze. The first steak marinade on our menu was a variation on one that Mom used at home.

Every time we opened a restaurant, my mother was there, shaping empanadas with the guys in the kitchen and doing whatever she could to help out. So much of what I feel about cooking, not to mention my taste buds and my love of a good party, came directly to me from my mother. I'm happy to share with you a few of her favorite recipes.

Beef Brisket

3½ pounds beef brisket

4 tablespoons paprika

Salt

1 teaspoon white pepper

¼ cup all-purpose flour

½ cup vegetable oil or chicken fat

2 medium onions, sliced

4 carrots, peeled and sliced

2 celery stalks, sliced

2 tablespoons tomato paste

3 bay leaves

1 teaspoon dried thyme

½ teaspoon cracked black pepper

Salt

3 quarts water

1. Preheat the oven to 350° F. Sprinkle the meat generously with paprika, 2 teaspoons of salt, and the pepper. Spread the flour on a large platter and dip the meat in it to evenly coat.

2. Heat the oil in a large Dutch oven over high heat. Brown the meat on all sides until crusty. Remove from the pan and reserve. Add the onions, carrots, and celery, and cook until softened, about 5 minutes. Add the tomato paste and cook for 2 minutes. Add the bay leaves, thyme, pepper, salt to taste, water, and meat, and bring to a boil. Cover, transfer to the oven, and bake for 1 to 1¼ hours on each side, or until the meat slips easily off a fork.

3. Transfer the meat to a cutting board and let rest for 10 minutes before slicing. Carefully skim and discard the fat from the cooking liquid in the pot. Discard the bay leaves. Puree the remaining sauce and vegetables in a blender (see Note), then strain through a sieve. Taste and adjust the seasonings. Slice the meat thinly across the grain, top with the warm sauce, and serve immediately.

NOTE: **Cool the sauce to warm before blending.**

Marinated Rib Eye Steaks

Four 10-ounce beef rib eye or
sirloin steaks

FOR THE MARINADE

1 cup olive oil

2 tablespoons dry mustard

1 tablespoon Worcestershire sauce

1 teaspoon minced garlic

1 teaspoon soy sauce

1 teaspoon fresh lemon juice

Dash of Tabasco

Salt and freshly ground pepper to
taste

1. Trim the steaks of all fat. Stir the marinade ingredients together in a container large enough to hold the steaks comfortably. Turn the steaks in the marinade, cover, and refrigerate at least 6 hours or as long as 24 hours. Remove the meat from the refrigerator 2 hours before serving time to enhance the flavors.

2. Preheat the grill or broiler.

3. Grill or broil the steaks for 5 minutes per side for medium-rare, longer for more well-done steaks. Serve with grilled onions and crumbled blue cheese.

Pantry Pickles

MAKES 1 GENEROUS QUART

6 pickling or Kirby cucumbers (see Notes), with skins

1 onion, thinly sliced across the width

1 red bell pepper, cored, seeded, and cut into thin strips

2 cups rice wine vinegar (see Notes)

½ cup sugar

1 tablespoon coarse salt

Cut the cucumbers crosswise on the diagonal into ¹⁄₁₆-inch slices. Combine all the ingredients in a medium saucepan. Bring to a boil over high heat, then lower to a simmer. Cook, uncovered, for 10 to 15 minutes. Store in the pickling liquid in the refrigerator for up to a month or so.

NOTES: Kirbies or pickling cucumbers are small, pale green cucumbers with fewer seeds and a milder flavor than larger cucumbers. They are available in supermarkets.

Rice wine vinegar is a full-flavored yellow Japanese vinegar made from rice wine. It is available in Asian markets and some supermarkets.

> **MOM'S TIP**
>
> *Add diced red, yellow, and green bell peppers if you'd like to give these pickles as Christmas gifts.*

Dill Pickles

15 small pickling or Kirby cucumbers (see Note on page 249)

FOR THE PICKLING LIQUID

3 cups water

2 cups white vinegar

¼ cup coarse salt

2 tablespoons sugar

1 teaspoon black peppercorns

¾ teaspoon ground cumin

½ teaspoon ground ginger

½ teaspoon turmeric

1 bay leaf

1 medium onion, sliced

1 celery stalk, sliced

½ carrot, peeled and sliced

1 jalapeño pepper, sliced with seeds

8 cloves garlic, peeled

1 bunch dill

1 sprig thyme

1.   Bring a large pot of water to a boil. Add the cucumbers and immediately remove the pot from the heat. Drain the cucumbers in a colander, rinse with cold water, and reserve.

2.   Combine all the pickling liquid ingredients in a medium saucepan and bring to a boil. Place the cucumbers in a large container along with the onion, celery, carrot, jalapeño pepper, garlic, dill, and thyme. Pour the hot pickling liquid over the cucumber mixture and set aside to cool. Cover with plastic wrap and let stand at room temperature for 1 day. Transfer to a sealed container and refrigerate for 3 days before serving. Store in the refrigerator indefinitely.

Poppy Seed Cake with Lemon Glaze

MAKES 8 TO 10 SERVINGS

I cup poppy seeds

⅓ cup honey

¼ cup water

12 tablespoons (1½ sticks) unsalted butter, softened

¾ cup sugar

I tablespoon grated lemon zest

I teaspoon vanilla extract

2 eggs

2¼ cups all-purpose flour

I teaspoon baking soda

I teaspoon baking powder

I teaspoon salt

2½ tablespoons fresh lemon juice

I cup sour cream

FOR THE LEMON GLAZE

I cup sugar

½ cup fresh lemon juice

1. Preheat the oven to 325° F. Butter and flour a 10-inch tube pan.

2. Combine the poppy seeds, honey, and water in a medium saucepan. Cook over moderate heat, stirring frequently, until the water evaporates and the mixture looks like wet sand. This will take about 5 minutes. Set aside to cool.

3. Cream together the butter and sugar until light and fluffy. Mix in the lemon zest and vanilla. Add the eggs, I at a time, beating well after each addition.

4. Stir the flour, baking soda, baking powder, and salt together in a separate bowl.

5. When the poppy seed mixture has cooled, stir in the lemon juice. Pour into the creamed butter mixture and stir until combined. Stir the dry ingredients and sour cream into the poppy seed mixture in 3 stages, alternating liquid and dry ingredients, and ending with the sour cream. Spoon the batter into the prepared pan, smooth the top with a spatula, and tap the pan vigorously on a counter to eliminate air pockets.

6. Bake until a toothpick inserted in the center of the cake comes out clean, about I hour and 15 minutes. Set aside to cool on a rack about 15 minutes.

7. Meanwhile, make the glaze: Combine the sugar and lemon juice in a small saucepan. Bring to a boil over medium heat and cook for 1 to 2 minutes, or until the sugar has dissolved. Remove from the heat.

8. Brush the top of the cake generously with the syrup. Remove the cake from the pan and brush the bottom and sides with the remaining syrup. Cool completely before serving.

GROWING UP IN MICHIGAN, with her mom's cooking a big part of her life, Mary Sue Milliken wasn't your average child. Other kids may have requested chocolate cake for their birthdays, but for Mary Sue, birthdays meant a boiled tongue dinner. (She especially looked forward to the cold tongue sandwiches the day after.) Around the fifth grade an unusual recipe in *Redbook* magazine caught her eye. The

next morning she climbed out of bed at four o'clock to work her way through a batch of apricot Danish so it would be ready by the time the rest of the family rolled out of bed. And it didn't stop there. As a young girl she and her mom would stage shrimp-eating contests with her cousins, including Tod, who, during one leave from his Navy base, won the event with a total of eighty-seven shrimp.

All through high school Mary Sue remained highly motivated when it came to food. She took every home economics course available, worked in pizza places, and even held a job at a local doughnut shop icing and filling doughnuts from four to seven in the morning before she headed off to class.

By the time Mary Sue was sixteen, she knew she wanted to be a chef, so she fast-tracked her high school classes and attended summer school in order to graduate high school in three years. After moving to

Chicago, Mary Sue worked in a bakery while waiting to be admitted to the culinary program at Washburne Trade School.

The first woman ever to join the staff at Chicago's prestigious Le Perroquet restaurant, Mary Sue was soon joined on the staff by Susan Feniger, her friend and business partner of twenty-five years. The rest, as they say, is history.

⚓

My mom, Ruth, is very adventurous with food. That's a bond we have always shared. Even when I was a young girl, we went out together to try different ethnic divey restaurants. Those little trips evolved into bigger trips, like the one we took to Scotland when I was seventeen specifically to have a traditional haggis dinner. That's a night I'll never forget. I drove through the pouring rain illegally; you had to be twenty-five for an international license, but I drove because my mom couldn't work a stick shift. I kind of backed up into a car, then ran off down a little hill while my mother slid into the driver's seat. After all the commotion, we called the restaurant to tell them what had happened and that we'd be late. (It never occurred to us to cancel; after all, we'd gotten that far.) I still remember stepping off the elevator into the restaurant and being met by a gentleman with two glasses of scotch, I guess to help calm us down from our ordeal.

Mary Sue Milliken and her mom, Ruth, at CITY Restaurant, c. 1982

I see a lot of my mom in me. She's really tenacious; that probably comes from being a single mom from the time I was twelve. She worked the graveyard shift at a local hotel and another job on top of that. I used some of that spirit getting into my first great kitchen, Le Perroquet in Chicago. The owner kept telling me that he wouldn't let a woman into the kitchen— it would be too distracting for the men. He actually suggested that I take a job checking hats! But I kept at it, phoning and writing letters, and I finally made it onto the staff.

And I'm as frugal as she is. My mom grew up during the Depression, when they learned to make the most out of everything. It has always felt true to me to use ingredients wisely and respect them.

After Susan Feniger and I opened CITY Restaurant in the mid-1980s, Mom left her real estate job (she was sick of the rat race) and moved out to work for us. That was interesting, to say the least, with poor Susan playing referee when necessary. My mother actually was a huge asset, right up to the day she gave notice and went to work for another restaurant.

So much of my mother's midwestern sensibilities showed through at work. She was in charge of making all our homemade foods that so many other restaurants just buy—pickles, sauerkraut, yogurt, and the like. She also got us into making our own sweetened condensed milk by boiling down milk in a huge pot. That homemade condensed milk is how we got the reputation for the best flan anywhere. And her frugality came through, too. I remember one time we asked her to separate a case of eggs for some ridiculous amount of hollandaise we needed. I found her wiping out the little bit of white that sticks to the broken shells. When I'm cooking at home, I catch myself doing that sometimes, and I just have to laugh. As I said, there's a lot of my mom in me.

Hamburger Buns

We've always had a "why buy it if you can make it yourself" kind of attitude in our restaurants. Like these buns and the yogurt and sauerkraut that Mom was in charge of during her stint as pastry chef at our first restaurant, City Café. She kept the crocks in her pastry station so she could keep an eye on their progress. MAKES 6 LARGE OR 10 SMALLER BUNS

I cup water

5 tablespoons unsalted butter

2 tablespoons sugar

1½ teaspoons salt

I tablespoon dry yeast

⅓ cup warm water

2 eggs

3½ cups all-purpose flour

Coarse salt and cracked black pepper for sprinkling

> **MOM'S TIP**
>
> *To make the best burgers, mix 3 pounds of ground beef with 1 diced onion and 3 minced garlic cloves. Divide into 6 patties, sprinkle with salt and pepper, and grill over high heat.*

1. Bring the I cup of water to a boil. Stir the boiling water into the butter, sugar, and salt in the bowl of an electric mixer. Set aside to cool to lukewarm, about 110° F.

2. Stir the yeast and the ⅓ cup of warm water together in a small bowl. Set aside until foamy.

3. Pour the dissolved yeast into the butter mixture. Add I egg, lightly beaten, and I cup of the flour. Beat at low speed until the batter is lump-free. Cover the bowl with plastic wrap and set aside in a warm place until the batter has doubled in size and is foamy, about 30 minutes.

4. Add the remaining 2½ cups of flour and beat until the dough becomes elastic, about 5 minutes. Transfer the dough to a buttered plastic container, cover, and refrigerate overnight. Check the dough occasionally and punch it down if it grows to more than double its size.

5. The next day, divide the dough into 6 or 10 pieces, depending on the size of your burgers. Lightly knead each piece into the shape of a bun and set aside to rest on a parchment-lined baking sheet at room temperature until doubled in size, about 30 minutes.

6. Preheat the oven to 375° F. Brush the tops of the rolls with the second egg, beaten lightly, and sprinkle coarse salt and cracked pepper over them. Bake until lightly browned, 15 to 20 minutes. Set aside to cool.

Fried Smelts

The smelt run in Michigan in May was a big deal in our family. There were so many of them and they were so easy to catch—just go down to the pier with a net. We never ate much fresh fish growing up, but for the two weeks when smelts were in season, we ate plenty. We used to do a version of this dish using strips of various fish fillets at CITY Restaurant. Fried smelts, or any fried fish for that matter, are the perfect vehicle for the fantastic tartar sauce that follows. MAKES 6 SERVINGS

I cup all-purpose flour, plus more for coating the smelts

2 teaspoons cayenne pepper

2 teaspoons salt

I teaspoon sugar

½ teaspoon baking powder

One 8-ounce bottle of beer, at room temperature

4 cups peanut oil for frying

1½ pounds fresh smelts, gutted and washed

Lemon wedges for garnish

Homemade Tartar Sauce (recipe follows)

MOM'S TIP

If you don't have a deep-fry thermometer, test the oil by sprinkling in a few drops of batter. If they immediately rise to the surface, the oil is ready.

I. Combine the flour, cayenne, salt, sugar, and baking powder in a medium bowl. Add the beer all at once, and whisk until smooth. Set aside, uncovered, at least I hour.

2. Pour the oil into a large saucepan and heat over medium heat to 350° F.

3. Dust the smelts lightly with flour, patting off the excess. Dip the smelts, I at a time, in the batter until thoroughly coated, then slip them into the oil. Fry 4 or 5 pieces at a time until crisp and golden, about 2 minutes. Remove with a slotted spoon and drain on paper towels. Serve immediately with lemon wedges and tartar sauce.

Homemade Tartar Sauce

MAKES I CUP

¾ cup mayonnaise (recipe follows)

2 tablespoons finely chopped dill pickle

2 tablespoons finely chopped red onion

2 tablespoons finely chopped capers

2 tablespoons finely chopped celery

2 tablespoons finely chopped parsley leaves

I tablespoon fresh lemon juice

I tablespoon stone-ground mustard

½ teaspoon salt

½ teaspoon freshly ground pepper

Stir all the ingredients together in a bowl until blended. This tartar sauce will keep in the refrigerator for up to I week.

Mayonnaise

MAKES I ½ CUPS

2 egg yolks

I teaspoon red wine vinegar

Juice of ½ lemon

½ teaspoon salt

¼ teaspoon white pepper

Dash of Tabasco

Dash of Worcestershire sauce

I cup vegetable oil

Whisk the egg yolks, vinegar, lemon juice, salt, pepper, Tabasco, and Worcestershire together in a bowl. Gradually add the oil, a drop at a time, whisking constantly. As the mixture begins to thicken and looks more like mayonnaise, you can add oil more generously. Adjust the seasonings and store in the refrigerator as long as 4 days.

Rhubarb Pie

MAKES 8 TO 10 SERVINGS

FOR THE PIE

Pie Pastry (recipe follows)

3 pounds rhubarb

1½–2 cups sugar, to taste

3 tablespoons tapioca

FOR THE STREUSEL

½ cup packed brown sugar

7 tablespoons unsalted butter, at room temperature

1 teaspoon cinnamon

¼ teaspoon salt

1 cup plus 2 tablespoons all-purpose flour

1. Lightly butter a 10-inch pie plate, preferably glass. Prepare the dough according to the recipe directions. On a generously floured board, roll the dough out to a 14-inch circle about ⅛ inch thick. Line the pie plate, leaving about a ¼-inch overhang. Pinch up the excess dough to form an upright fluted edge. Chill about 1 hour.

2. Preheat the oven to 350° F. To prebake the pie shell, line the dough with a sheet of parchment paper or aluminum foil and fill with pie weights, beans, or rice. Bake for 25 minutes, remove the paper and weights, and set the shell aside while you prepare the filling.

3. Clean the rhubarb and cut the stalks into ½-inch slices. Toss with the sugar in a large bowl and let sit at room temperature for 15 minutes. Sprinkle the tapioca over the filling, toss well, and let sit an additional 15 minutes.

4. Meanwhile, make the streusel: Cream together the sugar and butter until smooth. Add the cinnamon and salt, and mix until blended. Add the flour and mix with your fingertips just until crumbly.

5. Pour the filling into the prebaked pie shell and sprinkle the streusel over the top. Bake until the top is browned and the juices bubble around the edges, about 1 hour and 15 minutes. Set aside to cool on a rack before serving.

Pie Shell

When making pie dough, you should be able to see chunks of fat—whether lard, shortening, or butter—in the completed dough. In the oven they will expand and release the steam that makes pie dough so flaky. Butter may be substituted for the lard, but for the best crust we still use lard.   MAKES ONE 10-INCH PIE SHELL

I cup all-purpose flour

¼ cup lard

1½ tablespoons unsalted butter

½ teaspoon salt

3–4 tablespoons ice water

1.   In a medium bowl, combine all but 2 tablespoons of the flour, the lard, butter, and salt. Mix lightly with your fingertips until the dough forms pea-size pieces. You should be able to see chunks of fat.

2.   Stir in the remaining flour, then stir in the water. Knead the dough lightly until it forms a ball. It is important to handle the dough as little as possible.

3.   Cover the dough with plastic wrap and refrigerate for a minimum of 1 hour or as long as 3 days. Pie dough may be stored in the freezer for up to 1 week.

TODD ENGLISH first entered the doors of a professional kitchen at age fifteen. At twenty he attended the Culinary Institute of America and graduated in 1982 with honors. He continued to hone his craft with Jean Jacques Rachou at New York's La Côte Basque and then in Italy, where he apprenticed at the well-established Dal Pescatore in Canto Sull O'lio and Ristorante Paraccuchi Locando Dell Angelo. After returning to the States at twenty-five, Todd was asked to be the executive chef of the award-winning Italian restaurant Michela's in Cambridge, Massachusetts.

In the spring of 1991 the James Beard Foundation named Todd their National Rising Star Chef; he went on to be named Best Chef: Northeast in 1994. In 2001, Todd was given *Bon Appétit*'s Restaurateur of the Year Award and was also named one of *People* magazine's 50 Most Beautiful People.

In May 1989, Todd opened Olives, featuring interpretive rustic Mediterranean cuisine, in Charlestown, Massachusetts. Since then he has opened Olives in New York, Las Vegas, Washington, D.C., Aspen, and, most recently, Tokyo.

Todd also has four Figs restaurants in the greater Boston area and one location at LaGuardia Airport in New York City. Among his other restaurants are Tuscany at Mohegan Sun in Connecticut; Bonfire, a steak house that is a celebration of ranch cooking around the world; and Kingfish Hall, Todd's first seafood concept, in Boston's Historic Faneuil Hall. Todd's second seafood concept, Fish Club, opened in Seattle in 2003. Two other ventures took off recently: The Cunard Line's *Queen Mary 2* welcomed the restaurant Todd English, and Disney World saw the opening of Blue Zoo at the Swan and Dolphin.

Todd's television credits include his public television series *Cooking In with Todd English* and appearances on *Iron Chef USA, Martha Stewart Living, In Food Today, Bobby Flay's Food Nation, Live with Regis and Kelly,* and the *Today* show. Todd has also authored the critically acclaimed cookbooks *The Olives Table, The Figs Table,* and *The Olives Dessert Table.*

Todd is very involved with several local and national charities, including Big Brother, the Anthony Spinazzola Foundation, Community Servings, Share Our Strength, the Boys and Girls Clubs, and City Year.

***

When I was growing up in Atlanta with my mother, grandmother, and a nanny, our dinners were made up of everything from fried chicken to rabbit cacciatore. All three women took turns cooking; what we ate depended on whose day it was in the kitchen.

One of my earliest and favorite memories is of my grandmother Giulieta Vergara, who was born in Oppido di Reggio in Calabria, making rabbit cacciatore in a big cast-iron kettle over the flames of a wood fire in our fireplace. She'd start by searing the rabbit in olive oil: then she'd add garlic, oregano, and hot

Todd English, with possibly his first taste of gooey chocolate cake.

pepper, and let it all cook together. In went the vinegar and white wine and the tomato and mushrooms, and it simmered over the coals until the whole house was filled with that aroma.

On Grandma's days in the kitchen, we'd have breaded veal cutlets or whole whitefish tossed in batter and fried, not individually but stuck together, more or less like a fish cake. Grandma liked to do things big: antipasti platters with a dozen different things on them, big spreads of food. She loved big flavors. I see now that that was the beginning of my own love of big flavors and personal style of cooking. Grandma even managed to get big flavors out of really simple dishes, such as the pork dish she made slowly, browning big chunks of pork in olive oil with onion, garlic, and bay leaves.

My mother, Patti, made some Italian specialties, too, like *uova in purgatorio* (eggs poached in tomato sauce), which was a lunchy-brunchy thing or something

Todd English and his mother, Patti.

she made to cure a hangover. But she was more of an American-style cook. Her chocolate cake that I have included here probably started with a Betty Crocker kind of recipe but evolved into this wonderful gooey cake. Mom also made great steaks on the barbecue, with red wine and mushroom sauce.

We had a garden when I was in high school. We grew potatoes, asparagus, Italian flat beans, and a lot of other vegetables we ate as long as the weather stayed warm. Shredded green beans, cooked slowly in lots of olive oil, garlic, and dried mint, were a summertime favorite, as was broccoli cooked with olive oil and anchovies. In our house we always made vegetables that were slow-cooked until really tender. These kinds of vegetables are my favorites—I never liked crunchy nouvelle cuisine vegetables—and still show up quite often on my menus.

I tried college for a year, but it wasn't for me. I really wanted to get into cooking, and going to the Culinary Institute seemed like a natural progression. Not long after I left the school, I headed to Italy to work. It all came together for me in Italy—the way they treat ingredients, the seasonality of their cooking, the simple, bold flavors. That, combined with my grandmother's and mother's cooking, with their big flavors and love for fresh ingredients, is what defined me as a chef.

Uova in Purgatorio

EGGS IN PURGATORY (POACHED IN TOMATO SAUCE)

MAKES 6 SERVINGS

3 tablespoons extra virgin olive oil

2 small white onions, thinly sliced

6 green onions (or more if making Tuscan toast; see Note), trimmed and sliced

4 cloves garlic, chopped

One 35-ounce can peeled Italian plum tomatoes, preferably San Marzano

¼ cup dry white wine

1 tablespoon lemon juice

Sea salt and freshly ground black pepper

2 tablespoons butter

6 eggs

Tuscan toast (see Note)

1. Heat the oil in a large, deep skillet over medium-low heat. Add the white and green onions and garlic, and cook, stirring, until softened, about 5 minutes.

2. Meanwhile, pass the tomatoes and their juice through a food mill fitted with the fine disc or through a coarse china cap or metal sieve. Discard the seeds.

3. Add the tomatoes, wine, and lemon juice to the skillet. Bring to a simmer and cook until lightly thickened, about 15 minutes. Add water as the sauce cooks, if necessary, to keep it at a slightly brothy consistency. Season the sauce with salt and pepper and stir in the butter.

4. Crack the eggs into the tomato sauce. Adjust the heat so that the sauce remains at a gentle simmer and cook the eggs to your desired doneness. (Whites will be set and the yolks still runny in about 5 minutes. Cook the eggs longer for completely set yolks.)

5. Taste the sauce for seasoning and add salt and pepper if you like. Sprinkle salt and pepper over the eggs and serve them in shallow bowls with some of the sauce and Tuscan toast.

> NOTE: Brush both sides of nice thick slices of Tuscan-style bread with olive oil. Season them with salt and pepper and toast in a 375° F oven until golden brown, about 15 minutes. Sprinkle chopped scallions and freshly grated Parmesan cheese over the top and serve.

Mama's Zucchini

It's always a push and pull of flavors when my mother and I get together to cook. My mom seasons this mix of potatoes, zucchini, and tomatoes with fresh basil and oregano. I like to use fresh basil and mint. MAKES 4 SERVINGS

3 tablespoons extra virgin olive oil

1 medium red onion, diced

3 cloves garlic, minced

2 medium Yukon Gold potatoes, peeled and cut into 1-inch chunks

Fresh mint, coarsely chopped

Fresh basil or oregano, coarsely chopped

2 medium zucchini, trimmed and cut into ½-inch rounds

3 ripe fresh tomatoes, cored, roughly chopped, and smashed with a fork

Salt and freshly ground pepper

1. Heat the oil in a large skillet over medium-low heat. Add the onion and garlic, and cook, stirring, until softened, about 8 minutes. Add the potatoes, sprinkle a generous amount of mint and basil or oregano over them, and cook a few minutes, stirring. Stir in the zucchini and cook until softened, about 2 minutes.

2. Add the tomatoes, season with salt and pepper, and bring to a simmer. Cover the pan and cook until the potatoes are tender, about 12 minutes. Check the seasoning and serve hot.

Rabbit Cacciatore

My mom, Patti, likes this served over polenta or fusilli pasta. A big bowl of freshly grated Parmesan mixed with grated pecorino Romano is an essential condiment for the table. There's always a bowl of that on my grandmother's table. MAKES 4 SERVINGS

¼ cup extra virgin olive oil, or as needed

2 medium Vidalia or Spanish onions, cut into 2-inch pieces

2 medium red onions, cut into 2-inch pieces

2 portobello mushrooms, stems and gills removed, cut into 1-inch pieces

8 ounces button mushrooms, trimmed and quartered

4 shallots, sliced

4 cloves garlic, thinly sliced

8 ounces each hot and sweet Italian sausage

One 3-pound rabbit, cut into 8 serving pieces

Salt and freshly ground pepper

1 to 2 pounds pork and/or veal bones

1 cup red wine

½ cup white wine

2 cups chopped canned Italian peeled plum tomatoes with their liquid, preferably San Marzano

1. Pour enough oil into a large, heavy skillet to coat the bottom. (If your skillet isn't large enough to hold all the vegetables, divide the vegetables between two skillets or work in batches.) Heat over medium heat for 1 minute or so, then add both kinds of onions, both kinds of mushrooms, the shallots, and garlic. Cook, stirring often, until well browned, about 20 minutes.

2. Meanwhile, pour enough oil into a large, heavy, prefer- ably cast-iron pan to lightly coat the bottom. Heat over medium- high heat for 1 minute, then add the sausage. Cook, turning as necessary, until well browned on all sides, about 6 minutes. Adjust the heat to low, cover the pan, and cook until no trace of pink remains in the center, about 10 min-

> **MOM'S TIP**
>
> *The more bones you use, the richer the finished dish will be.*

utes. Drain the grease from the pan and set the vegetables and sausages aside.

3. Preheat the oven to 350° F. Pat the rabbit pieces dry with paper towels and season with salt and pepper. Pour enough of the remaining oil into a large, wide Dutch oven or casserole to generously coat the bottom. Heat over medium heat, then add as many of the rabbit pieces and bones as will fit comfortably. Cook the rabbit and bones, working in batches so you don't crowd the pan, until browned on all sides, about 12 minutes. Remove the rabbit and bones from the Dutch oven and spoon off the drippings.

4. "Chunk up" the sausages (as Mom says) and add them and the vegetables to the Dutch oven. Return the rabbit and bones. Pour in the wines and chopped tomatoes. Bake until the rabbit is tender, about 45 minutes. Remove the bones and serve.

Gooey Chocolate Cake

My mom and I made this cake at the restaurant not long ago. A minute after it came out of the oven, about ten cooks and two gallons of milk appeared. It's just that kind of cake.   MAKES 12 SERVINGS

I pound (4 sticks) unsalted butter cut into 2-tablespoon pieces, plus more for greasing the pan

2 cups all-purpose flour, plus more for coating the pan

I cup water

¾ cup plus 2 tablespoons unsweetened cocoa powder

2 cups granulated sugar

I teaspoon salt

I teaspoon baking powder

½ cup buttermilk

2 large eggs

I tablespoon vanilla extract

One I-pound box confectioners' sugar

I teaspoon cinnamon

1.   Preheat the oven to 400° F. Grease a 9 × 11-inch baking pan with butter and sprinkle a light coating of flour over the bottom and sides of the pan.

2.   Heat ½ pound of butter, water, and ½ cup of cocoa in a small pan over very low heat, stirring, until the mixture is glossy and smooth.

3.   Meanwhile, stir the flour, granulated sugar, salt, and baking powder together in a mixing bowl. Add the buttermilk, eggs, and vanilla, and mix on low speed. Add the melted chocolate mixture and mix until smooth. (Set the pan aside; you'll use it again.) Pour the batter into the prepared pan and bake until almost set in the center (a cake tester will come out not quite clean) and just beginning to pull away from the edges of the pan, about 20 minutes. Cool the cake on a rack for 10 minutes.

4.   While the cake is cooling, place the confectioners' sugar in a clean mixing bowl. Stir the remaining ½ pound of butter with the remaining ¼ cup plus 2 tablespoons of cocoa in the saucepan over very low heat. Stir in the cinnamon. Heat

the cocoa mixture until it is runny (when it registers about 200° F on an instant-read thermometer), but don't allow it to burn.

5. Pour the hot cocoa mixture into the confectioners' sugar and mix until smooth. If the glaze becomes too thick as you mix it, add warm water one table-spoon at a time until the icing is a thick pouring consistency. Pour the glaze over the semi-cooled cake. Serve the cake immediately, while warm, or cool it completely to room temperature.

CHEF MICHAEL LOMONACO started his professional life as an actor and singer. However, his passion for cooking, food, and wine prompted him to enter New York City College of Technology's hotel and restaurant management program, from which he graduated in 1984.

Michael Lomonaco

In 1986 he joined the staff at Manhattan's famous Le Cirque, where he worked under master chefs Alain Sailhac and Daniel Boulud, and in 1987 helped to reopen the newly renovated "21" Club. After a stint as executive sous-chef at the legendary Maxwell's Plum, Michael returned to the "21" Club as executive chef in 1989, at which time he created the culinary leadership that inspired a kitchen staff of thirty-four and brought about the revitalization of that decades-old restaurant.

In 1997, Michael was appointed executive chef/director of Windows on the World, including the main dining room and the boisterous Greatest Bar on Earth. (The more intimate Wild Blue opened later.) Through Michael's leadership Windows on the World was transformed into one of America's best-loved restaurants and the highest-grossing restaurant three years in a row. Serving as consulting chef, Michael has recently opened Noche, a Latin American restaurant and nightclub located in the heart of New York City's Times Square, and Shore House, a casual seafood restaurant in Stamford, Connecticut.

Michael has a passion for teaching what he loves, having served as a distinguished visiting professor at CUNY New York City. He also often participates in events that benefit a world of good causes, including Share Our Strength, City Meals on Wheels, City Harvest, and the March of Dimes. He is a principal founder and officer of the Windows of Hope Family Relief Fund, which has gathered nationwide momentum and support.

Michael is the co-host of the Travel Channel's popular cooking program *Epicurious*. He also hosted the much-loved *Michael's Place* on Food Network for three years. Michael has been a regular guest on *Late Night with David Letterman*, NBC's *Today* show, *CBS Saturday Morning*, ABC's *Good Morning America*, and *Live with Regis and Kathie Lee*. He has also been seen on *In Julia's Kitchen with Master Chefs* with host Julia Child. Michael is a regular guest on food- and lifestyle-oriented radio programs nationwide.

Michael Lomonaco is coauthor of the best-selling *The "21" Cookbook* and *Nightly Specials*, due to be published in 2004.

⁓

My mother, Mary, was born in New York, but her family came from Castiglione di Sicilia, a small town on the northeastern slopes of Mount Etna. She and my father—he's from the same town—showed me at an early age the rustic cooking of southern Italy and Sicily.

What my mother loved best was to have a house filled with people and to be moving around cooking and feeding them all. It wasn't unusual to have thirty people for the holidays, including family, roommates my brothers brought home from college, and neighbors. Sometimes the crowd was so large that we'd remove all the furniture from the living room and fill it with several large dinner tables. I don't remember my mother ever sitting down during those dinners, but rather working diligently as a chef, host, and maître d'.

I always had an interest in what was going on in the kitchen. As a grade school student I did my homework there because it smelled so good and was so cozy. And the kitchen was my mother's headquarters, the place where we caught up after school. When I finished my third-grader's homework (I was seven or eight at the time), I'd shell cranberry beans, slice potatoes, peel onions, and whatever else needed to be done, loving the chance to help her, even in my small way. I learned so much about food and cooking through that time I spent with my mother.

My mother made lasagna with beef, sausage, and three kinds of cheese; pizza rustica; and lots of other dishes with cheese—even though she didn't eat cheese herself. She spent hours making these dishes, especially when company was coming. That kind of generosity and her creativity are the reasons I went into the restaurant business. Creativity and generosity are the keys to good cooking.

When I first told my mother I was going to switch from acting to cooking, she was disappointed. Acting had been a longtime dream of mine. I was a committed home cook at that point, making meals as a way to please my wife and friends. When I explained how happy it made me to think about cooking for a living, she backed me one hundred percent.

By the time I decided to change careers I had already met and married my wife, Diane. Diane's family welcomed me and made me a part of their family, and because they were all terrific cooks—especially her grandmother Josephine and mother, Vicenza ("Vee")—I grew and became a better cook. Their cooking is also Sicilian, but because they came from Palermo, where the food is more sophisticated, I learned not only a whole new repertoire of dishes, but (mostly from Diane's grandmother) a whole new sense of pride in cooking.

Diane's grandmother "Grandma" was an adventurous cook with an encyclopedic knowledge of the cuisine of her homeland. She also had tremendous spirit, energy, and drive, and a personality that was strong and big. Every day in my restaurants I try to bring the same generosity of spirit and exuberance that my mother, Mary, and Vee and Grandma brought to their cooking, their family, and their table.

Sfincione ONION AND ANCHOVY PIZZA

Real Sicilian street food, this easily made dish is readily found at large family gatherings as a late-night snack after all the serious cooking and eating is but a memory until the next holiday or wedding.

My wife Diane's grandmother Josephine Spadaro made this dough by hand on a wooden board, starting with a mound of the flour and salt, making a well in the center, and adding all the ingredients to the well. Then she'd fold the ingredients together and work the dough by hand for 10 to 12 minutes, until the ball of dough was ready to rest.

This was originally made with *estratto*—homemade sun- or oven-dried tomato paste, whose taste and character is richer, darker, and more intensely tomatoey than store-bought tomato paste. MAKES TWO 13 × 9-INCH SFINCIONE, ABOUT 20 PIECES TOTAL

FOR THE DOUGH

2 cups all-purpose flour

1 cup semolina flour

1 teaspoon sea salt

1 envelope active dry yeast

1 cup warm water

1 large egg

3 tablespoons extra virgin olive oil

FOR THE TOPPING

⅓ cup olive oil

3 large sweet onions, finely sliced (about 4 cups)

3 ounces (about 1½ cans) oil-packed flat anchovy fillets, drained and coarsely chopped

One 6-ounce can tomato paste

½ tablespoon freshly ground black pepper

1 cup Italian-style bread crumbs (dry, unseasoned crumbs made from bread with the crust left on)

I. Make the dough: Combine the flours and salt in the bowl of an electric mixer or a food processor fitted with the plastic dough blade. Dissolve the yeast in the water and add to the flour on low speed or pulse briefly if using a food processor. While continuing to mix on low speed, add the egg and oil. Mix until the dough forms a ball and has completely pulled away from the sides of the bowl, about 6 to 7 minutes in an electric mixer and less time in a food processor. Place the dough in a clean bowl, cover with a cloth, and place in a warm area until the dough doubles in size, 50 to 60 minutes.

2. To make the topping: Place a 10- to 12-inch pan that is about 3 inches deep over low heat. (If your pan is smaller than this, cook the onions in batches.) Pour in all but 2 tablespoons of the oil. Heat for 1 minute before adding the onions. Cook the onions, stirring and turning them occasionally to prevent burning or sticking, until soft, translucent, and sweet without being dark or caramelized, 10 to 12 minutes. Add the anchovies, stir to combine, and cook for several minutes before adding the tomato paste and pepper. Cook until the mixture resembles a thick, moist onion sauce, about 8 minutes. Remove from the heat and set aside.

3. Preheat the oven to 450° F. Brush two 13 × 9-inch baking pans with ½-inch sides with the remaining 2 tablespoons of oil, coating the bottom of the pans.

4. Punch down the dough and divide it in half. Roll out the dough on a lightly floured surface to the size and shape of the pans. Fit the dough into the pans, pressing it gently into the corners. Bake until the bottom turns pale golden, 10 to 12 minutes.

5. Divide the onion mixture evenly between the 2 dough shells, leaving ½ inch of uncovered dough as a border around the edges. Sprinkle the bread crumbs over the topping, covering both sfincione evenly. Bake until the bottom is dark golden but not burned and the top is a richly colored caramel, 15 to 20 minutes. Remove and allow to cool for a few minutes before cutting into portions.

> **MOM'S TIPS**
>
> *Even better than canned anchovies are the imported Italian salt-packed anchovies. Rinse them under cold water and remove their heads and bones, a simple task, before using them. Even if you're using canned anchovies, drain the oil they're packed in and rinse briefly under cool water. You'll freshen up the flavor. Store any unused anchovies in fresh olive oil.*

> **MOM'S TIP**
>
> *Baking the crusts before adding the onion topping will ensure a dry, crisp bottom for your sfincione.*

Pizza Rustica

I learned this dish, a real crowd pleaser, from my mother, Mary Lomonaco. She often made it around the holidays. The name *pizza* refers more to the shape than what we usually think of as a pizza here in the States. In southern Italy these were more typically made with hard salami than the Genoa salami I call for here. And the mozzarella in the filling would be either *fiore di latte* (made from cow's milk) or *bufala*, made from water buffalo milk and a little tangier than cow's milk mozzarella. There is a similar dish called *pizza grana*, a pie filled with cooked whole grains and sweet custard, made in the same sort of shape, that my mother made during the Lenten season. MAKES 8 TO 10 SERVINGS

2 cups all-purpose flour, plus more for kneading the dough

½ cup sugar

¼ pound (1 stick) sweet butter, cut into pieces

¼ cup cold water

6 egg yolks

1 teaspoon salt

1¼ teaspoons ground black pepper

1 pound fresh ricotta cheese, preferably made from sheep's milk

8 ounces sliced Genoa salami, chopped

8 ounces fresh mozzarella, diced into ¼-inch pieces

4 ounces sliced prosciutto coarsely chopped

¼ cup grated pecorino Romano cheese

Olive oil

1. Set a rack in the center of the oven and preheat the oven to 375° F. Combine the flour, sugar, butter, water, 3 egg yolks, salt, and ¼ teaspoon of pepper in the work bowl of a food processor. Process until they form a ball of dough. Remove the dough, place on a floured work surface, and knead for 5 minutes, adding

flour as necessary to prevent the dough from sticking to your hands and the work surface. Cover the ball of dough with plastic wrap and refrigerate until firm, at least 1 hour.

2. In a bowl, stir together the ricotta, salami, mozzarella, prosciutto, Romano cheese, the remaining 3 egg yolks, and 1 teaspoon of pepper until well blended. Refrigerate while you prepare the pastry shell.

3. Remove the dough from the refrigerator and cut one-third off to be used as the top crust. Roll the larger piece out on a floured work surface, to a 12-inch-wide circle. Brush the inside of a 10-inch springform pan with oil and transfer the circle of dough to the pan. Using your fingertips, press the dough evenly into the bottom of the pan, making sure the dough has a flat bottom and is tucked into the seam of the pan. Pull the dough up the side to reach the top edge of the pan. Pour the filling into the dough and rap the pan sharply on the countertop once or twice to settle and distribute it evenly. (See Note.) Roll the remaining smaller piece of dough into a 10-inch circle and place this over the filling. Pinch the edges of the two pieces of dough together to seal the edge completely. Cut a cross into the top crust so that steam can escape during baking. Set the pan on a baking sheet and bake until the top is well browned, 45 to 55 minutes.

4. Remove the pizza from the oven and cool for 10 minutes. Run a sharp knife around the edge to loosen the crust from the pan and open the springform pan. Cool completely before serving at room temperature.

NOTE: Depending on the thickness of the ricotta, you may have to spread the filling into an even layer with a metal spatula.

Arriminati PASTA WITH SAFFRON-CAULIFLOWER SAUCE

If *pasta con sarde* (pasta with sardines) is one of the most famous Sicilian dishes, this dish is one of that island's best-kept secrets. Italians are fond of vegetable-pasta combinations, and there is hardly a vegetable that hasn't found its way into the idiom. This recipe takes the unappreciated, blandly colored cauliflower and turns it into a brilliantly hued dish that resembles its better-known cousin—the above-mentioned pasta with sardines. In Sicily this dish is traditionally made with a light green variety of cauliflower. If that is available at your market, then by all means use it here. MAKES 4 TO 6 APPETIZER SERVINGS

I large head cauliflower, dark leaves and thick stems discarded, but head left whole

Salt

I teaspoon loosely packed saffron threads

¼ cup olive oil

I medium onion, finely chopped (about ¾ cup)

4 to 5 anchovy fillets, roughly chopped

I tablespoon tomato paste

I pound buccatini or perciatelli pasta

⅓ cup dried Zante currants

¼ cup pine nuts

Freshly ground black pepper

MOM'S TIP

Zante currants are actually tiny raisins— dried grapes—not currants at all.

I. Choose a pot large enough to hold the cauliflower and an ample amount of water in which to cook it. A 4- to 5-quart pot should do it. Fill the pot two-thirds of the way with water, bring it to the boil, and add I teaspoon of salt. Add the cauliflower and return to a boil. Cook the cauliflower at a simmer until the floret stems are tender when pierced by a knife but have not yet become soft and mushy, 12 to 15 minutes. Try not to overcook the cauliflower; remember, it will cook again in the sauce. Pour off I cup of the cooking liquid. Drain the cauliflower carefully and set it aside to cool. When cool, break the head into large pieces. Soak the saffron in ¼ cup of the cooking liquid and set the remaining ¾ cup aside to finish the sauce.

2. Bring an 8-quart pot of salted water to a boil.

3. Heat the oil in a large skillet over medium heat for 1 minute. Add the onion and cook until translucent, 6 to 7 minutes. Add the anchovies and stir to combine.

4. Add the cauliflower florets, stir to combine, and cook for 5 minutes. Add the saffron water, half of the remaining cooking water, and the tomato paste. Bring to a boil, then adjust the heat so that the sauce is simmering. Simmer for 5 minutes.

5. Meanwhile, stir the pasta into the boiling water and cook, stirring occasionally, until *al dente*, about 10 minutes.

6. Add the currants and pine nuts to the sauce and season with pepper. Continue simmering the sauce over low heat until the pasta is cooked.

7. When the pasta is cooked, drain it and place it in a large serving bowl. Add half of the sauce and toss until the pasta is coated. If there is not enough sauce to coat the pasta evenly but lightly, add the reserved cauliflower cooking liquid little by little until there is. Serve topped with additional sauce.

Tonno Agrodolce TUNA MARINATED SICILIAN STYLE

Tuna belly—the thinner, paler tuna known as *toro* in Asian markets—is delicious, as sashimi and sushi lovers know. But it's also wonderful used in this recipe with its sweet-and-sour character (*agrodolce*), which offsets the luscious mouth-feel and cuts through the fattiness of this cut of tuna. Tuna belly is hard to find because so much of it heads to Asian restaurants first, but it is worth the trouble to seek out. That wasn't the case when I was a boy. This was a typical meatless Friday night meal that was popular with my family, and it was made extra delicious with our homegrown mint. This can be served as either a main dish or as part of an appetizer salad. A dinner of *tonno agrodolce* was often followed by homegrown peaches in wine as dessert.

MAKES 4 TO 6 SERVINGS

1½ pounds fresh fatty tuna belly, cleaned of all skin, bones, and cartilage, or tuna steaks

¼ cup olive oil

Salt and freshly ground pepper

2 medium white onions, thinly sliced (about 1¾ cups)

¼ cup sugar

¼ cup red wine vinegar

10 to 15 fresh, clean mint leaves, freshly chopped moments before use

I.   Have your fishmonger clean any skin or cartilage from the tuna. Cut the tuna into 4- to 5-ounce steaks. Pour half of the oil into a large frying pan or casserole and heat over medium heat for 2 minutes. Lightly season the tuna with salt and freshly ground black pepper. Turn the heat to high and add several pieces of tuna to the pan in a single layer. Do not crowd the fish because this will cool the pan too quickly, and the fish will not brown but instead will steam and overcook. Brown the steaks quickly on both sides, then remove them to a serving platter large enough to hold all of them in 1 layer and with a lip to prevent the sauce from spilling over. Cook the fish in several batches using the remaining oil.

2. After all the fish has been cooked, add the onions to the pan, lower the heat to medium, and cook, stirring often, until they are a golden, caramelized color, about 10 minutes. Add the sugar and stir for a couple of minutes, but be careful not to allow the sugar to burn or turn to caramel.

3. Add the vinegar to the pan, being careful of dangerous splattering, bring it to a simmer, and stir to intermingle the flavors. Cook for 2 to 3 minutes until the sauce is slightly reduced before adding half of the mint leaves. Stir to cook the leaves and release their flavor. Remove the pan from the heat, pour the contents over the cooked tuna, and let marinate for 15 to 20 minutes. Garnish with the remaining mint and enjoy this dish at room temperature.

BORN IN CANTON, China, to parents who ran a restaurant and a grocery store, Martin Yan possessed a passion for cooking at an early age. His formal induction into the culinary world began at age thirteen with an apprenticeship at a popular Hong Kong restaurant.

In 1978, Martin pioneered a daily television show featuring Chinese cuisine, the now classic *Yan Can Cook,* and infused it with his characteristic warmth, humor, and vitality. To date Martin has hosted more than eighteen hundred cooking shows that have been broadcast around the world.

Martin enjoys distinction as a certified master Chinese chef, a highly respected food consultant, restaurateur, professional instructor, and prolific author. His diverse talents have found expression in twenty-five cookbooks (in three languages), most recently in *Martin Yan's Chinatown Cooking,* which has an introduction by Julia Child; *Martin Yan's Feast,* and the award-winning *Chinese Cooking for Dummies.*

Chef Yan holds a master's in food science from the University of California at Davis and an honorary doctorate degree of culinary arts from Johnson & Wales University. He has received numerous honors, including two James Beard Foundation Awards and a daytime Emmy.

In 2001, Martin was inducted into the James Beard Foundation's Who's Who of Food and Beverage, which honors professionals for significant advancements in the field. He has also been awarded a 1996 James Beard Foundation Award for Best TV Food Journalism and a 1994 James Beard Foundation Award for Best TV Cooking Show.

⟞⟝

I learned so much from my mother, Lim. It shouldn't be surprising that the lessons that stand out most bring me back to food and the kitchen.

Martin; his mother, Lim; and his brother, Michael.

The first lesson my mother taught me was to be frugal but without skimping. When you grow up in a house that does not have a refrigerator, you are forced to cook with what is fresh in the market. That means a single chicken ended up on our family's dinner table in a few different dishes, much like a trained chef uses various parts of a duck in different ways for a Peking duck feast.

Perhaps the most important lesson I learned in my mother's kitchen, though, was to use ingredients when they are in season and in abundance. Without refrigeration we did not have the luxury of grocery shopping once a week; instead, we frequented community markets, fish stores, and butchers daily. We bought fresh ingredients every morning and used them the same day. My mother never followed recipes; she followed nature and cooked from what the seasons have to offer.

My mother's daily trips to the markets and the way she cooked with the seasons inspired me to be the kind of person and cook I am today. I think of my mother while walking through my local farmers' market, with ideas for this evening's meal running through my head—just as she must have done. I think of her, too, when I open my refrigerator and challenge myself to make a wholesome meal for my family from its contents. (I have it easier than my mother did when she was raising a family—I have a refrigerator!) This care and nurturing of a family is something every home cook does on a daily basis. Those of us who cook for a living do it, too, for the people who eat in our

Martin and his mother, Lim.

restaurants, read our books, and watch our television shows. It's a gift that most of us learned from the person who brought us into this world . . . our mother.

Grilled Cantonese Shrimp

My mother taught me how to cook at a very young age. We all had to help with family chores, and I luckily ended up more often than not in the kitchen. In the time we spent together preparing the family meals, I learned how to use the ingredients that were in abundance. We never followed recipes, we just blended flavors to enhance the primary ingredient, whether it was a large freshly caught fish or a root vegetable from the garden. In this recipe I use Cantonese flavorings with sweet and mild shrimp. MAKES 8 SKEWERS

32 large raw shrimp (about 1¼ pounds), shelled and deveined

1 tablespoon Chinese rice wine or dry sherry

1 teaspoon vegetable oil

½ teaspoon sesame oil

2 cloves garlic, minced

1 teaspoon minced ginger

¼ teaspoon ground white pepper

1 onion, cut into 2-inch cubes

MOM'S TIP

If you're using wooden skewers, soak them in water for about half an hour before assembling the skewers. That will prevent the skewers from burning while grilling.

1. Toss together the shrimp, wine, oils, garlic, ginger, and pepper in a bowl until the shrimp are evenly coated. Set aside for 10 minutes.

2. Thread the marinated shrimp on skewers, alternating them with pieces of onion. Grill over medium heat until the shrimp are pink, about 2 minutes per side.

Spicy Black Bean Swiss Chard

It was a surprise to some of my friends to hear that I grew up on this leafy green. My mother planted this fast-growing vegetable in our family garden. The weather was mild in southern China, and Swiss chard flourished. Salted black beans were always in our pantry, and the pungency of the fermented bean pairs exquisitely with the chard. We also used the garlic and black bean flavor combination with other leafy greens that grew in our plot. MAKES 4 SERVINGS

1 tablespoon vegetable oil

2 cloves garlic, minced

3 dried whole chilies

1 pound Swiss chard, trimmed, cleaned, and chopped

½ cup chicken stock or canned chicken broth

1 tablespoon black bean garlic sauce (see Note)

1. Heat a large pan that has a lid over high heat until hot. Add the oil, swirling to coat the bottom. Add the garlic and chilies, and stir until fragrant, about 30 seconds.

2. Add the chard, stock, and black bean garlic sauce. Cover the pan and lower the heat to medium. Cook, stirring occasionally, until the chard is wilted and tender, about 5 minutes. Served topped with Grilled Cantonese Shrimp (page 288).

NOTE: Black bean garlic sauce is available in Asian groceries and some supermarkets.

Simple Cabbage Soup

Chinese mothers believe that soups help cleanse the body, are good for the spirit, and will help cure what ails you. Mother encouraged me to eat and drink soup at every meal; I would eat *jook* (a slow-simmered thick rice porridge) for breakfast and this simple cabbage soup for lunch and dinner. We would always have a big pot of it on the fire. Mom would use not only cabbage and daikon but also fuzzy melon, zucchini, and any other seasonal squash. If available, we would add dried squid to add a more intense Cantonese ocean flavor.   MAKES 4 TO 6 SERVINGS

5 dried Chinese black mushrooms

5 cups chicken stock or canned chicken broth

3 green onions, roots removed, green and white parts cut into 2-inch segments

4 quarter-size slices of ginger

¼ cup dried shrimp

½ head napa cabbage, cored and cut into 1-inch pieces (about 4 cups)

8 ounces daikon, peeled and cut into ¼-inch-thick rounds

1 teaspoon salt

½ teaspoon ground white pepper

1.   Soak the mushrooms in warm water to cover until softened, about 10 minutes. Drain and discard the stems.

2.   Bring the broth, onions, ginger, and shrimp to a boil in a soup pot. Add the mushrooms, cabbage, daikon, salt, and pepper. Lower the heat to a simmer and cook until the vegetables are tender, about 10 minutes. Serve with steamed rice.

BORN IN THE TOWN of Mieres, in Asturias, Spain, in July 1969, José Andrés's cooking skills are deeply rooted in his Mediterranean heritage. At the age of fifteen, encouraged by his father, he applied to a new culinary school, the renowned Escuela de Restauracio I Hostalatge of Barcelona, where he studied from 1985 to 1988. As a student, José acquired practical experience by apprenticing in several important restaurants, including El Bulli, near Barcelona (one of the few non-French restaurants with three *Michelin Guide* stars), under the world-renowned master chef Ferrán Adriá. (José still visits Chef Adriá at El Bulli for a few weeks every summer.)

José Ramón Andrés

In 1990 José moved to New York City to work at the Barcelona-based restaurant El Dorado Petit. In 1993, he moved to Washington, D.C., to become a chef/partner at Jaleo in the Penn Quarter of downtown Washington. This opportunity quickly expanded, with José becoming executive chef at Café Atlantico; executive chef/partner at the second Jaleo in Bethesda, Maryland, and executive chef/partner in Zaytinya, which opened in October 2002.

José has won many honors and awards during his ten years in Washington. Nominated three times for the James Beard Foundation's Best Chef: Mid-Atlantic Region, he captured the coveted award in May of 2003. His latest culinary venture, Zaytinya, was one of only five restaurants in the country nominated for "Best New Restaurant" by the James Beard Foundation. *Condé Nast Traveler* selected Zaytinya as one of the seventy-five best new restaurants in the world in the May 2003 issue, and the restaurant won "Best New Restaurant" for the June 2003 Restaurant Association of Metropolitan Washington's Capital Restaurant & Hospitality Awards.

José is also chair of the board of D.C. Central Kitchen, a nonprofit organization that feeds the homeless and trains people for careers in food service.

———

The association between cooking and women is a very old one indeed. Where I came from, the Asturias region of Spain, women traditionally played a very important role in feeding the family, and the same is true today. (Sometimes, more often than not, this was out of necessity, rather than a love and passion for cooking.)

People speak of creative cooking. In my opinion, there has never been more creativity in the kitchen than that shown by the women of Spain after the Spanish Civil War. There was not much to eat, yet women somehow managed to serve their families hot food day after day. Necessity always brings the best out in mankind. Or in this case, womankind.

Women's cooking has always had a very big influence on me personally. I guess that from the moment we are fed by our mothers, without even knowing it, we are caught in a net that brings us comfort, something we always feel when a special woman cooks for us. It is something unique and personal—it is something we want to keep for ourselves. Maybe that's the reason that society has kept women's cooking for one's own household, rather than sharing it with the restaurant world (until recently, that is).

Nothing comforted me more than the smells that came from my mother's kitchen when I came back from school or a short trip. Still today, when I'm away from home, it brings me comfort to try to recreate those aromas and flavors from my childhood: my mother's roasted peppers, or the bonito with tomato that my godmother, Maria del Mar, whom I loved and miss, made in her kitchen in Santander. Or the smells in the kitchen of my grandmother Pia or my aunt Florentina, in San Vicenc de Castellet, where we get together on the twenty-sixth of December to eat *escudella and carn d'olla*, a very traditional soup enjoyed in three courses, with all the aromas flowing around the house. I've spent so many good moments in a kitchen around a table.

It gives me joy to see my wife trying hard day to day—even with her busy schedule—to always have a plate of lentils or a stew of chickpeas ready to share with me when I come back from work. I guess all these experiences are part of my genes. Because if something gives me a happy face it is when I see my two daughters, Carlota and Ines, cooking with me, as we did last Christmas, making a traditional paella in a garden in the Pyrenees Mountains. The girls fought over who would add the rice, or who would stir the mushrooms. All fights were forgotten when we all sat together to eat.

I have a third daughter on the way. And I guess I understand now why God is sending another woman into my life. The joys of my culinary experiences with women, past and present, will be perpetuated in the years to come by these new women of my life.

Buey con Cabrales Como le Gusta a Mi Madre BEEF WITH CABRALES "MAMA MARISA"

My mother and I were born in Mieres, Asturias, the most beautiful region you'll ever see in Europe and the home of Cabrales, a great blue cheese made in the Asturian mountains. When I was young, we moved to Barcelona. Whenever my mother was homesick for Asturias, she'd eat a little piece of Cabrales to bring her closer to Mieres. To this day, every time I want to feel like I'm in Asturias, I eat some Cabrales, by itself or in this beef recipe.

MAKES 4 TO 6 SERVINGS

10 tablespoons Spanish extra virgin olive oil

2 pounds beef tenderloin roast

Sea salt

Freshly ground black pepper

3 heads of garlic, roasted (see Note)

3 ounces Cabrales cheese (or any other blue cheese)

1½ tablespoons brandy

1 bunch chives, chopped

1. Preheat the oven to 250° F.

2. Heat 6 tablespoons of the olive oil in an ovenproof skillet over medium heat. Rub the beef on all sides with salt and pepper. Add the beef to the skillet and cook, turning it as necessary, until browned on all sides, about 10 minutes.

3. Roast the beef tenderloin until the inside reaches 145° F at its thickest point, about 30 minutes. Let it rest 5 minutes before cutting.

4. Meanwhile, mash the peeled roasted garlic and mix with the Cabrales and brandy.

5. Carve the tenderloin into ½-inch slices. Sprinkle the slices with sea salt to taste and spread a little of the Cabrales mix on each. Sprinkle the chives over the beef and serve.

NOTE: To roast garlic, first cut a thin slice from the top of each head to expose the tips of the cloves. Arrange the heads side by side in a small baking dish and drizzle a little olive oil over them. Roast in a 375° F oven until the garlic is browned and the cloves are very tender when poked with a fork, about 30 minutes. Cool to room temperature, then squeeze the softened garlic cloves out of their skins.

Chorizo a la Sidra "Chita y Marga"

SPANISH CHORIZO COOKED IN CIDER FROM ASTURIAS

My aunts, Chita and Margarita, are the sisters of my grandfather Ramon, who died when I was very, very young. (My aunts always remind me of how much I resemble my grandfather.) Both of them are very good cooks. Every year when I go to visit them in Mieres, in Asturias, we get together in the old part of town (before our "real" lunch) to eat this dish of chorizo made with the traditional Asturian cider in the local bars. No one eats and drinks more than Chita and Marga, and they are in their nineties! MAKES 4 SERVINGS

2 tablespoons olive oil

½ pound Spanish chorizos (see Note)

1 cup El Gaitero cider, or any hard cider

Salt

Heat the olive oil in a pan over medium heat. Add the chorizo and cook, turning, until very lightly browed, about 2 minutes. Pour in the cider, bring to a boil, and cook until the cider is reduced by half, about 2 minutes. Add salt to taste and serve in a *cazuela* (a small, shallow bowl) with good bread on the side for dipping in the sauce.

NOTE: If you are using *cantimpalitos* (small chorizos, about 1 inch each), you don't need to cut them. If you start with larger, softer chorizo sausages, cut them into ¾-inch pieces.

Endivias con Braña, Naranjas, y Almendras al Gusto de Pilar

ENDIVES WITH ORANGES, ALMONDS, AND GOAT CHEESE, PILAR STYLE

This recipe becomes one of the most popular tapas at Jaleo whenever we put it on the menu. Every summer we go to Algeciras, my wife's hometown, to spend time with her family—Pilar Canovas, her mother, and Carmen, Maria, and Piluca, her sisters. Pilar loves almonds or anything made with almonds. One day I had in hand good oranges and good goat cheese. Pilar said why don't you add almonds? Well I did, and here we have one of my most popular tapas ever! MAKES 6 PIECES

6 medium endive leaves

1 orange, peeled and cut into segments (see Note)

1 tablespoon toasted sliced almonds

2 ounces crumbled Spanish goat cheese (about ½ cup)

Pinch chopped chives

1 tablespoon Vinagreta de Ajo Tostado (recipe follows)

Salt

Arrange the endive leaves curved side down on a plate. Divide the orange segments among the leaves and top those with toasted almonds and goat cheese. Sprinkle the chives over everything, then drizzle the vinaigrette over them. Salt to taste and serve right away.

NOTE: Cut the peel and white pith from the orange with a paring knife, cutting into the fruit as little as possible. Remove the segments by cutting them free from the membrane that divides them.

Vinagreta de Ajo Tostado

ROASTED GARLIC VINAIGRETTE

MAKES ABOUT I CUP

¾ cup Spanish extra virgin olive oil

¼ cup peeled garlic cloves

2 tablespoons sherry vinegar

I tablespoon chopped shallots

Salt and freshly ground white pepper

I. Heat the oven to 375° F. Stir ¼ cup of the oil and the garlic together in a small baking dish until the garlic is coated with oil. Roast until the garlic is very tender and browned, about 30 minutes. Allow to cool slightly.

2. Scrape the garlic and oil into a blender. Add the sherry vinegar and shallots. Blend until smooth. With the motor running, gradually pour in the remaining ½ cup of olive oil. Season to taste with salt and pepper.

Gazpacho Andaluz Como lo Hace Mi Mujer

TRADITIONAL GAZPACHO AS MY WIFE "TICHI" MAKES IT

MAKES 4 TO 6 SERVINGS

2 pounds very ripe tomatoes, cored and cut into medium dice

½ medium green pepper, seeded and diced

1 medium cucumber, peeled and diced

2 cups bread torn into small pieces

6 tablespoons Spanish extra virgin olive oil, plus more for drizzling over the soup

2 tablespoons sherry vinegar

1 clove garlic

Salt

Spring water, if necessary

Croutons

1. Reserve a little of the diced tomatoes, green pepper, and cucumber. Blend all the remaining ingredients except the water and croutons in a blender in small batches until very smooth. You may have to add a little water to make the soup smooth, as the water content in the ingredients may vary. Strain through a coarse strainer and chill.

2. Serve cold in bowls and sprinkle the diced vegetables and croutons over the top. Drizzle a little olive oil over the top of each serving.

DURING THE SIX MONTHS I spent compiling and editing *Mom's Se-cret Recipe File*, many people, intrigued by the idea, related memories and recipes from the inspirational women in their lives. These dozen recipes, each with a history, come from across the country and around the world, and are just a sampling of the many recipes we received.

Other Moms Across the Country

We hope these recipes inspire you to search out, enjoy, and preserve the recipes, secret or not, that are part of your her-itage.

Poor Man's Rich Borscht

I learned how to make this soup from my mom. (*Her* mom made it this way, too.) I grew up on this soup in winter. The prunes and mushrooms are unusual. I think people used what they had, and not having meat or chicken broth, they turned to other ingredients for flavor and richness. *Prunes give the soup a sweetness and body. The dried mushrooms give it real depth of flavor.* It's a very thick soup, so feel free to thin it out toward the end of cooking.—*Sam Firer*

MAKES 10 SERVINGS

2 ounces sliced dried mushrooms

2½ pounds lean beef, cut into cubes, or one 2½- to 3-pound chicken, quartered

10 cups cold water, or more for a thinner soup and less for a thicker soup

2 large red onions, chopped

1 carrot, peeled, trimmed, and chopped

½ celery stalk, chopped

2 tablespoons dried parsley

1 bay leaf

8 black peppercorns

2 cloves garlic, chopped

Salt to taste

4 cups shredded cabbage (green, red, or both)

3 medium potatoes, cut into eighths

8 beets, peeled and cubed

8 ounces pitted dried plums

One 16-ounce jar or can sliced pickled beets

Two 6-ounce cans tomato paste

¼ cup sugar, or to taste

Freshly cracked pepper

¼ cup finely chopped fresh dill

¼ cup finely chopped green onions

½ cup sour cream

1. Soak the mushrooms in water to cover overnight. Drain the liquid and set the mushrooms aside.

2. Place the beef and water in a large soup pot. Bring to a boil, then adjust

the heat so the liquid is simmering. Cook for 20 minutes, skimming the fat and foam from the surface occasionally.

3. Add the onions, carrot, celery, parsley, bay leaf, peppercorns, garlic, and 1 teaspoon of salt. Cover and simmer over low heat until the carrot is tender, about 30 minutes. Check for salt from time to time as the soup cooks.

4. Stir in the cabbage and cook for 20 minutes. Add the potatoes, beets, and prunes. Cook for 20 minutes, then add the pickled beets and tomato paste. Cook until the potatoes are tender, about 10 minutes.

> **MOM'S TIP**
>
> *Empty the cans of tomato paste into a small bowl and whisk in some of the liquid from the soup. That will make it easier to dissolve the tomato paste in the soup.*

5. Add some water if the soup is too thick for your taste. Add the sugar and taste. Add more sugar if you like, depending on the sweetness of the beets. Add the cracked pepper to taste. Turn the heat to low. Stir in the dill and green onions.

6. Both the chicken and beef should be fall-apart tender at this point. Serve the soup—whatever lands in the ladle—in warm bowls. Add a dollop of sour cream to each bowl. If you made the soup with chicken, be careful of the tiny bones.

[From the Secret Recipe File of Tina Klein]

Country-Style Lentil Soup

My mother is an amazing cook. She transforms an ordinary lentil soup into something wonderful with a simple *condimento* of sautéed garlic. *Frying the garlic in oil and stirring it into the soup at the end give a livelier and fresher note of garlic flavor.* This soup is delicious with grilled country-style bread.—*Steven Petrecca*

MAKES 6 SERVINGS

I cup lentils, picked over and debris removed

2 large potatoes, peeled and cut into I-inch cubes

2 carrots, peeled, trimmed, and diced

I stalk celery, trimmed and diced

Salt and freshly ground pepper to taste

¾ cup extra virgin olive oil

2 cloves garlic

Freshly grated pecorino Romano or other cheese

I. Place the lentils, potatoes, carrots, and celery in a saucepan large enough to hold them easily. Pour in enough cold water to cover by 2 inches and bring to a boil. Adjust the heat to simmering and cook, spooning off any foam that rises to the surface, until the lentils are very tender, about 45 minutes. Season with salt and pepper about halfway through the cooking.

2. Heat the oil in a small skillet over medium heat. Add the garlic and cook, shaking the pan, until light golden brown, about 3 minutes. Stir the garlic and oil into the soup. Taste the soup and add salt and pepper as needed.

3. Ladle into generous bowls that have been warmed. Sprinkle with freshly grated cheese and pepper over each bowl.

[From the Secret Recipe File of Cenzina Petrecca]

Frozen Cheese Soufflé

This recipe was passed on to me from my mother more than forty years ago, and it is still one of my favorites. *The beauty of this cheese soufflé is that it can be prepared as long as two months in advance and then used for a delicious brunch and/or dinner whenever desired.* MAKES 4 SERVINGS

4 tablespoons butter, plus more
for greasing the soufflé dish

4 tablespoons all-purpose flour

1 cup whole milk

1½ cups grated sharp Cheddar
cheese

½ teaspoon dry mustard

½ teaspoon salt

¼ teaspoon pepper

4 large eggs, separated

1. Grease a 1½-quart (6-cup) soufflé dish.

2. Melt the butter in a medium saucepan over medium heat. Add the flour and cook, stirring, until well blended. Stir in the milk and cook, stirring, until the mixture is very thick. Stir in the cheese, mustard, salt, and pepper. Remove from the heat and let cool slightly.

3. Beat the egg yolks until lemon-colored and gradually add them to the cheese mixture. In a separate bowl, beat the egg whites until stiff. Gently fold the cheese mixture into the beaten egg whites. Turn this mixture into the prepared soufflé dish and cover with aluminum foil. Freeze immediately. Keep in the freezer at least 24 hours or up to 2 months.

4. Preheat the oven to 300° F. Take the soufflé from the freezer, uncover it, and put it directly in the oven. Bake until golden brown and nicely puffed, about 1½ hours. Serve at once, including some of the crust and creamy center with each serving.

[From the Secret Recipe File of Linda Perlman]

Vegetarian Stuffed Grape Leaves

When many of my cousins became vegetarian (a practice unheard of in Egypt), my aunt Lily Menasha developed a recipe for vegetarian-stuffed grape leaves that has as much flavor as meat-stuffed leaves and puts to shame the canned ones stuffed with rice that you find at restaurants in America. *The secret behind the full flavor of these grape leaves is the combination of the tart taste of the lemon and cardamom with the sweetness of the carrot and slow-cooked onions.* The rolling of the leaves can be time-consuming, but it is also an opportunity to sit around with your family and tell stories as you share the task.

1 tablespoon olive oil

4 large onions, grated

2 stalks celery, grated

8 carrots, peeled and grated

2 cups uncooked converted rice

One 16-ounce jar of preserved grape leaves, preferably large

Juice of one lemon

6 whole cardamom seeds

2 tablespoons coriander seed

1 clove garlic, minced

1.   Heat the oil in a large skillet over medium heat. Add the onion and cook over very low heat until it turns very soft and brown, about 20 to 30 minutes. Stir in the celery, carrot, and rice. Set aside.

2.   Rinse the grape leaves quickly under cold water. Cut off the stems with a sharp knife. Lay the leaves flat, with the ridged side facing up. Use only the whole leaves. Place the torn leaves flat on the bottom of a medium pot. Place 1 teaspoon of the rice mixture in the bottom center of a grape leaf and fold in the sides of the leaf over the filling. Roll the leaf up into a cylinder and place in the pot. Fill and roll the remaining leaves and place in the pot so that they fit very snugly. This will keep them from unrolling as they cook. Pour a small amount of water in the pot

My mother came to the United States in 1966 as an Egyptian-Jewish refugee. She came with her mother, father, and seven brothers and sisters. In this strange land they learned to make their native dishes with slightly different ingredients, and they learned how a taste or smell could recall a place so vividly that they were temporarily transported back to Egypt. But in reality they could not go back, so they went forward. My mother married a Russian man, and as my father likes to say, she learned all the ways of Russian cooking and made them better—by which he means she made them more Egyptian. She cooked cabbage soup without meat and with a tomato broth instead. She added parlsey to borscht, and dill to the simple dish of fried potatoes. And she and my grandmother taught me the secrets of Egyptian cooking as well. A squeeze of lemon brings out the nutty taste of lentils. Put a clove of garlic in the pot when cooking the rice. Never stop stirring the m'halabeya, or it will become clumpy. Always cook grape leaves with the water just covering the bottom of the pot, and always cook them slow, slow, slow. Some things just can't be rushed. And they taught me that food is not just fuel for the body but is also part of the thin and fragile web that connects me to my past.—LAURA FURMANSKI

along with the lemon juice. Sprinkle the cardamom, coriander, and garlic on top of the stuffed leaves. Place an overturned plate on top of the leaves to keep them secure. Cover the pot and cook on very low heat for 2 hours. As the water is absorbed, add more warm water to keep the level stable but low. Serve warm or cold.

[From the Secret Recipe File of Laura Furmanski]

Cucumber Sandwiches

These are a staple of my afternoon teas, and over the years they have evolved. *When my three-year-old grandson saw me shake the seasoned salt over the cucumber slices, he exclaimed, "That's the secret ingredient!"* And so it has remained. Now, at age twenty-three, he claims those sandwiches are still his "best favorite."

MOM'S TIP

To keep the sandwiches from drying out before you serve them, cover them with the damp paper towels used to drain the cucumbers.

1. To begin with, slice the cucumber ahead of time, placing the thin slices in single layers between paper towels to absorb the excess moisture. (Otherwise the bread becomes soggy.) I use very thinly sliced bread; Pepperidge Farm's thin type works well.

2. Put the sandwiches together not more than an hour before serving: Spread softened butter on one slice of bread and mayonnaise on the other. Arrange the cucumber slices in one layer over one of the slices and sprinkle them with your favorite seasoned salt. Cover with the other slice of bread. Press the sandwiches together and then slice off the crusts. Cut the sandwiches in triangles.

[From the Secret Recipe File of Joanne Hamlin]

Burgers Deluxe

We make these burgers a lot during the summer, since they are so good with lettuce, Jersey tomatoes, corn on the cob, and other summer produce. I got the idea from a cabbage roll I make with ground meat that has brown sugar and raisins in it. I also thought that barbecue sauces use sugar (most of the time), and *the sweetness seems to enhance the other flavors without really tasting "sweet."*

We like grilled zucchini on the side with these as well. They're ideal for company, since they can be made into patties ahead of time and then thrown on the grill when we're ready. We've been making these for several years now and never get bored with the taste, no matter what kind of cheese we top them with or which fresh herb we throw in.

When the weather is cooler, I make a meat loaf with this mix, which is delicious. I haven't made stuffed peppers with the ground meat mix yet, but will probably give it a try, using red peppers. MAKES 6 SERVINGS

2 pounds ground sirloin

½ cup quick-cook oatmeal

3 tablespoons light brown sugar

2 tablespoons crushed garlic

2 tablespoons soy sauce

2 tablespoons Worcestershire sauce

1¼ teaspoons ground ginger

Swiss cheese

6 kaiser rolls

1.   Crumble the ground sirloin into a bowl. Sprinkle the oatmeal, sugar, garlic, soy sauce, Worcestershire sauce, and ginger over the beef and work them gently into the beef until they are evenly mixed throughout. Shape the mix into six 1-inch-thick burgers.

2.   Grill or fry the burgers to the doneness you like and top them with the cheese after you flip them. Serve on the rolls.

[From the Secret Recipe File of Cindy Abbott]

Salmon Cakes

These salmon cakes are good enough (and easy enough) to keep a can of salmon on hand, just in case you find yourself with a little leftover mashed potatoes. *The secret is to keep the mixture nice and loose, not firm enough to form patties. That's why I use two eggs.* That makes them a little tricky to flour, but once you get the knack, there's really nothing to it.

I learned this recipe from my stepmom, who used to make it on Fridays, back when Catholics couldn't eat meat on that day. She served them with coleslaw and stewed tomatoes, but I think they'd be nice with a green salad and toast.   MAKES TWENTY 3-INCH CAKES

One 14-ounce can of salmon, drained

1 cup cold mashed potatoes

1 small yellow onion, finely chopped (about ½ cup)

2 eggs

3 tablespoons chopped parsley (optional)

Salt

Freshly ground pepper

All-purpose flour

Vegetable oil

1.   Pick over the salmon to remove any bones and pieces of skin. Crumble it into a mixing bowl. Add the mashed potatoes, onion, eggs, and parsley. Mash everything together until well blended. Season to taste with salt and pepper.

2.   Spread a thick layer of flour on a plate. Pour enough oil into a wide, heavy skillet to generously coat the bottom. Heat over medium heat until a little flour sizzles when you flick it into the pan. While the oil is heating, drop a rounded tablespoon of the salmon mixture into the flour. Turn it over to coat the other side, using a fork if you find that easier. What you'll have is a roughly shaped lump of the salmon mixture completely coated in flour.

3. Slip the cake into the oil. It will spread out a little bit. Continue making and flouring the cakes until the skillet is full. (Leave a little space between the cakes so they brown up nicely.) Fry, turning once, until golden brown on both sides, about 8 minutes. Repeat with the remaining batter. Drain them on paper towels and serve them hot.

[From the Secret Recipe File of Delores Fenton]

MOM'S TIP

Adjust the heat under the skillet so that the cakes are sizzling along at a steady clip. They shouldn't just lie there, but they shouldn't be hissing and spitting, either. If the heat gets too high and some of the flour that falls into the oil starts to burn, take a second to pour off the old oil and add new.

Pollo Guisado di Tía Amelia

(AUNT AMELIA'S CHICKEN IN SPICED TOMATO SAUCE)

When I was a little girl, I was the world's most finicky eater. There wasn't a fish or a vegetable that my mother could get me to eat. When it came to chicken or meat, I was *very* particular. You can see where this would be a problem in a Puerto Rican household, where we ate beans in various guises at least three times a week, and chicken or meat six days out of the week. (As Catholics, we still observed the "fish on Fridays" decree.) My mother tried disguising them in various ways, but I was just *not* having it.

It was a different story when we visited Tía Amelia's house. Tía Amelia was my grandmother's aunt who lived in a cute little apartment in the Bronx. Her son, my dad's cousin Freddie, was a merchant marine, and she had treasures all over her house that he had brought her from around the world! Tía Amelia would patiently tell me stories about these treasures, where they came from, and all the adventures Freddie had had while collecting them.

Tía Amelia made the most incredible *pollo guisado* with yellow rice that I have *ever* tasted. I would carefully pick up every grain of rice on my plate, because it was so good. My mother would watch me in amazement and Tía Amelia would rib her that she wasn't feeding me enough. Mami begged Tía for the recipe, and while she was reluctant to reveal her secrets, I believe she did so for my benefit. *It turns out, the secret to her delicious* pollo guisado *was cinnamon and cloves, not usually on the list of ingredients in this Latino classic. She had another trick up her sleeve—she used to sneak a tablespoon of palm sugar (like brown sugar) into the sofrito when she made her yellow rice to serve with the chicken.* MAKES 6 TO 8 SERVINGS

FOR THE SOFRITO

1 medium Spanish onion, cut into large chunks

1 to 2 cubanelle peppers (not regular green peppers)

8 to 10 cloves garlic, peeled

7 to 10 *ajices dulces* (or any small, mildly hot peppers; jalapeños will do in a pinch)

1 to 2 large plum tomatoes

1 small sweet red pepper, cored, seeded, and cut into large chunks

1 small bunch of cilantro, thick stems removed

2 leaves of culantro, optional (see Notes)

FOR THE CHICKEN

Two 3- to 4-pound chickens, each cut into 8 serving pieces

Salt and pepper

¼ cup canola oil

3 tablespoons achiote oil (see Notes)

Splash of dry white wine

¼ cup *alcaparrado* (bottled olive-caper salad) or 3 tablespoons chopped pimiento-stuffed green olives and 1 tablespoon capers

1 bay leaf

1 whole clove

¼ teaspoon cinnamon

½ cup canned Spanish-style tomato sauce

½ cup chicken broth

1. To make the sofrito: Combine the onions and cubanelle peppers in a food processor. Process until finely chopped. With the motor running, add the remaining sofrito ingredients, one at a time, and process until the mixture is pureed.

2. Season the chicken pieces with salt and pepper. Heat the canola oil in a skillet or Dutch oven large enough to hold all the chicken over medium-high heat until hot. Add as many of the chicken pieces to the skillet as will fit without crowding. Cook, turning as necessary, until they're browned on all sides, about 10 minutes. Set aside to drain on paper towels. Repeat with the remaining chicken. Keep the heat adjusted as the chicken cooks so there is always a lively sizzle, but be careful the chicken doesn't burn. Toss the browned chicken and the achiote oil together

> **MOM'S TIP**
>
> *Cubanelle peppers are long, thin, light green peppers that look a bit like Italian frying peppers. They have a mild kick and a complex flavor.*

in a large bowl until the chicken is coated. Drain all but 1 tablespoon of oil from the skillet.

3. Add the sofrito to the skillet and lower the heat to medium. Cook the sofrito, stirring often, until most of its liquid is evaporated, about 10 minutes. Add the wine, bring it to a boil, and cook until evaporated. Stir in the *alcaparrado*, the bay leaf, clove, and cinnamon. Bring to a nice bubble, then stir in the tomato sauce and broth.

4. Return the chicken to the skillet, turning to coat with the spice-scented sofrito. Make sure that the tomato sauce is at a happy bubble, lower the heat to simmer, cover the chicken, and cook for about 45 minutes. Rotate the chicken from top to bottom about halfway through the cooking. Serve hot with rice.

NOTES: Culantro, related to but not the same as cilantro, is an herb with long leaves and a pungent aroma similar to but stronger than cilantro. It is available in Latin markets.

To make achiote oil, heat ½ cup canola oil and 2 to 3 tablespoons of achiote (annatto) seeds together in a small saucepan over medium-low heat. There should be just a gentle sizzle—if you heat it too much, the seeds will burn and the oil will turn a nasty color. Let the oil cool a little, then strain it. Use leftover achiote oil to season other dishes.

[From the Secret Recipe File of Daisy Martinez]

Arroz con Pollo CHICKEN WITH RICE

One of my most vivid childhood memories is my mother with a can of beer in one hand and a large wooden spoon in the other, towering over a pot in the kitchen of our Manhattan apartment. No, she wasn't preparing to go to a Giants game or getting geared to reprimand my father. She was in the last phase of completing her delicious chicken with rice.

My grandmother Maria Diaz—who had about five names, which was mandatory if you were born in Asturias, Spain—taught my mother at a very early age how to cook and, most important, how to make a great chicken and rice, a pillar of Spanish cuisine. My grandmother traveled frequently to Havana and loved it so much that she eventually moved there, where she gave birth to three daughters. After Castro's rise, she left for her new and last home, the United States. My grandmother had a very distinctive style of cooking. She took the flavors of her birthplace and incorporated what she learned in the two countries of which she was a resident alien (literally and figuratively). *Until her passing she continued using her secret ingredient—a can of beer; it went into every pot of* arroz con pollo *she made, a tradition she handed down to her daughters.*

My mother, Nora Seoane (she has three names but uses only two), is a true New Yorker. She says that she doesn't want to live anyplace where you can't walk to where you shop and talk to people along the way. She taught both of my sisters to cook and how to make a great chicken and rice, which has become a staple in their homes. I was completely uninterested in learning how to cook. I was too preoccupied with when the next great disco song would be released.

My mother feels fortunate to have been offered the opportunity to live in this great country and continues to take the very best flavors it has to offer to create her own unique way of cooking. Whatever else she might come up with, she continues to add a can of beer to her *arroz con pollo*, a tradition *she* handed down to my sisters and, eventually, to me. Cheers!—*Joseph Seoane*

MAKES 6 SERVINGS

Olive oil

One 3½-pound chicken, cut into 12 pieces

Salt and freshly ground pepper

1 large onion, finely chopped

1 green pepper, finely chopped

2 cloves garlic, finely chopped

One 8-ounce can tomato sauce

1 teaspoon dried oregano

1 bay leaf

One 12-ounce can of beer

1½ cups shelled green peas or one 10-ounce package frozen peas, defrosted

3 cups long-grain rice

2 whole pimientos, cut into 1-inch pieces

1. Pour enough oil into a large (6-quart or so) heavy pot to coat the bottom evenly and heat over medium heat. Season the chicken with salt and pepper and add it to the pot. Cook, turning the chicken pieces, until browned on all sides, about 10 minutes. Transfer them to a plate.

2. Add the onion and pepper to the pot and cook, stirring, until lightly browned, about 6 minutes. Stir in the garlic and cook 1 or 2 minutes. Stir in the tomato sauce, oregano, and bay leaf. Return the chicken to the pot, pour the beer over it, and then pour in 4 cups of water. Add the peas, bring the liquid to a boil, and stir in the rice. Adjust the heat so that the liquid is barely simmering and cover the pot. Cook until the rice is tender and the chicken is cooked through, about 25 minutes.

3. Stir in the pimientos gently and let the chicken and rice stand 1 or 2 minutes before serving.

[From the Secret Recipe File of Nora Seoane]

Pecan Bars

In the early 1930s, in Merrill, Wisconsin, my mother's best friend, Dode, an excellent cook, called my mother and said, "Elsie, I just tried a new cookie recipe, and it is so good I've eaten the whole batch." Here is the recipe. *The secret behind these cookies is that they're really more like pecans perfectly toasted in butter and sugar, with just enough flour to keep them together.*—Marjorie Greenberger MAKES ABOUT 3 DOZEN

½ pound (2 sticks) butter

¼ cup confectioners' sugar, plus more for rolling the cookies

2 teaspoons vanilla extract

2 cups bread flour

2 cups pecan halves, broken into small pieces

1. Beat the butter and sugar together until blended. Beat in the vanilla. Stir in the flour to form a smooth dough, then stir in the pecans. Cover the dough with plastic wrap and chill until firm.

2. Preheat the oven to 300° F. Pull off a golf-ball-size piece of dough and roll it on a smooth surface to form a long rope of dough about as thick as your finger. Cut into 1½-inch lengths and arrange them on a baking sheet, leaving about an inch between them. Repeat with the remaining dough, using 2 baking sheets if you have them.

3. Bake until the cookies are straw-colored, 20 to 25 minutes. Cool the cookies for 10 minutes.

> **MOM'S TIPS**
>
> *Break the pecans by hand into pea-size pieces; any larger and the dough will be hard to roll out. Bake these cookies slowly to bring out the flavor of the toasted nuts.*

4. Meanwhile, spread a thick layer of sugar on the bottom of a shallow bowl. Roll the still-warm cookies in the sugar, then cool completely. Roll them in the sugar again once they are cool.

[From the Secret Recipe File of Dode Weiss]

Mema's Mandelbrot

Mema, my grandmother, moved from her birthplace in the Bronx, New York, to Atlanta, Georgia, more than fifty years ago. This is her signature dish. Everybody thinks his own Jewish grandmother makes the best mandelbrot, but I *know* that my mema really does: *Her secret is that instead of double-baking these crunchy bar cookies, she triple-bakes them.*—*Kelly Alexander* MAKES ABOUT 40 COOKIES

I cup sugar, plus more for dusting the cookies

I cup canola oil

3 eggs

I teaspoon pure vanilla extract

3½ cups all-purpose flour

1½ teaspoons baking powder

I cup chopped walnuts

Cinnamon

1. Preheat the oven to 300° F.

2. Mix the sugar and oil together well in a large bowl. Beat in the eggs one at a time. Mix in the vanilla. Add the flour and baking powder, and combine well. Mix in the walnuts and turn the dough out onto a work surface. Knead the dough into a rough ball. The dough should be very sticky, but if it is too sticky to handle, you can add more flour (by the pinch).

3. Divide the dough into thirds and form each piece into an 8 × 2-inch strip. Place the strips on a baking sheet and sprinkle the tops lightly with cinnamon and sugar.

4. Bake, watching closely, until the dough is just beginning to brown, about 30 minutes. Remove from the oven and let rest until cool enough to handle. Cut the dough diagonally into ½-inch slices. Turn the slices on their sides. Return to the oven and brown the mandelbrot to your liking, watching carefully so they don't burn, about 15 minutes.

> **MOM'S TIP**
>
> *For extra-crunchy mandelbrot, stand the pieces up again and brown on top, about 3 more minutes.*

5. Flip the strips over again so that the underside is now facing up. Dust the strips again with cinnamon and sugar. Bake until brown on this side, watching carefully, about 15 minutes. Cool the mandelbrot completely before serving. They'll keep in a covered container for up to one week.

[From the Secret Recipe File of Lil Pachter]

Poppy Seed Cake

This poppy seed cake—one of my mother's most requested—is very tasty and quite easy to make. (It uses a cake mix [!] as its base.) *Sherry and sour cream are the secret ingredients that add complexity to the flavor as well as extra moistness.*—Jennifer Cohan MAKES 12 SERVINGS

¼ pound (I stick) butter, softened

4 eggs

I box Pudding in the Mix or Butter Recipe yellow cake mix

I box French vanilla pudding (instant or regular)

8 ounces (I cup) sour cream

¼ cup sherry

¼ cup poppy seeds, or less if you prefer

Confectioners' sugar

I. Preheat the oven to 350° F. Butter a bundt cake pan, preferably a fabulous retro '70s pan.

2. Beat the butter in the bowl of an electric mixer or with a handheld mixer until light and fluffy. Beat in the eggs. Add the cake mix, pudding, sour cream, sherry, and poppy seeds, and mix to combine well.

3. Pour the batter into the prepared pan and spread the top into an even layer. Bake until golden and a cake tester inserted in the center comes out clean, about 45 minutes.

4. Remove from the oven and cool for 20 minutes. Carefully slide a knife around the edges, cover the top of the cake with a plate, and with one quick motion invert the cake onto the plate. Lift off the pan and cool the cake completely. Sift confectioners' sugar over the top of the cake just before serving.

> **MOM'S TIP**
>
> *A gerbera daisy or any bunch of edible flowers look marvelous springing from the center of the cake.*

[From the Secret Recipe File of Diane Cohan]

My Mom's Favorite Recipe

_____
_____
_____
_____
_____
_____
_____
_____
_____
_____
_____
_____
_____
_____
_____
_____
_____
_____
_____
_____
_____
_____
_____
_____
_____
_____
_____
_____

The Women's Commission
for Refugee Women and Children

One story of the work done by the Women's Commission for Refugee Women and Children:

Angelina Atyam of northern Uganda has experienced a mother's nightmare. Her fourteen-year-old daughter was abducted in 1996 from her boarding school one night, taken by the Lord's Resistance Army, a rebel group fighting the Ugandan government. She has not seen her since. Since that time, Angelina, who was a midwife, has become an international activist, co-founding an organization for parents of the more than 14,000 children who have been kidnapped during eighteen years of war, and advocating for their release. Her dedication to these children is steadfast. The rebels once offered to release her daughter if she would stop her advocacy efforts. Angelina refused, saying, "All these children are my children now." The Women's Commission for Refugee Women and Children has been working since 1998 to help Angelina bring this ongoing tragedy to the attention of the international community.

Around the globe today, more than 32 million women and children have been driven from their homes. Fleeing from armed conflict and persecution, they face rape, abduction by armed groups, hunger, and fear. Even in refugee camps, women and children are not safe from forced marriage, exposure to HIV/AIDS, sexual exploitation, and many forms of violence. Children are no longer innocent bystanders caught in the crossfire, but are now targets for calculated acts of genocide, military recruitment, torture, and trafficking.

The Women's Commission was founded in 1989 to document these dangers and abuses, inform the international community, and advocate for solutions. Over the last fifteen years, the Women's Commission staff have traveled to war-torn countries like Bosnia, Angola, Sierra Leone, and Afghanistan; interviewed refugee women and children; given them the chance to tell their stories at the United Nations and the U.S. Capitol; and helped make real and lasting improvements in their lives.

Refugee women are not only victims; they are resourceful, resilient, and brave. Often, the only things that refugee women carry in flight, besides the clothes on their backs and the children at their sides, are their cooking pots—and the tenacious will to hold their families together. The center of life for refugees—in tents, in fields, under tarps—remains the hearth, where mothers and daughters do their best to prepare familiar foods and recreate a sense of home. The Women's Commission for Refugee Women and Children affirms the power that women possess to restore and protect their families' well-being. On their behalf, the commission thanks the thirty-three chefs who donated their time, energy, and memories to create *Mom's Secret Recipe File.*

Every time Mangala Sharma, a refugee from Bhutan, looks at her two daughters, she feels indescribable joy—and relief. Mangala, who gained asylum in the United States in 2001, was separated for three years from her young daughters and husband as they waited for approval to live in the United States. Mangala fled persecution in Bhutan and lived for many years in a refugee camp in Nepal, but the separation from her family was the most difficult time in her life. "I missed them so much at times it was unbearable," says Mangala, who now lives with her family in Georgia. "But being with them again has brought me so much happiness. For our first meal together I prepared a traditional Bhutanese dish that my daughter loved. It's a simple dish we make when someone is sick, which we needed because we had to heal after so much pain. I hope the bond we forged at that meal will never be broken again." The Women's Commission for Refugee Women and Children worked with Mangala to make policymakers and the public aware of the plight of separated refugee families.

The Women's Commission is an affiliate of the International Rescue Committee, which is now the largest nonsectarian organization in America devoted to the cause of refugees worldwide. To find out more about women and children refugees, to learn how you can get involved, or to offer financial support, please visit the commission's website: *www.womenscommission.org.*

Index

stuffed, 16–17
Swiss chard cannelloni with chanterelle sauce,
234–35
mussels, salad of zucchini and, 220

Nathan, Joan, 77–79
noodles, *see* pasta and noodles

okra and tomato gumbo, 149
Oliver, Jamie, 163–65
onion
and anchovy pizza (sfincione), 276–77
soft scrambled eggs with tomato, pepper, and
("tunk-a-lee"), 142
tsimmes, 176

pasta and noodles
arriminati (pasta with saffron-cauliflower sauce),
280–81
baked chicken thighs with port and fresh
mushroom sauce, 211–12
baked macaroni, 106
fettuccine di biete rosse al sugo d'agnello (beet
fettuccine with lamb sauce), 217–19
Hungarian cabbage and noodles, 139–40
noodle kugel, 178–79
pasta e piselli (pasta and peas), 47
pasta for breath only a mother could love, 130
spaghetti with tomatoes, basil, and green
peppercorns, 186–87
pear and cranberry cobbler, 116–17
peas, pasta and (pasta e piselli), 47
pecan
bars, 317
pie, my grandmother's, 38
Pépin, Jacques, 27–29
pepper(s), bell
green, and potato frittata, 131
soft scrambled eggs with tomato, onion, and
("tunk-a-lee"), 142
in tomato sauce (peperoni a giambotella), 46
Perdue, Jim, 203–5
pickles
dill, 250
pantry, 249

pie
pecan, my grandmother's, 38
rhubarb, 260
shell, 261
pineapple, grilled, grilled ham steaks with
pineapple glaze and, 229–30
pizza
onion and anchovy (sfincione), 276–77
rustica, 278–79
polenta gratin with mushroom Bolognese, 237–38
poppy seed cake, 320
with lemon glaze, 251–52
pork
and ginger pot stickers, 158–59
hoisin, tenderloin sandwiches, 160
Tuesday night meatball soup, 69–70
potato(es)
cagoots, and sun-dried tomatoes, 97
country-style spring chicken with olives and
(pollastrella alla campagnola con cipolle,
patatine rosse ed olive), 8–9
dumplings (gnocchi), 4–5
and green pepper frittata, 131
lace, 33–34
and porterhouse alla Mamma, 132–33
and rice soup (riso e patate), 10
salad, Babe's, 64
Sunday at Cricketers: roast beef, best spuds, and
huge yorkies (Yorkshire puddings), 166–67
pot stickers, pork and ginger, 158–59
poultry
harvest turkey, 208–9
see also chicken
puddings
my grandmother's ginger-jam bread and butter,
198–99
pound, 168

rabbit cacciatore, 269–70
Raichlen, Steven, 221–24
relish, Frances Raichlen's cranberry-kumquat,
228
rhubarb
daisy cake, 169–70
pie, 260

rice
    chicken with (arroz con pollo), 315–16
    and potato soup (riso e patate), 10
    spiced apple, Swedish roast chicken with,
        88–89
    vegetarian stuffed grape leaves, 306–7
rock candy, 54–55

Sailhac, Alain, 273
salads
    Babe's potato, 64
    beet, 238–39
    Mom's healthful but delicious coleslaw,
        58–59
    of mussels and zucchini, 220
salmon cakes, 310–11
Samuelsson, Marcus, 85–87
sandwiches
    cucumber, 308
    hoisin pork tenderloin, 160
sauces and dressings
    homemade tartar sauce, 259
    mayonnaise, 259
    vinagreta de ajo tostado (roasted garlic
        vinaigrette), 298
sauerkraut and franks, my mother's, 80
sausages
    chorizo a la sidra "Chita y Marga" (Spanish
        chorizo cooked in cider from Asturias), 296
    Italian, with lentils, 194–95
scallops
    Chinese fire pot, 156–57
    coquilles St.-Jacques, 104–5
Schlesinger, Chris, 119–21
Schwartz, Arthur, 181–84
seafood
    brandade de morue de Nîmes, 75
    Chinese fire pot, 156–57
    codfish à la highlife, 76
    coquilles St.-Jacques, 104–5
    fried smelts, 258
    fried Virginia spots, 148
    grilled Cantonese shrimp, 288
    my home-style salt cod, 74
    salad of mussels and zucchini, 220

salmon cakes, 310–11
salt-seared swordfish with garlic and mint,
    188–89
shrimp with thyme butter, 39
tonno agrodolce (tuna marinated Sicilian style),
    282–83
shrimp
    Chinese fire pot, 156–57
    grilled Cantonese, 288
    with thyme butter, 39
smelts, fried, 258
Smith, Art, 109–11
soufflé, frozen cheese, 305
soups
    cold beet borscht, 22–23
    country-style lentil, 304
    gazpacho andaluz como lo hace mi mujer
        (traditional gazpacho as my wife "Tichi"
        makes it), 299
    mushroom-barley, 177
    poor man's rich borscht, 302–3
    rice and potato (riso e patate), 10
    simple cabbage, 290
    Tuesday night meatball, 69–70
spinach and sun-dried tomato strata, 67–68
spoon bread with Smithfield ham and Cheddar
        cheese, 122–23
spreads, see dips and spreads
squash
    fettuccine di biete rosse al sugo d'agnello (beet
        fettuccine with lamb sauce), 217–19
    see also zucchini
stew, Grandma Sarah's lamb and prune, 56–58
strata, spinach and sun-dried tomato, 67–68
Styler, Chris, 61–63
Swiss chard
    cannelloni with chanterelle sauce, 234–35
    spicy black bean, 289
swordfish, salt-seared, with garlic and mint, 188–89

tartar sauce, homemade, 259
tomato(es)
    gazpacho andaluz como lo hace mi mujer
        (traditional gazpacho as my wife "Tichi" makes
        it), 299

Permissions